The Big Read
Book of books

LONDON, NEW YORK,
MELBOURNE, MUNICH, AND DELHI

Project Editor Nicky Munro
Project Art Editors Clive Hayball; Gillian Andrews
Picture Research Louise Thomas
DTP Designer Jackie Plant
Production Controller Joanna Bull

Managing Editor Adèle Hayward
Managing Art Editor Karen Self

Art Director Peter Luff
Category Publisher Stephanie Jackson

For the BBC Big Read:
Creative Director Mark Harrison
Project Producer
Hannah Beckerman

First published in 2003 by
Dorling Kindersley Limited
80 Strand, London WC2R 0RL

A Penguin Company
2 4 6 8 10 9 7 5 3 1

A CIP catalogue record for this book is available
from the British Library

ISBN 1 4053 0405 7

Colour reproduction by Colourscan, Singapore
Printed and bound by Butler and Tanner, Frome, UK

See our complete catalogue at
www.dk.com

INTRODUCTION

What is your best loved book? The one that feels like an old friend; the one you grew up with; the one that gets you through hard times; even the one that changed your life? This is the question the BBC asked the British public on 5 April 2003 when we launched The Big Read.

The nominations period lasted for two weeks, and people could vote by telephone or on the internet. Only novels were eligible, but they could be from any country or time, and a series of books, such as *The Lord of the Rings*, could count as a single title as long as it had been published in a single volume. With sophisticated measures in place to identify and discount any attempts at multiple voting we were able to ensure that the results were genuine.

When the poll closed after two weeks, nearly 140,000 votes had been cast, making The Big Read the biggest ever survey of Britain's literary loves. Nearly 7,000 different titles were nominated. The most popular of the books feature here in the Top 100. They are listed in the order in which you, the public, voted for them – from 100 down as far as number 22. The remaining Top 21 titles are listed in alphabetical order only. These are the titles that formed the basis of a BBC Two documentary series, with seven films, each featuring three books. These books were also the contestants for a second round of voting: to find the best-loved book of all.

But the aim of The Big Read is not only to find our most popular book; it is also to celebrate in public the private joy that all wonderful stories bring. This Book of Books is a part of that huge celebration.

Mark Harrison, Creative Director for Arts, BBC Television

THE TOP 100 TITLES

Here are the books that the British public voted their Top 100 favourite novels of all time. You will find classics, children's books, novels translated into English, popular fiction and modern literary novels – all of which have touched the nation's heart.

TOP 21
page 14

TOP 21 page 16	**TOP 21** page 18	**TOP 21** page 20	**TOP 21** page 22	**TOP 21** page 24	**TOP 21** page 26	**TOP 21** page 28	**TOP 21** page 30	**TOP 21** page 32
TOP 21 page 52	**TOP 21** page 54	**NO. 22** page 58	**NO. 23** page 60	**NO. 24** page 61	**NO. 25** page 62	**NO. 26** page 64	**NO. 27** page 66	**NO. 28** page 68
NO. 38 page 86	**NO. 39** page 88	**NO. 40** page 90	**NO. 41** page 91	**NO. 42** page 92	**NO. 43** page 94	**NO. 44** page 96	**NO. 45** page 98	**NO. 46** page 100
NO. 56 page 113	**NO. 57** page 114	**NO. 58** page 116	**NO. 59** page 117	**NO. 60** page 118	**NO. 61** page 120	**NO. 62** page 121	**NO. 63** page 122	**NO. 64** page 123
NO. 74 page 136	**NO. 75** page 137	**NO. 76** page 138	**NO. 77** page 139	**NO. 78** page 140	**NO. 79** page 142	**NO. 80** page 144	**NO. 81** page 145	**NO. 82** page 146
NO. 92 page 160	**NO. 93** page 161	**NO. 94** page 162	**NO. 95** page 163	**NO. 96** page 164	**NO. 97** page 165	**NO. 98** page 166	**NO. 99** page 167	**NO. 100** page 168

THE TOP 100

TOP 21

BIRDSONG SEBASTIAN FAULKS

CAPTAIN CORELLI'S MANDOLIN LOUIS DE BERNIERES

CATCH-22 JOSEPH HELLER

THE CATCHER IN THE RYE J. D. SALINGER

GONE WITH THE WIND MARGARET MITCHELL

GREAT EXPECTATIONS CHARLES DICKENS

HARRY POTTER AND THE GOBLET OF FIRE
J. K. ROWLING

HIS DARK MATERIALS PHILIP PULLMAN

THE HITCHHIKER'S GUIDE TO THE GALAXY
DOUGLAS ADAMS

JANE EYRE CHARLOTTE BRONTE

THE LION, THE WITCH AND THE WARDROBE
C. S. LEWIS

LITTLE WOMEN LOUISA MAY ALCOTT

THE LORD OF THE RINGS J. R. R. TOLKIEN

NINETEEN EIGHTY-FOUR GEORGE ORWELL

PRIDE AND PREJUDICE JANE AUSTEN

REBECCA DAPHNE DU MAURIER

TO KILL A MOCKINGBIRD HARPER LEE

WAR AND PEACE LEO TOLSTOY

THE WIND IN THE WILLOWS KENNETH GRAHAME

WINNIE THE POOH A. A. MILNE

WUTHERING HEIGHTS EMILY BRONTE

22-100

HARRY POTTER AND THE PHILOSOPHER'S STONE
J. K. ROWLING

HARRY POTTER AND THE CHAMBER OF SECRETS
J. K. ROWLING

HARRY POTTER AND THE PRISONER OF AZKABAN
J. K. ROWLING

THE HOBBIT J. R. R. TOLKIEN

TESS OF THE D'URBERVILLES THOMAS HARDY

MIDDLEMARCH GEORGE ELIOT

A PRAYER FOR OWEN MEANY JOHN IRVING

THE GRAPES OF WRATH JOHN STEINBECK

ALICE'S ADVENTURES IN WONDERLAND
LEWIS CARROLL

THE STORY OF TRACY BEAKER JACQUELINE WILSON

ONE HUNDRED YEARS OF SOLITUDE
GABRIEL GARCIA MARQUEZ

THE PILLARS OF THE EARTH KEN FOLLETT

DAVID COPPERFIELD CHARLES DICKENS

CHARLIE AND THE CHOCOLATE FACTORY ROALD DAHL

TREASURE ISLAND ROBERT LOUIS STEVENSON

A TOWN LIKE ALICE NEVIL SHUTE

PERSUASION JANE AUSTEN

DUNE FRANK HERBERT

EMMA JANE AUSTEN

ANNE OF GREEN GABLES L. M. MONTGOMERY

WATERSHIP DOWN RICHARD ADAMS

THE GREAT GATSBY F. SCOTT FITZGERALD

THE COUNT OF MONTE CRISTO ALEXANDRE DUMAS

BRIDESHEAD REVISITED EVELYN WAUGH

ANIMAL FARM GEORGE ORWELL

A CHRISTMAS CAROL CHARLES DICKENS

FAR FROM THE MADDING CROWD THOMAS HARDY

GOODNIGHT MISTER TOM MICHELLE MAGORIAN

THE SHELL SEEKERS ROSAMUNDE PILCHER

THE SECRET GARDEN FRANCES HODGSON BURNETT

OF MICE AND MEN JOHN STEINBECK

THE STAND STEPHEN KING

ANNA KARENINA LEO TOLSTOY

A SUITABLE BOY VIKRAM SETH

THE BFG ROALD DAHL

SWALLOWS AND AMAZONS ARTHUR RANSOME

BLACK BEAUTY ANNA SEWELL

ARTEMIS FOWL EOIN COLFER

CRIME AND PUNISHMENT FYODOR DOSTOYEVSKY

NOUGHTS AND CROSSES MALORIE BLACKMAN

MEMOIRS OF A GEISHA ARTHUR GOLDMAN

A TALE OF TWO CITIES CHARLES DICKENS

THE THORN BIRDS COLLEEN MCCULLOUGH

MORT TERRY PRATCHETT

THE MAGIC FARAWAY TREE ENID BLYTON

THE MAGUS JOHN FOWLES

GOOD OMENS TERRY PRATCHETT AND NEIL GAIMAN

GUARDS! GUARDS! TERRY PRATCHETT

LORD OF THE FLIES WILLIAM GOLDING

PERFUME PATRICK SUSKIND

THE RAGGED TROUSERED PHILANTHROPISTS
ROBERT TRESSELL

NIGHT WATCH TERRY PRATCHETT

MATILDA ROALD DAHL

BRIDGET JONES'S DIARY HELEN FIELDING

THE SECRET HISTORY DONNA TARTT

THE WOMAN IN WHITE WILKIE COLLINS

ULYSSES JAMES JOYCE

BLEAK HOUSE CHARLES DICKENS

DOUBLE ACT JACQUELINE WILSON

THE TWITS ROALD DAHL

I CAPTURE THE CASTLE DODIE SMITH

HOLES LOUIS SACHAR

GORMENGHAST MERVYN PEAKE

THE GOD OF SMALL THINGS ARUNDHATI ROY

VICKY ANGEL JACQUELINE WILSON

BRAVE NEW WORLD ALDOUS HUXLEY

COLD COMFORT FARM STELLA GIBBONS

MAGICIAN RAYMOND E. FEIST

ON THE ROAD JACK KEROUAC

THE GODFATHER MARIO PUZO

THE CLAN OF THE CAVE BEAR JEAN M. AUEL

THE COLOUR OF MAGIC TERRY PRATCHETT

THE ALCHEMIST PAULO COELHO

KATHERINE ANYA SETON

KANE AND ABEL JEFFREY ARCHER

LOVE IN THE TIME OF CHOLERA
GABRIEL GARCIA MARQUEZ

GIRLS IN LOVE JACQUELINE WILSON

THE PRINCESS DIARIES MEG CABOT

MIDNIGHT'S CHILDREN SALMAN RUSHDIE

BIG READ TRIVIA...

- There are **75 DIFFERENT AUTHORS** in the Big Read Top 100; **12** have more than one book in the Top 100 and between them they account for more than a third of the list.
- **2 AUTHORS** have **5 TITLES** in the Top 100: **Charles Dickens** and **Terry Pratchett**.
- **3 AUTHORS** have **4 TITLES** in the Top 100 (all children's books): **Roald Dahl**; **J. K. Rowling** and **Jacqueline Wilson**.
- **WOMEN'S TOP 3 FAVOURITE BIG READ BOOKS**: *Rebecca, Pride and Prejudice, Jane Eyre*. **MEN'S TOP 3 FAVOURITE BIG READ BOOKS**: *Catch-22, Nineteen Eighty-Four, The Hitchhiker's Guide to the Galaxy*.
- The biggest-selling novel of all time is **J. R. R. Tolkien's *The Lord of the Rings***; having sold more than **100 MILLION COPIES** to date (sales of the book have rocketed since the release of the films).
- **30 OF THE TOP 100 BOOKS** were written for children (but lots of adults voted for them too...).
- **MORE THAN A QUARTER OF THE 75 AUTHORS** in the Top 100 were once teachers.
- **2** of the 75 Big Read authors are buried at Westminster Abbey: **Thomas Hardy** and **Charles Dickens**.
- **8** of the Top 100 books have been translated into English from a foreign language: ***The Alchemist*** (Portuguese); ***Anna Karenina*** (Russian); ***The Count of Monte Cristo*** (French); ***Crime and Punishment*** (Russian); ***Love in the Time of Cholera*** (Spanish); ***One Hundred Years of Solitude*** (Spanish); ***Perfume*** (German); ***War and Peace*** (Russian).
- The longest book in the Top 100 is ***A Suitable Boy*** by **Vikram Seth**, running to **1,474 PAGES** It is the longest single-volume novel ever published in English and took **Seth 8 YEARS TO WRITE**.
- The shortest book in the Top 100 is ***The Twits*** by **Roald Dahl**, running to just **87 PAGES**.
- **SOME BIG READ AUTHOR PSEUDONYMS/PEN NAMES**: Boz, Timothy Sparks, Charles Tringham **(Charles Dickens)**; Jean-Louis Incogniteau, Richard Lupoff **(Jack Kerouac)**; Richard Bachman, John Swithen **(Stephen King)**; C. B., Currer Bell, Marquis of Douro, Genius, Lord Charles Wellesley **(Charlotte Brontë)**; C. L. Anthony, Charles Henry Percy **(Dodie Smith)**.
- When voters were asked which books they had read 4 times or more, the 5 that came out on top were (in alphabetical order): ***Harry Potter and the Goblet of Fire***; ***Harry Potter and the Prisoner of Azkaban***; ***The Hitchhiker's Guide to the Galaxy***; ***Jane Eyre***; ***The Lion, the Witch and the Wardrobe***.
- **5 OF THE 75** authors were one-hit wonders – these were the only novels they wrote: ***Black Beauty*** by **Anna Sewell**; ***Gone With the Wind*** by **Margaret Mitchell**; ***The Ragged Trousered Philanthropists*** by **Robert Tressell**; ***To Kill a Mockingbird*** by **Harper Lee**; ***Wuthering Heights*** by **Emily Brontë**.
- **THE OLDEST BOOK** in the Top 100 is ***Pride and Prejudice*** by **Jane Austen**, **PUBLISHED IN 1813**.
- **THE OLDEST CHILDREN'S BOOK** in the Top 100 is ***Alice's Adventures in Wonderland*** by **Lewis Caroll**, **PUBLISHED IN 1865**.

- 5 AUTHORS IN THE TOP 100 were 30 OR YOUNGER when their book was first published: **Douglas Adams (27)** *The Hitchhiker's Guide to the Galaxy*; **F. Scott Fitzgerald (28)** *The Great Gatsby*; **Donna Tartt (28)** *The Secret History*; **Emily Brontë (29)** *Wuthering Heights*; **Stella Gibbons (30)** *Cold Comfort Farm*.

- 3 of the books in the Top 100 appear on the BBC's list of the top 10 books chosen by castaways on Desert Island Discs: **War and Peace** by **Leo Tolstoy** (no. 3); **The Lord of the Rings** by **J. R. R. Tolkien** (no. 8); **Alice's Adventures in Wonderland** by **Lewis Carroll** (no. 9). The complete works of **Charles Dickens** (5 titles in the top 100) comes in at no. 10.

- Only 1 per cent of the books we purchase were written before 1900, although 22 of the Big Read Top 100 titles were written before that date.

- **SOME BIG READ TITLES THAT WERE AT FIRST REJECTED BY PUBLISHERS:** *Ulysses, Pride and Prejudice, Lord of the Flies, Catch-22, The Wind in the Willows, Tess of the D'Urbervilles, Animal Farm, Dune, The Catcher in the Rye.*

- More than **40** of the Top 100 books were published in the last **30 YEARS** – the most popular decades for Top 100 books are the **1980s** and the **1990s** (16 titles each).

- 3 of the 75 Big Read authors have won the Nobel Prize for Literature: **John Steinbeck** (1962); **Gabriel Garcìa Màrquez** (1982) and **William Golding** (1983).

- 2 of the Top 100 books are Booker prize-winners: **Midnight's Children** by **Salman Rushdie** and **The God of Small Things** by **Arundhati Roy**. Both are by Indian writers and are set in India.

- **SOME CLASSIC PUTDOWNS**: Truman Capote on **On the Road** . . . "That's not writing, it's just typing"; Elizabeth Bowen on **Aldous Huxley** . . . "A stupid person's idea of a clever person"; Norman Mailer on **J. D. Salinger** . . . "The greatest mind ever to stay in prep school"; Tom Stoppard on **James Joyce** . . . "An essentially private man who wished his total indifference to public notice to be universally recognised"; Henry James on **War and Peace** . . . "A loose, baggy monster".

- In 1998, a rare first edition of **Alice's Adventures in Wonderland**, with 10 original drawings by John Tenniel, sold at auction for **1.5 MILLION DOLLARS** – the most ever paid for a children's book.

- **TOP 3 FAVOURITE BIG READ BOOKS BY AGE GROUP:**
0–9: *Harry Potter and the Goblet of Fire*; *Winnie the Pooh*; *The Lion, the Witch and the Wardrobe*; **9–13**: *Harry Potter and the Goblet of Fire*; *His Dark Materials*; *The Lord of the Rings*; **14–16**: *His Dark Materials*; *Harry Potter and the Goblet of Fire*; *The Hitchhiker's Guide to the Galaxy*; **17–21**: *Nineteen Eighty-Four*; *The Catcher in the Rye*; *The Hitchhiker's Guide to the Galaxy*; **22–31**: *Nineteen Eighty-Four*; *The Catcher in the Rye*; *Catch-22*; **32–41**: *A Prayer for Owen Meany*; *To Kill a Mockingbird*; *Captain Corelli's Mandolin*; **42–51**: *Tess of the D'Urbervilles*; *Birdsong*; *Middlemarch*; **52–61**: *The Grapes of Wrath*; *Middlemarch*; *The Wind in the Willows*; **62+**: *Gone With the Wind*; *Little Women*; *War and Peace*.

TOP 21

BIRDSONG CA
MANDOLIN CATCH-2
THE RYE GONE WITH
EXPECTATIONS HARI
GOBLET OF FIRE HIS
THE HITCHHIKER'S G
JANE EYRE THE LION
THE WARDROBE LITT
OF THE RINGS NINET
PRIDE AND PREJUDI
A MOCKINGBIRD WA
THE WIND IN THE WI
THE POOH WUTHERI

PTAIN CORELLI'S
THE CATCHER IN
HE WIND GREAT
Y POTTER AND THE
ARK MATERIALS
IDE TO THE GALAXY
HE WITCH AND
E WOMEN THE LORD
N EIGHTY-FOUR
E REBECCA TO KILL
AND PEACE
LOWS WINNIE
G HEIGHTS

SEBASTIAN FAULKS
1953–

Born in Newbury in Berkshire, Sebastian Faulks was educated at Wellington College and then Emmanuel College, Cambridge. His ambition was to become a novelist, but he began his working life as a teacher, at the same time writing freelance book reviews and newspaper articles. In 1978 he turned to journalism, working successively on the *Daily Telegraph*, the *Sunday Telegraph*, the *Independent* and the *Independent on Sunday*. His first novel, *A Trick of the Light*, was published in 1984. He wrote and presented the 1999 Channel 4 TV series *Churchill's Secret Army*, and still writes articles and reviews. Faulks lives in London with his wife and three children. He was awarded the CBE in 2002.

Other books by Sebastian Faulks:
A Trick of the Light
The Girl at the Lion d'Or
A Fool's Alphabet
The Fatal Englishman: Three Short Lives
Charlotte Gray
On Green Dolphin Street

BIRDSONG
SEBASTIAN FAULKS
Publication date 1993

From the lazy boulevards of pre-war France to the stifling heat, terror and filth of the trenches, Stephen Wraysford's journey takes him deeper and deeper into the horror of the First World War. *Birdsong* is a stunning tale of passion and war, which never loses sight of the essential frailty of human life and love.

▲ **First World War poster**
This British recruitment poster, by Alfred Leete, circa 1916, depicts Lord Kitchener, the Secretary of State for War. Under the 1916 Conscription Act, men between the ages of 18 and 41 were liable to be called up.

TRUTH IN LIFE AND DEATH

The harrowing story of *Birdsong* brings us war and love at their most evocative. This is no dashing tale of derring-do and manly bravado, but "an exploration of how far men can be degraded", or an examination of the physical and mental limits to which a man can be taken and still survive. Just as the war in Faulks' book is passionate and physical, so is the love affair that precedes it. Love, and its end, shapes Stephen's character and his view of war, as he and his comrades struggle to live with the inevitability of death. Faulks researched the reality of life in the trenches meticulously; the result is a haunting description of never-ending shell bombardment and endless waking hours. He tells his story through a small group of characters whom we come to know well – and to care about deeply.

▲ **Current edition**
Reviews of *Birdsong* were resoundingly favourable. "Magnificent – gorgeously written, deeply moving, rich in detail", wrote *The Times*.

Troops prepare their rifles with bayonets before going "over the top", Western Front, Somme, 1916

Did you know?
In the first 30 minutes of the Battle of the Somme, 30,000 British soldiers were killed. The battle claimed more than a million lives from all sides.

THE STORY IN A NUTSHELL

It is 1910, and 20-year-old **Stephen** travels from his native England to Amiens in northern France to learn about the French textile trade. His early life has not been easy, but it seems to be entering a better phase. Then he falls passionately in love with **Isabelle**, the wife of his host. They embark on an affair that is to leave them both indelibly enriched ~ and heartbroken. The story shifts to 1916, and Stephen is again in northern France as a soldier in the endless muddy, bloody, lice-ridden trenches and battlefields of the First World War. He is by now an embittered man, hardened to life yet possessed of an intense will to survive. The bulk of the book is taken up with the despair of the war years in the trenches. Finally Stephen is trapped underground, with little hope of rescue. Interwoven with his tale is that of his granddaughter **Elizabeth**, who, in 1970s England, finds his diaries and a history unravels. The discovery changes her life and enables her to keep a promise on Stephen's behalf.

"JACK FIREBRACE LAY FORTY-FIVE FEET UNDERGROUND WITH SEVERAL HUNDRED THOUSAND TONS OF FRANCE ABOVE HIS FACE. HE COULD HEAR THE WOODEN WHEEZING OF THE FEED THAT PUMPED AIR THROUGH THE TUNNEL. MOST OF IT WAS EXHAUSTED BY THE TIME IT REACHED HIM."

"Those of us who did not know the First World War cannot imagine it: Birdsong requires us to do so. It helps to define the nature and the limits of human endurance."
William Hague

First World War military cemetery at Douaumont, France

CAPTAIN CORELLI'S MANDOLIN
LOUIS DE BERNIERES

Publication date 1994

▲ First edition
Captain Corelli's Mandolin found a huge audience for its gentle lyricism and wit.

LOUIS DE BERNIERES
1954–

De Bernières was brought up in Surrey. At the age of 15, he decided to follow his father into the army and won a military scholarship. However, at 18, after just "four disastrous months" in the army, his pacifist inclinations had tarnished the appeal of a military career and he resigned, leaving his father to pay the school fees. Shamefaced, he left for Colombia to be an English teacher and cowboy for a year, before returning to read philosophy at Manchester University. During his 20s, he took a variety of jobs before settling down to write – a decision forced on him when he was immobilised in plaster for six months following a motorcycle accident.

Other books by Louis de Bernières:

The War of Don Emmanuel's Nether Parts

Señor Vivo and the Coca Lord

The Troublesome Offspring of Cardinal Guzman

Labels

Sunday Morning at the Centre of the World

Red Dog

When it was published this rich, complex book became the ultimate sleeper hit. Gradually, word spread about de Bernière's charming story full of light touches and dark incidents and propelled it to bestseller status – a classic story of love, hope and war.

LOVE IN THE TIME OF WAR

An epic tale following the Greek island of Cephallonia through peace, war and a painful recovery, *Captain Corelli's Mandolin* is a sparkling book that ambushes the reader with the horrors of war. The characters' many charms and the comedy of their stories are no preparation for the violence to come. De Bernières's skill is such that he blends the gently pastoral with the grimly serious.

In tackling the big themes of love, death, heroism and cowardice, he wrings his readers' emotions dry; but even at its bleakest this story is never without optimism or humour. This is a moral tale with the destruction of war at its heart. Corelli, with his distaste for fighting, and Dr Iannis, who is unable to kill even a wounded bird, are noble heroes set against the fisherman, Mandras, who seeks to prove his worth by fighting, but is destroyed by it. De Bernières's narration is unflaggingly passionate and often moving, showing us the viewpoints of everyone from dictator to goatherd.

▲ The setting
It is on a beach such as this one that the action takes place. Tourism frequently booms in the places where novels are set. In Cephallonia, cafes were renamed after the hero and tourist maps referred to "Captain Corelli's beach".

A German military convoy overtakes a group of Greek peasants, May 1941

If you like this, you may also enjoy books by:

Pat Barker

Julia Blackburn

Joseph Conrad

Christopher Hudson

Mario Vargas Llosa

STORY IN A NUTSHELL

It is the 1940s. **Pelagia** and her father, **Iannis**, the local doctor, live on the idyllic Greek island of Cephallonia. The fisherman **Mandras** wants to marry Pelagia. When Italy invades Greece, he decides to show off to her by joining the resistance. However, Pelagia's letters to him go unanswered and her love wanes, turning to revulsion when Mandras returns filthy, emaciated and mad. The Italian forces reach Cephallonia, but prove to be fairly benign occupiers. The mandolin-loving **Captain Antonio Corelli** is billeted with Dr Iannis and his daughter. His heart is in music more than in war, and he deflects their best efforts at frostiness, charming the father and bewitching the daughter. Soon, Pelagia and Corelli fall in love and embark on a cautious affair. A second invasion, this time by the Germans, is more sinister and, when Italy signs an armistice with the Allies, Germany takes horrific revenge, massacring a huge number of Italian soldiers on the island. Corelli survives, and is smuggled to Italy. As the war drags on, Pelagia and her father suffer terrible deprivations. Pelagia studies medicine and begins to rebuild her life, but all the time hoping for Antonio Corelli's return.

> "Captain Corelli's Mandolin is a story of powerful love – and hurt, the cruelty and stupidity of war and the capacity of people to be kinder, to endure and rebuild."
> Clare Short

"LOVE ITSELF IS WHAT IS LEFT OVER WHEN BEING IN LOVE HAS BURNED AWAY, AND THIS IS BOTH AN ART AND A FORTUNATE ACCIDENT."

Did you know?

One real survivor of the Cephallonian massacres bears a remarkable resemblance to de Bernières' hero. Amos Pampaloni was, like Corelli, a captain in the 33rd artillery regiment who had an affair with a Cephallonian girl. He is remembered as a folk hero on the island. De Bernières denies Corelli was based on a real person.

▶ **On the big screen**
The 2001 film, directed by John Madden, features Nicholas Cage as Captain Corelli and Penelope Cruz as Pelagia. Christian Bale plays Pelagia's suitor, the handsome but illiterate Mandras, and John Hurt plays her father, Dr Iannis.

JOSEPH HELLER
1923–99

Born in New York City into a Jewish family, Heller enlisted in the US Army Air Force in 1942. Sent into combat over Italy, he flew 60 missions as a wing bombardier. After the war he graduated from Columbia University, was a Fulbright scholar at Oxford University and taught at Pennsylvania State University. He began *Catch-22* in 1953, while working as an advertising copywriter; it took him almost eight years to write. Its success was never quite matched by his later novels. Heller also wrote the absurdist play, *We Bombed in New Haven* (1968). In his later years he suffered and recovered from Guillain-Barre syndrome, a paralysing nerve disorder, which he described in *No Laughing Matter* (1986). He died of a heart attack in 1999.

Other books by Joseph Heller include:

Something Happened

God Knows

Closing Time

CATCH-22
JOSEPH HELLER

Publication date 1961

Are you mad enough to live? Or sane enough to die? That's the catch. Catch-22. Heads they win, tails you lose. What's a man to do when the unholy powers of military bureaucracy threaten to destroy freedom and the human spirit? This exhilarating comedy blasted its way out of the futility and fear of the Second World War.

HUMOUR FROM HORROR

The protagonist of *Catch-22*, Captain Yossarian, spends all his time trying to survive the war, surrounded as he is by a cast of ludicrous characters, comprising power-mad freaks, oddballs, incompetents and other assorted lunatics. Their lives are intertwined in a series of ridiculous and tragic situations, with both author and characters wisecracking their way from one memorable moment to the next. *Catch-22* is probably the best (and certainly the funniest) comedy to come out of the Second World War – very dark, very satirical, bleak, profound and profane. Inspired by Heller's own wartime experiences, its subversive humour, anti-authority stance and snappy dialogue caught the spirit of the 1960s and later stood as an ironic counterpoint to the Vietnam war. It became a surprise bestseller and a cult classic, giving the English language the ultimate expression for a situation that can only turn out badly.

◄ **First edition**
On publication, *Catch-22* attracted a mixed press. *The New York Times* called it "wildly original... a dazzling performance that will outrage as many readers as it delights", while *The New Yorker* accused Heller of drowning in his own laughter.

"Catch-22 is not only the funniest black comedy ever written about young men at war, it rings true for everyone who works in a large organisation."
John Sergeant

Second World War recruitment poster

▶ **Bombing missions in 1944**
Part of the US Army Air Force's job was to disrupt German communications in Italy by laying strings of explosives across their lines. Heller drew on his own experiences in the Air Force when writing *Catch-22*.

> "ORR WOULD BE CRAZY TO FLY MORE MISSIONS AND SANE IF HE DIDN'T, BUT IF HE WAS SANE HE HAD TO FLY THEM. IF HE FLEW THEM HE WAS CRAZY AND DIDN'T HAVE TO; BUT IF HE DIDN'T WANT TO HE WAS SANE AND HAD TO. YOSSARIAN WAS MOVED VERY DEEPLY BY THE ABSOLUTE SIMPLICITY OF THIS CLAUSE OF CATCH-22 AND LET OUT A RESPECTFUL WHISTLE."

THE STORY IN A NUTSHELL

Based on Pianosa, a small island off Italy, the story follows the ordeals and frustrations of a group of American airmen from 256 Bombing Squadron, and in particular the wartime career of the cynical anti-hero **Captain Yossarian** who is desperate to escape the war. Among the multitude of characters that people *Catch-22*'s crazy world, Yossarian has to contend with the ambitious **Colonel Cathcart**, whose main goal is to become a general; the wheeler-dealing **Milo Minderbinder**, who goes too far when he bombs his own base on behalf of the Germans; the ineffectual and accidentally promoted **Major Major** and hordes of otherwise twisted individuals. During the novel, Yossarian's various attempts to avoid missions by any means possible – skiving in hospital, feigning insanity by walking backwards and turning up naked to collect a medal – all fail. During the mayhem, he finds himself confronting military bureaucracy in all its manifestations – including the dreaded clause Catch-22. Finally, his superiors, worried by Yossarian's effect on morale, offer him a deal that will return him home a hero, but compromise his principles. However, inspired by the news that a fellow airman, Orr, has "escaped" to Sweden, Yossarian decides the only way to leave is to go AWOL.

If you like this you may also enjoy books by:

Saul Bellow
Tibor Fischer
John Irving
Norman Mailer
Tim O'Brien
Thomas Pynchon
Tom Robbins
Derek Robinson
Philip Roth
Leslie Thomas

▶ **US troops in Italy**
The Allied troops landed in Sicily in July, capturing Palermo and Rome. Heller's inside knowledge of the mundane side of army life – queueing for meals – as well as its terror and mayhem brings *Catch-22* to life.

▲ **On the big screen**
In 1970 *Catch-22* was made into a film, directed by Mike Nichols and starring Alan Arkin as Yossarian. It was too dark for many people's tastes and was compared unfavourably to Robert Altman's *M*A*S*H* of the same year. It bombed at the box office. One critic described it as being "as hot and heavy as the original was cool and light".

J. D. SALINGER
1919–

Jerome David Salinger, the son of a Jewish cheese importer and a Scots-Irish mother, was born in Manhattan, New York City. He was educated at private schools and New York University, where he fell madly in love with Oona O'Neill (daughter of the playwright, Eugene) – she later married Charlie Chaplin. In 1939 Salinger took a class in short-story writing at Columbia University before being drafted into the army during the Second World War. From 1946 he devoted himself full-time to writing, and was soon contributing to *The New Yorker*, which published nearly all his later stories. Salinger's reputation, however, rests on his first (and only full-length) novel, *The Catcher in the Rye*. The public attention that followed its success led Salinger to retreat to the hills of Cornish, New Hampshire, where he continues to live as an enigma and a recluse.

Other books by J. D. Salinger:
Nine Stories
Franny and Zooey
Raise High the Roof Beam, Carpenters
Seymour: An Introduction

THE CATCHER IN THE RYE
J. D. SALINGER
Publication date 1951

First edition

For every mixed-up, moody teenager who ever felt out of sorts with the world, *The Catcher in the Rye* has become a rite of passage. With a rebellious teenage anti-hero who shares as much with James Dean as with Huckleberry Finn, it's the definitive cult novel of adolescence – funny and moving, and as relevant today as it was over 50 years ago.

TEENAGERS UNDERSTOOD

Despite its obvious appeal to teenagers, *The Catcher in the Rye* should not be pigeonholed – it is truly one of the great American novels. Written as a monologue, it uses the lively slang of its 17-year-old narrator, which still sounds edgy today and continues to keep it on lists of banned books in the US. While the narrative seems casual and unforced, the apparent effortlessness is both eloquent and underpinned by a skilful structure and a careful style. The comedy of the novel places it in the tradition of Mark Twain – hence critical comments linking it to *Huckleberry Finn* – but its world view is very much of its time. The humour derives from the narrator's acute observations of the people around him, especially his contemporaries, whom he despises for their lack of sincerity and for striving to ape the "phoney" values of a hypocritical adult world. The novel made an immediate impact. Though initial reviews were mixed, most critics considered the writing brilliant. It became an international success and still sells around a quarter of a million copies annually.

◀ **Robert Burns**
The book's title is taken from a misquoted line from "Comin' through the rye" by the Scots poet Robert Burns. When his sister asks him what he would like to be Holden imagines himself as "the catcher in the rye" after overhearing a boy singing some lines from the poem.

"This is a book that everyone believes was written just for them."
Ruby Wax

Did you know?
Despite its screen potential and a leading role to die for, no one has yet turned *The Catcher in the Rye* into a film. This is due to Salinger's protective control of his estate, although there have been many imitators.

◀ **Central Park**
Holden Caulfield obsesses about what the ducks in Central Park do when the lagoon freezes over – even asking a mystified cab driver for the answer.

THE STORY IN A NUTSHELL

Recalling the events of three days over the previous Christmas, *The Catcher in the Rye* is narrated by 17-year-old **Holden Caulfield** while he recovers from a nervous breakdown. After being expelled from his private school in Pennsylvania for flunking his exams he decides to leave school early and hang out in New York for a few days. This is the latest in a series of schools from which Holden has been expelled, so he is understandably reluctant to face his parents. In New York Holden holes up in a hotel and passes several days in a strange jumble of adventures involving a prostitute, taxi drivers, his ex-girlfriend **Sally Hayes**, an elevator man and a former teacher. After enjoying breakfast with two nuns, he buys a record for **Phoebe**, his kid sister. On the way he notices a boy singing "If a body catch a body coming through the rye", which cheers him up. Holden is considering running away from his problems, and also from himself, when Phoebe arrives.

The home of the reclusive J. D. Salinger, Cornish, New Hampshire

MARGARET MITCHELL
1900–49

Margaret Munnerlyn Mitchell was born in Atlanta, Georgia. She grew up surrounded by family stories and local history of the Civil War. Engaged in 1918 to Lt Clifford Henry, she suffered her first heartbreak when he died in battle. Mitchell then married and divorced a violent man, became a feature writer on the *Atlanta Journal Sunday Magazine* and married her ex-husband's best man, John Marsh. While recuperating from a broken ankle early in 1927, Mitchell began work on *Gone With the Wind*. Lacking confidence in her work, Mitchell let the manuscript gather dust for eight years. When finally published, the novel pre-sold more than 50,000 copies, and Mitchell was awarded the Pulitzer Prize.

GONE WITH THE WIND
MARGARET MITCHELL

Publication date 1936

The definitive blockbusting epic, *Gone With the Wind* has lost none of its pulling power. Nearly 60 years after it was published, it goes on selling, its readers still thrilling to this huge, sweeping tale of love and loss, passion and tragedy, set against the dramatic backdrop of the American Civil War.

Margaret Mitchell's house

MASTER OF HER ART

Margaret Mitchell's novel may have a 19th-century setting and lashings of love interest, but *Gone With the Wind* is far from a mere historical romance. Of course, many people have come to the story through the immensely popular film but, for all its appeal, it couldn't hope to capture the details and nuances of the book. Mitchell's Pulitzer prize-winning story – her only novel – is as skilfully constructed as any "serious" work, with a complex plot and satisfying character development underpinned with historical and social authenticity. She weaves the narrative strands with a master's touch, drawing her readers into a panorama of events and the human relationships at its centre. Her two main characters are indelibly printed on our collective subconcious. However, the prickly, combative relationship between Scarlett O'Hara, the archetypal strong but thwarted woman, and the aloof, macho Rhett Butler are far from the romantic stereotypes many imagine them to be.

Margaret Mitchell Marsh

▲ **First edition**
Gone With the Wind sold one million copies in the first six months after its publication. It was reprinted 100 times while still in its first edition.

> "Gone With the Wind, Scarlett O'Hara; this is where girl-power really began."
> Arabella Weir

▲ **A southern plantation**
Gone With the Wind was set against a backdrop of wealthy plantations, elegantly columned homes and a glittering society to match. The plantations' downfall came about because they were largely based on a single crop – cotton – and relied upon the use of slaves. After the Civil War, the Deep South was changed forever, and Scarlett's struggle for survival reflects the aftermath.

EPIC ROMANCES

Telling of extreme passion, lovers torn apart and love affairs set against dramatic historical events, it is no wonder the epic romance has always proved popular with readers and film audiences. Such stories encompass whole lives or generations, with the grand passions of the protagonists interwoven with events of the day, including war and political upheaval. This is romance on a grand scale, and it often makes the transition to big and small screens – from love in the bleak Russian landscape of *Doctor Zhivago* to the brooding passions and religious intrigue of *The Thorn Birds* and, of course, "the greatest story ever told", *Gone With the Wind*.

THE STORY IN A NUTSHELL

Sixteen-year-old **Scarlett O'Hara**, a spoilt and strong-willed Southern belle, lives with her family on the Tara plantation. She flirts outrageously with the local beaux, but gives her heart to the dreamy **Ashley Wilkes**. She is devastated when he marries the sweet and unselfish **Melanie Hamilton**. Undeterred, Scarlett soon meets her match in the worldly, roguish **Rhett Butler**, and is affronted by his insolence. War clouds have been gathering and, when conflict finally breaks out, Scarlett's cocooned world disappears forever. She marries twice, on neither occasion for love, and is widowed twice. Throughout her trials and tribulations among the horrors of war, Rhett somehow remains a presence in her life Scarlett is forced to flee the burning city of Atlanta and return to Tara, where she finds the place stripped bare. With everything gone and little to eat, life becomes a sheer struggle for survival. From now on, Scarlett has to keep the tattered remnants of her household together and work to the limits of her strength, driven on by a ruthless determination not to be beaten. Her path crosses Rhett's again, but can love ever run smooth for them?

Battle scene from the American Civil War, 1861–65

Did you know?

In 1936, the film rights to *Gone With the Wind* were sold for $50,000, then the highest price ever paid for an author's first novel. F. Scott Fitzgerald was one of the – uncredited – screenwriters employed to work on the script. He was worried that the production would bankrupt MGM studios, but the film went on to win a total of ten Academy Awards. Hattie McDaniel was the first black actress to win an Oscar (for Best Supporting Actress). Best Screenplay went to Sidney Howard.

In new screen splendor...
The most magnificent picture ever!

DAVID O. SELZNICK'S PRODUCTION OF MARGARET MITCHELL'S

"GONE WITH THE WIND"

CLARK GABLE
VIVIEN LEIGH
LESLIE HOWARD · OLIVIA de HAVILLAND

▲ **On the big screen**
National polls in the US helped decide who should play the lead roles. Clark Gable was a certainty, but 32 actresses were screen-tested for Scarlett before Vivien Leigh was chosen.

"I'M TIRED OF SAYING, 'HOW WONDERFUL YOU ARE!' TO FOOL MEN WHO HAVEN'T GOT ONE-HALF THE SENSE I'VE GOT, AND I'M TIRED OF PRETENDING I DON'T KNOW ANYTHING, SO MEN CAN TELL ME THINGS AND FEEL IMPORTANT WHILE THEY'RE DOING IT."

"My dear, I don't give a damn!"

The Big Read
TOP TWENTY-ONE

CHARLES DICKENS
1812–70

Dickens was born at Portsea, near Portsmouth, Hampshire. The family moved to London, where his father was jailed in the Marshalsea Prison for debt. At 12 the sensitive, intelligent Charles was forced to work in a blacking (shoe polish) factory to help support the family. The experience scarred him for life. Dickens went to school, but soon left to work as a parliamentary reporter. He wrote humorous sketches for magazines, which met with huge success. Meanwhile Dickens married and had 10 children. Against the backdrop of an often turbulent personal life, Dickens wrote 14 novels between 1837 and his death. A gifted performer, Dickens also made lucrative and highly acclaimed tours of Britain and the US in the late 1860s, reading from his work. He died leaving his 15th novel, *The Mystery of Edwin Drood*, unfinished.

Other books by Charles Dickens include:

David Copperfield
(Big Read no. 34)

A Christmas Carol
(Big Read no. 47)

A Tale of Two Cities
(Big Read no. 63)

Bleak House
(Big Read no. 79)

Oliver Twist

GREAT EXPECTATIONS
CHARLES DICKENS

Published UK 1860–61

This masterpiece by one of the world's greatest storytellers is considered by many to be the pinnacle of Dickens' achievements. *Great Expectations* exceeded the promise of its title: a convoluted but thrilling plot, unforgettable characters, wrenching pathos and exuberant comedy – all infused with the depth and maturity of true psychological insight.

▲ **First edition**
Printed in dark green morocco and light green cloth with gilt ruling and lettering, first editions are rare because most were bought by libraries.

EXPECTATIONS FULFILLED

With 12 hugely successful novels to his name, the public could be forgiven for thinking that Dickens' best work was behind him. This book would prove them wrong. Dickens took the bold step of first publishing it in weekly, rather than monthly episodes, hoping to boost the flagging sales of his weekly magazine, *All the Year Round*. He knew how taxing it was to keep up this accelerated schedule, and the creative challenge was enormous. Thankfully, all his travails paid off: from the first episode in December 1860 the series was an immediate success, as was the subsequent book. In 1861 *Atlantic Monthly* declared "Altogether we take great joy in recording our conviction that *Great Expectations* is a masterpiece." It seems that today's audience wholeheartedly agrees.

Did you know?
Dickens' public readings were legendary. His recitation of *Oliver Twist* was so realistic and dramatically effective that members of the audience regularly fainted during the murder scene.

◄ **On the small screen**
Charlotte Rampling played Miss Havisham in a BBC adaptation in 1999. The deranged and solitary old lady – one of the spookiest literary creations – is the source of most of young Pip's misunderstandings.

"Great Expectations is a vivid portrait of violence, hatred, scorn and revenge. A subtle tale of unrequited love. A masterpiece of English writing at its most powerful."
David Dimbleby

"IT WAS NOW TOO LATE AND TOO FAR TO GO BACK,
AND I WENT ON. AND THE MIST HAD ALL SOLEMNLY
RISEN NOW AND THE WORLD LAY SPREAD BEFORE ME."

THE STORY IN A NUTSHELL

Pip, a poor young orphan, meets and helps an escaped convict, **Magwitch**. Several years later, he is told he has "great expectations" – a mysterious benefactor is to provide for him so that he can become a gentleman. Pip assumes that the reclusive and bitter **Miss Havisham**, whom he has been visiting, is his sponsor, and that he is being groomed to marry **Estella**, Miss Havisham's beautiful adopted daughter. These experiences form a series of events that change the orphaned Pip's life forever, and he eagerly abandons his humble origins to begin his new life. As he grows up he falls in love with Estella, who callously rejects him. One night, Pip receives a strange visitor who reveals the true identity of his benefactor. Horrified by this revelation, Pip takes desperate measures first motivated by loathing and then gradually by love. His education and development through adversity eventually lead him to the true nature of his "great expectations".

▲ **On the big screen**
Jane Wyatt and Phillips Holmes star as Estella and Pip in the Universal film, directed by Stuart Walker and made in 1934. Estella, the haughty beauty, addresses Pip, who has become a gentleman. Many thought the film "too Hollywood" for a Dickens adaptation.

◄ **On the big screen**
The 1945 film adaptation by David Lean was nominated for an Oscar. It starred John Mills (right) as Pip and Alec Guinness as his good-hearted friend, Herbert Pocket. Estella was played by Jean Simmons. The film was considered by many to be the classic adaptation of a Dickens tale, transforming literary gems into potent screen characters.

J. K. ROWLING
1965–

Joanne Katherine Rowling grew up in Chipping Sodbury near Bristol; the family moved to the countryside when she was nine. Jo loved school even though she was put in the "dim" row by a teacher (who influenced the character of Snape). She studied French at Exeter University, then worked as a secretary before moving to Portugal. Here she met her first husband and had a baby, Jessica. When her marriage broke up, Jo returned to Edinburgh, deciding to train as a teacher, but first she wanted to finish a story she had begun in Portugal. Famously, she completed *Harry Potter and the Philosopher's Stone* in a cafe. Its success changed her life; she became the world's best-selling author, and one of its wealthiest women.

Other books by J. K. Rowling:

Harry Potter and the Philosopher's Stone (Big Read no. 22)

Harry Potter and the Chamber of Secrets (Big Read no. 23)

Harry Potter and the Prisoner of Azkaban (Big Read no. 24)

Harry Potter and the Order of the Phoenix

HARRY POTTER AND THE GOBLET OF FIRE
J. K. ROWLING

Publication date 2000

This fourth part of the Harry Potter story came out in the biggest blaze of publicity ever seen for a book – not to mention a frenzy of media attention. No one was allowed a copy until one minute past midnight on 8 July 2000. Fans were not disappointed – *The Goblet of Fire* is a dazzling story packed with humour and excitement.

HARRY POTTER SUPERSTAR

By the time *Harry Potter and the Goblet of Fire* was published, J. K. Rowling had topped bestseller lists all over the world, and Harry Potter had evolved from fictional hero to international sensation. Although published for children, the books had been taken up by adults who loved the adventures as much as younger readers. "Pottermania" was a worldwide phenomenon. This episode took longer to write, but readers were rewarded for their patience – the book has all the magic of the previous titles, and even more excitement and suspense. Harry is growing up and taking an interest in girls as well as continuing his struggle against the forces of evil. As promised, the book is darker and scarier than earlier instalments, and extends the author's exploration of prejudice and tolerance, a central theme of all four titles.

▲ **Current edition**
After all the hype, the book was published to rave reviews from critics and readers.

Did you know?
Harry Potter and the Goblet of Fire was released on a Saturday to stop children from taking a day off school to start reading it. More than one-third of a million copies were sold in the UK on the book's first day on sale.

"Harry Potter fires my imagination like no other book. You fall straight into the fantasy world of Hogwarts as soon as you open the book." Fay Ripley

THE STORY IN A NUTSHELL

Together with his best friends **Ron Weasley** and **Hermione Granger**, **Harry Potter** goes to the Quidditch World Cup. The games are fantastic and the atmosphere electric, but there are dark forces around and Harry knows that **Lord Voldemort** is getting bolder, more powerful and – most scarily – nearer. Back at school for their fourth year, Harry, Ron and Hermione find schoolwork is increasing, especially their studies of Defence Against the Dark Arts. But there's now more to Hogwarts than lessons and Quidditch: it is to be host to the Triwizard Tournament, an international competition between wizarding schools. Despite being officially too young to represent Hogwarts, Harry's name mysteriously appears in the Goblet of Fire, meaning that he must compete alongside the other three school champions. Meanwhile, the powers of darkness creep ever nearer.

> "HARRY DIVED. BEFORE THE DRAGON KNEW WHAT HE HAD DONE, OR WHERE HE HAD DISAPPEARED TO, HE WAS SPEEDING TOWARDS THE GROUND AS FAST AS HE COULD GO... HE HAD TAKEN HIS HANDS OFF THE FIREBOLT – HE HAD SEIZED THE GOLDEN EGG."

▲ **The post owl**
Harry Potter's snowy owl, Hedwig, appears in all the books. She delivers parcels and letters for Harry and is very important in carrying communications between Harry and Sirius Black, his godfather, who was wrongly implicated in the murder of Harry's parents.

▲ **Cover artwork**
The cover for *Harry Potter and the Goblet of Fire*, illustrated by Giles Greenfield, depicts Harry on his broomstick facing the first of his mysterious challenges in the Triwizard Tournament: a Hungarian Horntail dragon.

◀ **The film location**
The cloisters at Gloucester Cathedral are regarded as one of the most beautiful architectural features in Britain, and provide the setting for several scenes in the Harry Potter films.

POTTERMANIA

After five books, Pottermania shows no sign of abating, making it the greatest publishing sensation in history. The release of a new title generates incredible excitement around the globe, not just from young (and not so young) fans, but from the media, and, of course, the book trade. The publication of the fifth title, *Harry Potter and The Order of the Phoenix*, was greeted with near hysteria, as the author and publishers fought to keep the story a secret from the waiting public. The publicity paid off as the book flew off the shelves to become the fastest selling book of all time.

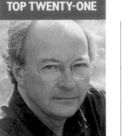

PHILIP PULLMAN
1946–

Philip Pullman was born in 1946 in Norwich. As a child he travelled widely, since his father and stepfather were in the RAF. He lived for a while in Australia, then from the age of 11, in North Wales. He read English at Exeter College, Oxford. After graduating in 1968 he became a teacher in Oxford and began writing for children. In 1970 he married Judith Speller; they have two sons. After teaching for 12 years he became a Senior Lecturer at Westminster College in Oxford and taught courses on the Victorian Novel, Creative Writing and The Traditional Tale. He became known as a specialist in folklore and oral storytelling. In 1996 he gave up lecturing to write full time. He is on the Board of Trustees for the Centre for the Children's Book, and his own work has won many awards.

Other books by Philip Pullman:
I Was a Rat!
Count Karlstein
The White Mercedes
The Tin Princess
The Ruby in the Smoke
The Shadow in the North
The Tiger in the Well

HIS DARK MATERIALS
PHILIP PULLMAN

Publication dates *Northern Lights* 1995; *The Subtle Knife* 1997; *The Amber Spyglass* 2000

▲ **Current edition**
All three parts are published in one volume of this crossover novel that appeals to children and adults alike.

▼ **Aurora borealis**
In the trilogy, the northern lights, or aurora borealis, are a bridge between alternative worlds. "And the Aurora swayed above... so close you'd think that you could step from this world to that."

Pullman's acclaimed and epic trilogy weaves myths and traditional sagas into dazzling theories about the universe. But the essence of his world, and of this astonishing story, is the importance of human experience and the search for truth.

THE QUEST FOR PARADISE

The title of this magical and entrancing tour de force comes from Milton's epic poem about the fall from grace of mankind, *Paradise Lost*: "…Unless the Almighty maker them ordain, His dark materials to create more worlds." Here Pullman is the creator of worlds that have dazzled millions of readers. He takes Milton's ideas about creation, temptation and rebellious angels and gives them a new spin. Young heroes Will and Lyra are the modern Adam and Eve, but the trilogy is really about a different kind of battle – the battle to understand the universe. Some see in Pullman's work a renouncement of the Church; the author, however, believes that The Fall was not the beginning of human misery, but the first day of freedom. One other thing is certain: *His Dark Materials* is a rollicking good read, whatever your beliefs might be.

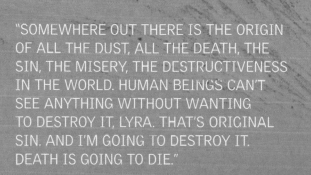

THE STORY IN A NUTSHELL

This trilogy pits good against evil in a world parallel to our own, and the mysterious entity called Dust just might have the power to unite the universes – if it isn't destroyed first. In *Northern Lights*, **Lyra** lives in an alternative world. Her search for her friend **Roger** takes Lyra to the far North, where she identifies her real parents and learns about Dust. Using an alethiometer, or truth-seeker, she journeys with fantastical characters, vowing to avenge Roger's death and discover the secret of Dust. In *The Subtle Knife*, **Will** lives in our world, but finds a window into Lyra's world. They return to Will's Oxford, where Lyra meets **Mary Malone**, a scientist researching Shadows – made of the same substance as Dust. Lyra's alethiometer is stolen and the ransom is a knife that cuts holes between universes. Will battles for the knife, and retrieves the alethiometer; but then Lyra is kidnapped. In *The Amber Spyglass*, Lyra is stalked by assassins but is also sought by those who are trying to save her. The two great powers of the many worlds are prepared for war, and Will must find Lyra and journey into the world of the dead in order to protect their future.

> "A dangerous epic of revolution, fantasy and the loss of innocence – devoured by our children, too important to be ignored by adults."
> Benedict Allen

Did you know?

Northern Lights won the Carnegie Medal and the Guardian Award in 1996. *The Amber Spyglass* was the first children's book to win the Whitbread Book of the Year in 2001. In his acceptance speech for the Carnegie Medal Pullman said, "We don't need lists of rights and wrongs, ...Thou shalt not is soon forgotten, but Once upon a time lasts for ever."

◀ **The Far North**
Norway's Svalbad Islands are north of the Arctic Circle, and have been the base for many Arctic expeditions. In Lyra's Svalbard, where her father is being held prisoner, "bear-smiths hammered out mighty sheets of iron and riveted them into armour".

THE PARALLEL OXFORD

Jordan College, where the story begins, seems to be a hybrid of several Oxford colleges. In *Northern Lights*, it is described as "the grandest and richest of all the colleges in Oxford", which points to Christ Church or New College. "You could walk from Oxford to Bristol in one direction and to London in the other, and never leave Jordanland"; this could be St John's, whose estates, it is said, stretch from Oxford to Cambridge. It becomes easier to place in *The Subtle Knife*. "That en't the Cornmarket? And this is the Broad. There's Balliol. And Bodley's Library down there." Pullman must be referring to his alma mater, Exeter College.

"SOMEWHERE OUT THERE IS THE ORIGIN OF ALL THE DUST, ALL THE DEATH, THE SIN, THE MISERY, THE DESTRUCTIVENESS IN THE WORLD. HUMAN BEINGS CAN'T SEE ANYTHING WITHOUT WANTING TO DESTROY IT, LYRA. THAT'S ORIGINAL SIN. AND I'M GOING TO DESTROY IT. DEATH IS GOING TO DIE."

DOUGLAS ADAMS
1952–2001

Douglas Adams was born in Cambridge in 1952. After school in Brentwood, Essex, he read English at St John's College, Cambridge, where he wrote and performed sketches for the comedy revue *Footlights*. Much of his early work was for BBC Radio, including collaborations with Graham Chapman of *Monty Python's Flying Circus*. With the first *Hitchhiker's Guide* radio series in 1978 he became a household name. Other novels followed, as well as work on behalf of endangered animals. In the 1990s, by now living in California, he co-founded a digital media company and produced *Starship Titanic*, a computer game, and the online guide h2g2. He died of a heart attack, aged just 49.

Other books by Douglas Adams include:

Dirk Gently's Holistic Detective Agency

The Meaning of Liff (with John Lloyd)

Last Chance to See... (with Mark Carwardine)

THE HITCHHIKER'S GUIDE TO THE GALAXY
DOUGLAS ADAMS
Publication date 1979

The glorious blend of mad humour, combining the everyday and the surreal with intelligent science fiction, has huge appeal far beyond the ranks of sci-fi junkies. The cult hit began life as a radio show in 1978, then developed into a best-selling four-part "trilogy" of novels – a stroke of contrary logic that characterises its tone.

▲ **Early edition**
Don't panic: it's just volume one of *The Hitchhiker's Guide*, in book form for humans.

FROM BABEL FISH TO THE ROLE OF TOWELS

The initial trilogy of four books, later compiled into a single volume, comprised *The Hitchhiker's Guide to the Galaxy*, *The Restaurant at the End of the Universe*, *Life, the Universe and Everything* and *So Long, and Thanks for all the Fish*. Adams later added a TV series, a fifth and sixth part, a computer game and a website. The idea for the books came to him in 1971, but "having had this thought I promptly fell asleep and forgot about it for six years." Like *Monty Python*, *The Hitchhiker's Guide* spawned a generation of catchphrase-quoting fans. Writing didn't come easy – Adams was notoriously bad with schedules: "I love deadlines. I like the whooshing sound they make as they fly by." To extract the fourth book, his editor checked into a hotel with him and stayed until Adams had finished.

Did you know?
In the 1970s Adams was a script editor on *Dr Who*. He wrote a number of the episodes that featured Tom Baker as the doctor, and is credited with introducing much of the fourth Doctor's surreal humour.

▲ **On the radio**
The series was written and recorded in episodes (or "fits", as they were called), and Adams always claimed that he made up the plot as he went along, not knowing what was going to happen from one show to the next. When production was at its most frantic, he would be in one room typing the script while the cast was recording in another.

THE STORY IN A NUTSHELL

At eight o'clock one Thursday morning, **Arthur Dent** wakes to find that his house is about to be demolished to make way for a bypass. His friend **Ford Prefect** reveals that he is an alien, a researcher for *The Hitchhiker's Guide to the Galaxy* (providing tips for the intergalactic traveller). He tells Arthur that the entire earth is about to be vaporised to make way for a hyperspatial express route. With just seconds to spare, Arthur and Ford hitch a ride on a spaceship. In deep space, they are picked up by an Improbability Drive spacecraft stolen by **Zaphod Beeblebrox**, two-headed ex-President of the Galaxy. On board, they meet paranoid android **Marvin** and Zaphod's astrophysicist girlfriend **Trillian**. Together they set off on a series on adventures in search of the answer to the "ultimate question" of life, the universe and everything.

"If you think that you've seen it all and you can prove it to me, then don't read this book. For everyone else, I'd say: read the book. It is an amazing ride."
Sanjeev Bhaskar

▲ **Zaphod Beeblebrox**
"If there's anything more important than my ego around, I want it caught and shot now."

▲ **Ford Prefect**
"You just come along with me and have a good time. The galaxy's a fun place. You'll need to have this fish in your ear."

▶ **Arthur Dent**
"This must be Thursday... I never could get the hang of Thursdays."

If you like this you may also enjoy books by:

Neil Gaiman
Rob Grant
Tom Holt
Terry Pratchett
Robert Rankin
Bob Shaw

"IN THOSE DAYS SPIRITS WERE BRAVE, THE STAKES WERE HIGH, MEN WERE REAL MEN, WOMEN WERE REAL WOMEN, AND SMALL FURRY CREATURES FROM ALPHA CENTAURI WERE REAL SMALL FURRY CREATURES FROM ALPHA CENTAURI."

CHARLOTTE BRONTE
1816–55

The third daughter of a clergyman, Charlotte lived in Haworth, a remote Yorkshire village. Her mother died young, and the children were raised strictly and in poverty by their father and an aunt. All five sisters were sent to boarding school, where harsh conditions destroyed the health of the two eldest girls, who died of TB in 1824. The surviving sisters, Charlotte, Emily and Anne, later worked as teachers and governesses. They jointly published a collection of poetry in 1846 under the male pseudonyms Currer, Ellis and Acton Bell. In 1847 Charlotte published *Jane Eyre* to immediate critical acclaim. Tragically, within 18 months Emily, Anne and their brother Branwell had all died. In 1854 Charlotte married her father's curate. She died a few months into her first pregnancy, aged 38.

Other books by Charlotte Brontë:

Villette

Shirley

The Professor

Mina Laury

JANE EYRE
CHARLOTTE BRONTE

Publication date 1847

This is one of the greatest, most passionate love stories in all English literature, the tale of a strong and uncomplicated woman who demands the right to love. *Jane Eyre* has intense emotion, vividly drawn characters, twists and turns of fate – and a romantic finale to satisfy even the hardest of hearts.

A WOMAN OF PRINCIPLE

In each of her novels Charlotte Brontë drew on her own life, haunted as it was by suffering and tragedy, and wove personal events into imaginative narratives of love, loss and hope. She insisted that women were the emotional equals of men – a controversial idea in the male-dominated society of her day. Jane herself seems an unlikely heroine: small, plain, downtrodden and looked down upon as a social inferior. But she is physically brave, morally steadfast and loyal. Despite a harsh, loveless upbringing, she insists on her right to love and to be loved in return, and it is this determination that has inspired the devotion of generations of readers. Jane is based very much on her creator's personality, but Charlotte went further, creating a whole cast of unforgettable characters and an atmospheric setting. With Jane, Brontë also gave birth to one of the emerging group of strong, independent heroines in English literature, and became one of our leading novelists.

▲ **Current edition**
Jane Eyre fulfilled its publisher's ambitions of success. It was an immediate hit on publication. It sold more copies than her sister Emily Brontë's *Wuthering Heights*, and her other sister Anne Brontë's *Agnes Grey*.

> " *Jane Eyre* is a thoroughly modern heroine, passionate, feisty, clever and brave. She is a truly good person, but never a prissy miss. "
> Lorraine Kelly

▲ **Strict schooling**
This mid-19th-century painting of a dame school, by Thomas Webster, from the Tate Gallery, shows an approach to classroom education typical of the period.

THE STORY IN A NUTSHELL

Jane Eyre, an orphan, is banished to Lowood, a harsh charity school, by her rich relations. Eight years later she is a governess at Thornfield, a remote country house, looking after a little girl, **Adèle**. Although Adèle's guardian, **Mr Rochester**, has a domineering and brusque manner, Jane falls in love with him, but he is expected to marry **Blanche Ingram**, a woman far superior to Jane in social class and wealth. When mysterious things start to happen in the house Jane proves herself honest and brave; she earns the respect and love of Mr Rochester, who asks her for her hand in marriage. Their wedding ceremony is dramatically interrupted by the arrival of a stranger claiming that Mr Rochester is already married. Mr Rochester drags the whole wedding party back to Thornfield and takes them up to a locked attic. Upon the revelation of a terrible secret, Jane is devastated and runs away. She is given sanctuary by the **Rivers** family. Has she any chance of happiness?

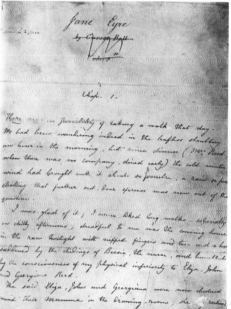

◀ **Author's manuscript**
The first page of the original manuscript of *Jane Eyre*, written in 1846, shows Charlotte Brontë writing under the male pseudonym Currer Bell, the initials corresponding to those of her own name.

▼ **On the small screen**
The BBC adaptation of *Jane Eyre*, made in 1983, starred Timothy Dalton as Mr Rochester and Zelah Clarke as Jane. It was directed by Julian Amyes.

◀ **On the big screen**
Joan Fontaine starred in the title role in 1944 opposite Orson Welles as Rochester. The most recent film version, in 1999, starred Charlotte Gainsbourg and William Hurt.

Did you know?

The most famous homage to Jane Eyre is Jean Rhys' *The Wide Sargasso Sea*, which tells the story of the first Mrs Rochester. The vivid descriptions of her childhood in the West Indies, her marriage and her subsequent descent into madness make this a modern classic.

"I AM NO BIRD AND NO NET ENSNARES ME. I AM A FREE HUMAN BEING WITH AN INDEPENDENT WILL."

C. S. LEWIS
1898–1963

Clive Staples Lewis (nicknamed "Jack") was born in Belfast. He had an older brother, Warnie, who was his best friend. They lived in Northern Ireland until their mother died when Jack was nine. Their father sent the boys to school in England, and later Jack went to Malvern College and then on to University College, Oxford. He fought in France during the First World War and when his friend Paddy Moore died he looked after Paddy's mother. When he started work at Magdalen College, Oxford he, Warnie and Mrs Moore moved in together, and during the Second World War they took in child evacuees. Lewis wrote a great deal about Christianity and was also a literary critic. His circle of Oxford friends, the Inklings, included J. R .R. Tolkien. In 1956 Lewis married an American divorcée, Joy Davidman.

Other Narnia titles by C. S. Lewis:

The Magician's Nephew

The Horse and His Boy

Prince Caspian

The Voyage of the Dawn Treader

The Silver Chair

The Last Battle

THE LION, THE WITCH AND THE WARDROBE
C. S. LEWIS

Publication date 1950

▲ **2000 edition**
To celebrate the 50th anniversary of the book a full-colour collector's edition was published.

This sparkling story has all the ingredients to stir a child's imagination. A hidden door to a magic land outside time, which is inhabited by creatures from myth and fairy tale, is discovered by four ordinary children who become the heroes of great adventures. For generations Narnia has meant a place of enchantment, and books to treasure.

THE TRUE SPIRIT OF NARNIA

Lewis was well known for his writing on Christianity, and *The Lion, the Witch and the Wardrobe* tells a story of sacrifice and return-to-life that recalls the crucifixion and resurrection of Jesus. Lewis probably put his own feelings about the seven Chronicles of Narnia into the penultimate title, *The Silver Chair*: "I'm on Aslan's side even if there isn't any Aslan to lead it. I'm going to live as like a Narnian as I can even if there isn't any Narnia…" Lewis's allegorical world was the inspiration for many other writers.

"When I realised that I was never going to be asked to tea by a half-man, half-goat, I knew that life was going to be a letdown."
Ronni Ancona

▲ **Into the wardrobe**
Lucy loves the feel of the fur coats that are hanging in the wardrobe, but is amazed to find that the racks of coats seem to go on forever.

▶ **Lucy meets Mr Tumnus, the faun**
Pauline Baynes illustrated all seven books in *The Chronicles of Narnia* series. Each book had a colour frontispiece like this one.

THE STORY IN A NUTSHELL

The four Pevensie children, **Peter**, **Susan**, **Edmund** and **Lucy** have been sent to live in a big old house in the country to escape the air-raids on London during the Second World War. While playing in the house one afternoon Lucy, the youngest of the children, climbs into a wardrobe and is amazed to find herself walking out of the back of it, into a whole new world covered in snow – Narnia. She meets **Mr Tumnus**, a faun, who tells her that Narnia is under a spell cast by the **White Witch**, and that Lucy is in great danger. The White Witch must keep humans out of Narnia because it has been foretold that she will lose her power when two Sons of Adam and two Daughters of Eve sit on the thrones of the castle Cair Paravel. Lucy finds she can return home through the wardrobe to everyday life as if she has never been away. Gradually, all four children enter the world of Narnia, but they do indeed find themselves in danger. Soon they realise that they cannot even trust each other. Only **Aslan**, the great lion and the true king of Narnia, has the power put all things right.

▲ **The White Witch**
Edmund was the first of the children to encounter the "Queen of Narnia". Pauline Baynes' illustrations were initially produced in black and white. Forty years later she coloured in the originals.

▶ **The map of Narnia**
Lewis planned the land of Narnia and its surrounding countries meticulously.

Did you know?

Although it was the first of the Narnia stories to be published, *The Lion, the Witch and the Wardrobe* is not the first book in the Narnia series. The first title is *The Magician's Nephew* in which the land of Narnia is created. In it Aslan sings the land of Narnia into being. Although all the books are complete in themselves, and can be read in any order, C.S. Lewis recommended that the books were read in order of events.

"I DON'T THINK IT WILL BE ANY GOOD TRYING TO GO BACK THROUGH THE WARDROBE DOOR... YOU WON'T GET INTO NARNIA AGAIN BY THAT ROUTE. YES, OF COURSE YOU'LL GET BACK TO NARNIA AGAIN SOME DAY... BUT DON'T GO TRYING TO USE THE SAME ROUTE TWICE. INDEED, DON'T TRY TO GET THERE AT ALL. IT'LL HAPPEN WHEN YOU'RE NOT LOOKING FOR IT."

LOUISA MAY ALCOTT
1832–88

Louisa May Alcott's father, Bronson Alcott, was a philosopher, teacher and a member of a transcendentalist group that included Ralph Waldo Emerson and Henry David Thoreau. He founded a utopian community called Fruitlands, and when Louisa was 11 the family lived on the commune for a year until it failed. Realising that her father was too impractical to provide for his family, Louisa began to take on financial responsibility. She started writing, but also worked as a teacher, a domestic and finally a nurse in the American Civil War in 1862, where she caught typhoid. Back at home she began writing dime novels and stories that appeared in *The Atlantic Monthly*. Louisa never married; her life's work was to look after her family. She died just two days after her father.

Other books by Louisa May Alcott:

Hospital Sketches
Rose in Bloom
Good Wives
Little Men
The Inheritance
Jo's Boys

LITTLE WOMEN
LOUISA MAY ALCOTT

Publication date 1868

The first American children's book to become a classic, *Little Women* was a hit from the day it was published. Girls could relate to the March sisters and their journey into womanhood: they were especially inspired by Jo, who rapidly became a role model for spirited young women everywhere.

▲ **First edition**
The title page of the first edition read *Little Women or Meg, Jo, Beth and Amy,* and was illustrated by Louisa's sister May.

Mr Alcott

Anna

May

Elizabeth

▲ **The Alcott family**
Louisa based the characters in *Little Women* on herself and her sisters: she was Jo; Meg March was Anna; Beth March was Elizabeth; and Amy March was based on May. Louisa was devoted to her idealistic, self-educated father, and wrote of him: "My father taught in the wise way which unfolds what lies in the child's nature, as a flower blooms, rather than crammed in, like a Strasbourg goose, with more than it could digest."

A CELEBRATION OF FAMILY VALUES

Louisa May Alcott drew on her own experiences of home and family to create her warm and loving fictional world. When she was first asked by a Boston publisher in 1867 to write a book for girls, she wasn't keen on the idea: "Never liked girls or knew many except my sisters." Three months later the finished story of *Little Women* was in proof. The first print run of the book sold out immediately and Louisa began to receive letters asking for more. Her readers wanted to know who the little women would marry. At first the proto-feminist Louisa was incensed by the idea of marrying off her characters, but she wrote a sequel, *Good Wives*. *Little Women* became popular as a family story that promoted American family values and the Protestant ethic. Young readers still respond to its simplicity, truth and good humour, while scholars regard it as a precursor of feminist literature.

The Alcott's home, Orchard House, in Concord, Massachusettts, US

"Louisa Alcott was telling girls they could do anything they wanted to: be actresses, writers, artists, wives or homebodies. That you could be a philosopher and still cook and look after people. And I thought that was wonderful."
Sandi Toksvig

▲ Jo's great sacrifice
This illustration was by Harold Copping for the 1912 edition of the book. Jo has her hair cut short, then sells it to raise money for her father, who is ill

STORY IN A NUTSHELL

There are four sisters in the March family: **Meg** is the rather vain beauty; **Beth** is delicate and musical; **Amy** is an artist; and tomboyish **Jo** (modelled on Alcott herself) wants to be an author. The sisters adore their mother, **Marmee**, who is cheerful even though the family is impoverished and the father is away from home as an army chaplain serving in the American Civil War. Rather than having an overall plot, the story of *Little Women* consists of a series of scenes in the family's life during the course of a year. The story begins as the Marches prepare to celebrate a spartan yet traditional family Christmas. Throughout the next 12 months the book follows the highs and lows of the events in the lives of the various family members, whose great strength of spirit binds them. The sisters get to know their neighbours, the **Laurences**, and as the story unfolds, the girls experience romance, ambitions realised, sickness and sacrifice, confronting them all with characteristic fortitude. The intimate details of the March family are set against the bedrock of family and home as the sisters develop into young women.

▲ Film poster
In the 1949 screen version the four sisters were all played by stars. June Allyson as Jo, Janet Leigh as Meg, Elizabeth Taylor as Amy and Margaret O'Brien as Beth. Mary Astor played Marmee.

▼ On the big screen
The 1994 version starred Winona Ryder as Jo, with Susan Sarandon playing Marmee.

"I HATE TO THINK I'VE GOT TO GROW UP, AND BE MISS MARCH AND WEAR LONG GOWNS... IT'S BAD ENOUGH TO BE A GIRL, ANYWAY, WHEN I LIKE BOYS' GAMES AND WORK AND MANNERS!"

"Life is my college. May I graduate well, and earn some honors."

Louisa May Alcott

THE LORD OF THE RINGS
J. R. R. TOLKIEN

Publication date 1954–55

John Ronald Reuel Tolkien, known as Ronald, was born in Bloemfontein in South Africa. In 1896 his father died; his mother took her sons back to England, but died herself in 1904. Taken in by a Catholic priest, Tolkien went to school in Birmingham. His talent for language earned him a first in English Language and Literature at Oxford, where he began to write. He fought in the Battle of the Somme as a second lieutenant in the Lancashire Fusiliers, but caught trench fever and was sent back to England. After an academic post at Leeds University, he was made professor of Anglo-Saxon, and later of English Literature, at Oxford University. He also worked on the *Oxford English Dictionary*, and is said to have compiled the 'W's.

Redefining the epic in modern literature, this sustained feat of imagination has had a colossal impact on writers, film-makers, song-writers, artists and even games developers. All have all been influenced by the huge scope of Tolkien's fantasy world. *The Lord of the Rings* is by far the best-selling novel of all time.

▲ **Current edition**
Ever since publication, *The Lord of the Rings* has been continuously in the bestseller lists.

THE MAGIC OF MIDDLE EARTH

The novel was first published in three parts: *The Fellowship of the Ring*, *The Two Towers* and *The Return of the King*. Critical reception varied from stinging sarcasm to triumphant praise, but the book-buying public all over the world voted with cash, giving Tolkien an incredible commercial success – over 150 million copies have so far been sold. *The Lord of the Rings* owed some of its popularity to the timing of publication, which coincided with radical social change in Britain and America. Tolkien's blend of Norse mythology, European fairy tales and Arthurian legend – complete with invented languages – found a welcome in 1960s alternative culture; *The Lord of the Rings* became "the hippy bible". For those of us under its spell, Middle Earth is a place of otherworldly escape, full of heroism, comradeship and good triumphing over evil.

One man cast a lingering spell of awe and wonder, of magical innocence overcoming evil, of simple courage conquering fear – he gave us the legend that will live forever in our minds.

J.R.R. Tolkien triumphed with the perception that a single dream is more powerful than a thousand realities.

Come to Middle-earth, a world beyond the furthest reaches of your imagination.

JRR Tolkien's
"the **Lord** of the **Rings**"

A SAUL ZAENTZ PRODUCTION
A RALPH BAKSHI FILM
J.R.R. Tolkien's "THE LORD OF THE RINGS" Music by LEONARD ROSENMAN
Screenplay by CHRIS CONKLING and PETER S. BEAGLE • Based on the novels of J.R.R. TOLKIEN
Produced by SAUL ZAENTZ • Directed by RALPH BAKSHI

DOLBY STEREO   A Fantasy Films Presentation   United Artists

◀ **Film poster**
The 1978 animated movie version of *The Lord of the Rings* was directed by Ralph Bakshi. Animation was the only way the book could be brought to the big screen until recent technological advances.

Did you know?
C. S. Lewis, author of the Narnia novels, was a friend of Tolkien. He was one of a group of friends, known as the Inklings, who read and commented on each other's manuscripts, including *The Lord of the Rings,* as they were written.

Other books by J. R. R. Tolkien include:

The Hobbit (Big Read no. 25)

Leaf by Niggle

The Adventures of Tom Bombadil

"Tolkien's epic isn't just a fabulous adventure. It's a tale that champions the values of long-lost ways of living and connects us to the very land that surrounds us."
Ray Mears

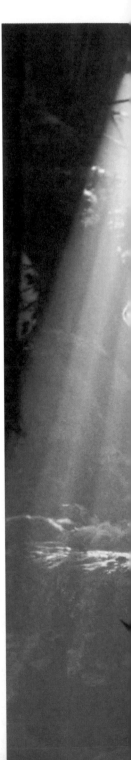

THE STORY IN A NUTSHELL

The hobbit **Frodo Baggins** has inherited a magic ring from his uncle **Bilbo** (hero of Tolkien's earlier work, *The Hobbit*), who had stolen it from a creature called **Gollum**. Frodo learns from the wizard **Gandalf** that this is "the one ring", with awesome power, forged in the mists of time by the evil **Sauron** then lost to history. Sauron is now aware of the ring's existence, and wants it back. It would give him the power to control – and ruin – Middle Earth; the only safe course is to destroy the ring by casting it into the inferno in the heart of Sauron's realm. Frodo (with fellow hobbits **Sam**, **Merry** and **Pippin**) sets off on the daunting journey, accompanied by a fellowship of elves, dwarves and men. But the insidious power of the ring splits the fellowship and Frodo continues with only Sam and the corrupt Gollum. Meanwhile, Middle Earth heads towards the ultimate battle between the forces of good and evil.

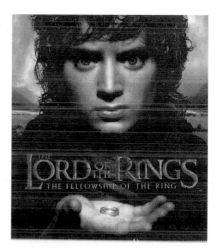

◀ ▼ **On the big screen**
The first part of Peter Jackson's trilogy of films was released in December 2001, to great acclaim and numerous awards. It stars Elijah Wood as Frodo and Ian McKellen as Gandalf, along with Liv Tyler, Viggo Mortensen, Sean Astin, Cate Blanchett, Billy Boyd, Dominic Monaghan and Christopher Lee. Shot in New Zealand, the trio of movies took 274 days of filming and a crew of more than 120 technicians to create Middle Earth.

"ONE RING TO RULE THEM ALL, ONE RING TO FIND THEM,
ONE RING TO BRING THEM ALL AND IN THE DARKNESS BIND THEM
IN THE LAND OF MORDOR WHERE THE SHADOWS LIE."

GEORGE ORWELL
1903–50

Eric Arthur Blair (Orwell's real name) was born in India, the son of a civil servant. After a scholarship to Eton he joined the Indian Imperial Police in Burma from 1922 to 1927. This inspired his first novel, *Burmese Days* (1934). Set on becoming a writer, he spent the next 15 years in poverty; the result was *Down and Out in Paris and London* (1933). In 1936 he fought in the Spanish Civil War against the fascists. During the Second World War he worked at the Ministry of Information, then became literary editor of *Tribune*. The devastating political allegory *Animal Farm* followed (1945). In 1946 he moved to the Scottish island of Jura, where he died of tuberculosis, aged 47.

Other books by George Orwell include:

Animal Farm (Big Read no. 46)

Down and Out in Paris and London

The Road to Wigan Pier

Homage to Catalonia

NINETEEN EIGHTY-FOUR
GEORGE ORWELL
Publication date 1949

A world of untruth and fear, where you are always watched, where thought can be a crime and where the clocks strike 13 – this is the world of *Nineteen Eighty-Four*, the realm of Big Brother, Newspeak, doublethink and unpersons. The date might have passed, but Orwell's chilling prophecy has lost none of its contemporary appeal.

THE VOICE OF CONSCIENCE

Orwell's nightmarish vision of an authoritarian, state-controlled future was also a grim warning against totalitarian regimes such as those of Nazi Germany and Soviet Russia. In *Nineteen Eighty-Four* he portrays a society based on brainwashing, systematic lying and deception and sucked dry of humanity. All thoughts and actions are controlled by the Party through extensive use of propaganda, surveillance (by Thought Police) and fear, themes later echoed in reality, particularly in Mao's China. The book is striking not only for its political message but also for its insight into the corruption of power and how people can be made to believe anything. The title is a rearrangement of the year it was written, 1948, suggesting that Orwell believed his vision was practically a reality.

▲ **First edition**
Publisher Frederick Warburg described *Nineteen Eighty-Four* as "...among the most terrifying books I have ever read". *The New York Times* said that "...it is probable that no other work has made us desire freedom more earnestly."

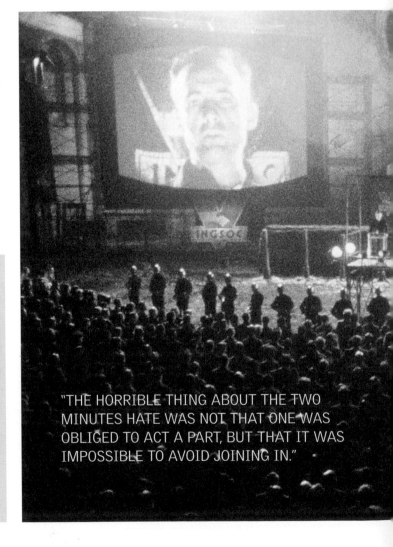

"THE HORRIBLE THING ABOUT THE TWO MINUTES HATE WAS NOT THAT ONE WAS OBLIGED TO ACT A PART, BUT THAT IT WAS IMPOSSIBLE TO AVOID JOINING IN."

FUTURE WORLDS

Future society has long been an inspiration for writers, who have in turn inspired film-makers. In particular, sci-fi author Philip K. Dick's intriguing and frightening futurescapes have been big money-earners. In *Do Androids Dream of Electric Sheep?* (adapted as the 1982 film *Blade Runner*) androids hide among humans, while in Steven Spielberg's *Minority Report* (2002) murder is punished in advance.

"It was a bright cold day in April

▲ On the big screen
Nineteen Eighty-Four has been made into a film twice (as "1984"). The 1955 adaptation, starring Edmond O'Brien and Michael Redgrave, softened the book's bleakest aspects to make it more palatable.

THE STORY IN A NUTSHELL

It is the year 1984, and the world is divided into three super-states, each permanently at war with one or both of the others. Britain has become Airstrip One, a province of Oceania, which is ruled by the Party as a repressive police state. Its "leader", Big Brother – the symbolic face of totalitarian power – stares down from a million posters. Anything that is beyond Party control, even the act of love, is considered subversive, and any dissidents in word, thought or deed are eliminated. **Winston Smith**, the novel's protagonist, works in the Ministry of Truth, where his job is to rewrite the past to fit the present, using a specially modified language known as Newspeak. But he is leading a double life, silently rebelling against the Party by keeping a secret diary as well as conducting an illicit love affair with **Julia**, a young woman who also works at the Ministry. So markedly does Winston see himself as the last bastion of humanity that the book's title was originally intended to be *The Last Man in Europe*. However, he is deceived into self-betrayal by a senior Party official, **O'Brien**, and is taken to the Ministry of Love (responsible for Law and Order), where he will be tortured in Room 101 in an attempt to remould him into a model citizen. Will he be able to resist? Or will he betray his beloved and learn to love Big Brother again?

WILL ECSTASY BE A CRIME

...IN THE TERRIFYING WORLD OF THE FUTURE?

Amazing wonders of tomorrow! Nothing like it ever filmed!

FROM THE STARTLING GEORGE ORWELL NOVEL!

"1984"

Edmond O'BRIEN · Michael REDGRAVE · Jan STERLING

Film poster from the 1955 film

◄ On the big screen
Neither of the two films of *Nineteen Eighty-Four* was wholly successful. However, Michael Radford's 1984 version was more faithful to the original. Its depressingly grey and nightmarish atmosphere is enhanced by the excellent performances of John Hurt as Winston and Richard Burton as party official O'Brien.

"Most people would choose Nineteen Eighty-Four because it is the most powerful and incisive analysis of political control ever written. I like it because it's got rats, torture and loads of sex in it."
Jo Brand

and the clocks were striking thirteen."

PRIDE AND PREJUDICE
JANE AUSTEN

Publication date 1813

JANE AUSTEN
1775–1817

Born in Steventon in Hampshire, where her father was vicar, Jane Austen was the seventh of eight children; her extended family played an important role throughout her life. Jane and her older sister Cassandra, to whom she was very close, went to boarding school, but otherwise Jane spent the first 25 years of her life in Steventon. She began writing as a teenager, although nothing was published until *Sense and Sensibility* in 1811. *Pride and Prejudice* began life as *First Impressions* in 1797, and was then rewritten and published in 1813. In 1801 the Austen family moved to Bath. After her father's death in 1805, his widow and daughters moved back to Hampshire. Jane resumed work, but recognition of her talent came slowly. She died in Winchester aged just 42 after a year-long debilitating illness, and was buried in the cathedral.

Other books by Jane Austen:

Persuasion
(Big Read no. 38)

Emma
(Big Read no. 40)

Mansfield Park

Sense and Sensibility

Northanger Abbey

"It is a truth universally acknowledged, that a single man in possession of a good fortune must be in want of a wife" – such is the premise of the brightest and most sparkling of all Jane Austen's novels. The five, single Bennet sisters compete for the attention of the most eligible men: but which is the most suitable, and for whom?

A MARRIAGE OF TRUE MINDS

Is it Elizabeth Bennet who is prejudiced and Fitzwilliam Darcy who is proud? A writer of such depth and subtlety as Jane Austen does not create one-dimensional figures, but characters that are complex, compelling and ambiguous. Austen reveals how the social whirl of the middle classes at the turn of the 19th century often hid real emotions: a truth that resonated for her contemporary audience. Elizabeth has her pride, and Darcy his prejudices, and during the dance of their courtship Elizabeth is revealed as an attractive, rather modern heroine, and Darcy a prototype of the brooding hero. But despite the later pastiches of popular romantic fiction, Austen was writing at a time when marriage for those of her class was a serious business, offering financial security and status, as well as romance. Austen's classic opening was an insight into a world of gossip and dalliance, and a statement of intent.

▲ **First edition**
Pride and Prejudice was originally published in three volumes. Jane Austen wrote to her sister Cassandra after its publication: "The work is rather too light... it wants shade... [to] form a contrast and bring the reader with increased delight to the playfulness of the general style."

▼ **Sudbury Hall**
This National Trust property at Ashbourne in Derbyshire was the location for Pemberley, Mr Darcy's home, in the most recent adaptation of *Pride and Prejudice*.

▶ **On the small screen**
Actor Colin Firth played Mr Darcy in the BBC's five-hour adaptation of *Pride and Prejudice*. The production was a huge success, particularly with female viewers – no more so than when Firth's Mr Darcy emerged dripping from the lake, a scene not in the novel, but a classic moment of television, if an irreverent one.

"FOLLIES AND NONSENSE, WHIMS AND INCON3I3TENCIES, DO DIVERT ME... BUT THESE, I SUPPOSE, ARE PRECISELY WHAT YOU ARE WITHOUT."

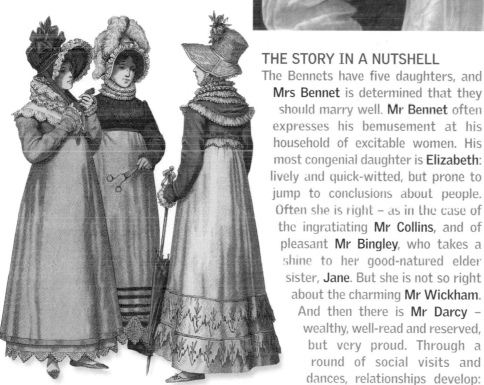

THE STORY IN A NUTSHELL

The Bennets have five daughters, and **Mrs Bennet** is determined that they should marry well. **Mr Bennet** often expresses his bemusement at his household of excitable women. His most congenial daughter is **Elizabeth**: lively and quick-witted, but prone to jump to conclusions about people. Often she is right – as in the case of the ingratiating **Mr Collins**, and of pleasant **Mr Bingley**, who takes a shine to her good-natured elder sister, **Jane**. But she is not so right about the charming **Mr Wickham**. And then there is **Mr Darcy** – wealthy, well-read and reserved, but very proud. Through a round of social visits and dances, relationships develop: Jane and Mr Bingley are doing nicely until someone turns him against her; Elizabeth rejects proposals from both Mr Collins and Mr Darcy, and then learns some uncomfortable truths about Mr Wickham; meanwhile the two youngest sisters, **Kitty** and **Lydia** party till they drop, and the reserved **Mary** struggles to find her place in the world. Elizabeth takes a trip to Derbyshire with her aunt and uncle, during which they discover another side to Mr Darcy. Then comes dramatic news: the headstrong Lydia has run off with Mr Wickham. What will become of them all?

"Pride and Prejudice is the DNA of all romantic comedy. It's an hilarious fairytale for cynics – an old-fashioned romance with a modern soul!"
Meera Syal

▲ **On the big screen**
Laurence Olivier and Greer Garson starred in the 1940 screen adaptation. Despite the fact that Garson was 36 and playing a 20-year-old girl, she was outstanding as Elizabeth Bennet, and the film was a huge hit for MGM.

DAPHNE DU MAURIER
1907–89

Daphne du Maurier was born in London into a wealthy theatrical family. Her first full-length novel, *The Loving Spirit*, was published in 1931. She married Major Frederick Browning in 1932 and had three children. Du Maurier spent most of the rest of her life living near the wild, rocky shores of Cornwall, which she loved passionately. From the 1930s she wrote prolifically, becoming a successful novelist and a household name. Many of her best-selling books and short stories, including *Rebecca*, were made into films. From the 1970s onwards she turned to writing plays, travel guides, biographies and her autobiography.

REBECCA
DAPHNE DU MAURIER

Publication date 1938

"Last night, I dreamt I went to Manderley again..." is one of the most memorable opening lines in fiction. With it, du Maurier sets the scene for a nightmarish tale of murder, obsession and jealousy. An international bestseller that has never gone out of print, *Rebecca* has enthralled readers with its masterful suspense, mystery and terror.

▲ **First edition**
Rebecca was published to rave reviews, although the similarities to Charlotte Brontë's *Jane Eyre* (1847) led to accusations of plagiarism, which were subsequently refuted.

A TALE OF TWO HEROINES

Unusually, Daphne du Maurier's novel has two strong heroines, although one is only a memory. The second Mrs de Winter is the central character but increasingly modern female readers have identified with the wild and now deceased Rebecca, Maxim de Winter's first wife. The Christian name of the narrator is never revealed. Du Maurier claimed that she couldn't think of one initially, and that later it became a technical challenge to complete the book without naming her. Adding to the novel's sense of mystery and expectation, this also emphasises the narrator's timidity and her struggle to find her own identity, living as she does in the shadow of Rebecca. There is more than a passing resemblance to du Maurier herself in the character of Mrs de Winter, and the author's experiences of certain relationships in her own life inspired the plot. However, she propelled the story beyond familiar realms, taking in murder, a devastating fire, a sinister servant in a house that seems to have a character of its own and a hint of the supernatural in the unquiet spirit of Rebecca. The ghostly heroine remains one of the most powerful female characters in fiction.

▲ **Dramatic landscape**
Du Maurier's association with Cornwall dated from her childhood. Many of her novels are set against this backdrop.

▲ **Du Maurier at Menabilly**
One day while out walking, du Maurier stumbled upon the beautiful old house of Menabilly near Fowey and vowed she would live there one day. In 1943, she leased the house from its owners and stayed until 1969. She wrote most of her romantic novels during this period and the house became, in part, the model for Manderley, the beautiful setting of *Rebecca*.

Did you know?
Alfred Hitchcock and producer David O. Selznick locked horns on their first collaboration, *Rebecca*. In the final scene, Selznick wanted smoke to form an 'R' in the sky. Hitchcock was appalled, and suggested a subtler image: the memory of Rebecca should go up in flames with an R embroidered on a bed pillow. Hitchcock won – and it proved to be a classic cinematic image.

"I'll never forget reading Rebecca and not realising until the end of the book that I didn't know the narrator's name. I can still feel the shivers going down my spine.**"**
Alan Titchmarsh

Other books by Daphne du Maurier include:

Jamaica Inn
Frenchman's Creek
Hungry Hill
My Cousin Rachel
The Birds
The Scapegoat
Don't Look Now

> "I PICTURED THEM ALL DOWN THERE IN THE BAY, AND THE LITTLE DARK HULL OF THE BOAT RISING SLOWLY TO THE SURFACE, SODDEN, DRIPPING, THE GRASS-GREEN SEAWEED AND SHELLS CLINGING TO HER SIDES."

"We can never go back to Manderley again. That much is certain..."

▲ On the big screen
Many well-known actresses auditioned for the part of the narrator in Rebecca, including Vivien Leigh, who had completed *Gone with the Wind* the year before, and Margaret Sullavan, who had starred in a radio adaptation of the book. However, the role was given to a relative newcomer, Joan Fontaine, seen above with Judith Anderson as the housekeeper.

THE STORY IN A NUTSHELL

The story opens with the narrator's dream of Manderley. She wakes to reality and her thoughts turn to the past. While working as a lady's companion in Monte Carlo, the narrator falls in love with a rich but mysterious widower, **Maxim de Winter**. He proposes and she is whisked away from her life of servitude and installed as the second **Mrs de Winter** at Manderley, Maxim's beloved family estate in Cornwall. She soon learns that Maxim's first wife, **Rebecca**, died in a boating accident, but her presence remains a powerful force in the house and the lives of those connected with it. The forbidding housekeeper, **Mrs Danvers**, is devoted to Rebecca's memory and is hostile to the new bride, making it clear that she thinks Maxim is still obsessed by his first wife. The atmosphere of the novel darkens like the stormy Cornish setting, and the tension at Manderley increases as the narrator imagines herself haunted by the dazzling, incomparable Rebecca. Then, one morning, the lives of the protagonists are turned upside down by a dramatic discovery, and the second Mrs de Winter realises that nothing in the world of Manderley was quite as she imagined. Her battle with Rebecca is only just beginning.

HARPER LEE
1926–

"Nelle" Harper Lee grew up in a small town in southwest Alabama. She studied law at Alabama University but withdrew six months before graduation. She moved to New York in 1949 and began to write while working as an airline reservation clerk. Friends, worried at her financial state, provided her with funds to quit her job and concentrate fully on her novel. Submitting her manuscript in 1957 to the publishers J. B. Lipincott, she was encouraged to rewrite it and *To Kill a Mockingbird* was finally published in 1960. The first editions carried an author photograph taken by her close friend and childhood neighbour Truman Capote, who is clearly the influence for the character of Dill in the novel. Apart from a few published essays, Lee has shunned the literary limelight and has not responded to the pleas to pick up a pen again – as the reclusive author says, "When you're at the top, there's only one way to go."

TO KILL A MOCKINGBIRD
HARPER LEE
Publication date 1960

A classic that grows in stature with the passing of time, *To Kill a Mockingbird* has become one of the best-loved of the great American novels. Through the eyes of children, it bears witness to racism and bigotry in the Deep South during the 1930s depression, and affirms the potential for one person to make a difference.

▲ **First edition**
The book was hailed by the *Chicago Tribune* as "A first novel of such rare excellence that it will no doubt make a great many readers slow down to relish more fully its simple distinction... A novel of strong contemporary national significance."

◄ **The Deep South**
Slave labour made cotton-growing lucrative in the southern US. An area known as the "Black Belt" – Georgia, Alabama, Mississippi and Louisiana – grew 80 per cent of the US cotton crop, tended by slaves. When *To Kill a Mockingbird* was published, the black civil rights movement was gathering strength and inspiration.

PRICKING THE NATION'S CONSCIENCE

Harper Lee's novel was certainly timely. When it was published in 1960, the black civil rights movement was gathering pace. While initial reviews were mixed, *To Kill a Mockingbird* sold more than 2.5 million copies in its first year, and won the 1961 Pulitzer Prize. Since then it has sold millions more. The 1962 film was highly acclaimed, winning an Academy Award for Gregory Peck as the incorruptible attorney Atticus Finch, and has served to fix the original work firmly in the minds and affections of readers worldwide. Harper Lee drew on parallels with her own upbringing in rural Alabama; she was the daughter of a respected attorney, Amasa Lee. Narrated by a young girl, the book uses the child's perspective to strike a lighter, more positive note despite a dark backdrop of racism and the struggle for equality. The narrator progresses from innocence to experience: she is helped by her father to understand that good and evil co-exist in people and that wisdom lies in appreciating one and understanding the other.

> "Above all this is the story of a decent man who stood up to an iniquitous system and made a difference – the perfect antidote for a cynical old hack like me."
> John Humphrys

Did you know?
Initially concerned that Gregory Peck's youthful good looks might hinder him in projecting the moral seriousness of Atticus Finch, Lee cast all doubts aside when she saw his performance. She presented Peck with her beloved father's gold watch, engraved "To Gregory from Harper".

CIVIL UNREST

Harper Lee grew up in a time of great civil unrest in America. One night she and her childhood companion, Truman Capote, persuaded an aunt to take them spying on a Ku Klux Klan rally. Cases such as the Scottsboro Trials, in which nine young black men were accused of assaulting

two white women in 1931, were widely reported during Lee's formative years. The jury ignored the evidence and, even after the judge went against public sentiment to protect the rights of the defendents, the men were sentenced to death. Although none of the men was actually executed, a number remained on Death Row for many years.

▼ **On the big screen**
The film was shot in black and white in 1962, at a time when other movies had switched to colour. Gregory Peck's Atticus was voted the most popular screen hero of all time in a national poll shortly after the actor's death.

THE STORY IN A NUTSHELL

The story covers three summers in the life of the narrator, **Scout Finch** (aged six at the start), and her older brother **Jem**. They live with their widower father, the attorney **Atticus Finch**, and their strong-minded black housekeeper, **Calpurnia**, in the small rural town of Maycomb, Alabama, in the 1930s. The two children and their friend next door, **Dill**, spend their summers getting into fights and light-hearted mischief, in particular investigating the recluse next door, the elusive **Boo Radley**. The harsh realities of life hit the children when their father is assigned to defend a Negro, **Tom Robinson**, accused of raping a white woman, **Mayella Ewell**. The Finch family is threatened by the passions aroused in the town, and the children find most support in the black community. Atticus faces down a lynch mob trying to attack the accused man, and in court provides compelling evidence of his innocence, proving Mayella a liar. However, the all-white jury convicts him. The girl's resentful father **Bob Ewell** then sets off a chain of events, at the end of which Scout learns one of the most important life-affirming lessons of her young life.

"MOCKINGBIRDS DON'T DO ONE THING
BUT MAKE MUSIC FOR US TO ENJOY...
THEY DON'T DO ONE THING BUT SING
THEIR HEARTS OUT. THAT'S WHY IT'S A
SIN TO KILL A MOCKINGBIRD."

LEO TOLSTOY
1828–1910

Count Leo Nikolayevich Tolstoy was born on his family's estate, Yasnaya Polyana, near Tula, 200 km from Moscow. He studied law and oriental languages, but did not graduate. In 1847 he inherited the estate and tried to lead an exemplary life as a farmer and ethical landowner. By 1850 he had given up, and went to fight in the Crimean War. After the war he moved to St Petersburg and started writing. In 1862 he married Sofya Behrs and moved back to Yasnaya Polyana, where they had 13 children. By this time he was already famous as an author, and the Tolstoys' home was a magnet for other writers. From the 1880s, however, he underwent a spiritual crisis, renouncing writing and material pleasures. He died of pneumonia at a railway station in 1910.

Other books by Leo Tolstoy include:

Anna Karenina
(Big Read no. 54)

Father Sergius

Childhood

Boyhood

Youth

Resurrection

WAR AND PEACE
LEO TOLSTOY

Publication date 1863–69

No other novel spans the breadth of human existence as *War and Peace* does. In telling the story of a group of Russian aristocrats during and after the Napoleonic wars of the early 19th century, Tolstoy's vast narrative dwells on affairs of the human heart as searchingly as it analyses the events of history.

▲ **First English edition**
"What an artist and what a psychologist! It seems to me there are some passages worthy of Shakespeare. I found myself crying out in admiration while reading." So wrote French writer Gustave Flaubert after reading *War and Peace*.

A MILESTONE IN WORLD LITERATURE

Although *War and Peace* only covers about 15 years of Russian history, it is a classic epic historical novel in terms of length, breadth and subject matter, and has been described by many as "the greatest novel ever written". Tolstoy gives perceptive and panoramic coverage to almost every aspect of humanity, and he confronts big issues: the possible causes of war, the role of women and the importance of family, the emancipation of Russian serfs in 1861 and the great debate of whether or not human beings act from free will. Such is Tolstoy's great attention to detail that readers can almost take part in the debates, smell the fear and confusion as Moscow burns, and feel the poignant atmosphere of a deathbed scene. Psychologically, too, Tolstoy examines the inner workings of his characters' minds, making them wholly believable and showing the reader in bleak human terms what the dire consequences of war can be.

MEETING OF DAZZLING MINDS

The Russian intelligentsia of the late 19th century was an extraordinarily creative milieu, both artistically and intellectually. Political discussion stirred thoughts of early socialism and Marxism. Famous authors met regularly and mixed with other luminaries. Tolstoy's house in Moscow frequently hosted soirées attended by, among others, Chekhov (with Tolstoy, above), Gorky and Bunin, and musicians such as Rachmaninov, Rimsky-Korsakov, Rubinstein and Scriabin.

▲ **Freemasons**
In *War and Peace*, Pierre Bezuhov meets a stranger who introduces him to the Order of Freemasons. Pierre is later invited to join the Order. He accepts the invitation, and Tolstoy describes the extraordinary initiation ceremony that Pierre experiences.

THE STORY IN A NUTSHELL

The setting is Moscow in 1805, and the city is buzzing with gossip. For some, the focus is the threat of invasion from Napoleon; for others, ordinary life continues in the form of social engagements and romances. The novel opens with a soirée at the residence of **Anna Pavlovna** in Petersburg, where talk is of the recent proclamation of **Napoleon** as Emperor. The cream of Petersburg society turn up at this party to parade themselves and their knowledge on general matters of the day, including politics. The three principal characters, **Pierre Bezuhov**, **Andrei Bolkonsky** and **Natasha Rostova** are first introduced at the party. Their actions are followed as they progress from youthful uncertainties towards a more mature view of life. Both Pierre

▲ **On the big screen**
Directed by King Vidor in 1956, this US screen version of *War and Peace* starred Henry Fonda as Pierre Bezuhov, Audrey Hepburn as Natasha Rostova and her husband Mel Ferrer as Prince Andrei Bolkonsky.

The French Invasion of Moscow depicted in 1812

and Andrei go to fight in the war, and both become caught in unhappy marriages; as they and the other characters seek meaning in life, the reader follows their fates through analytical discussions, the battle scenes of Austerlitz and Borodino, births, deaths, love affairs and family business. In the aftermath of the war, those who are left must follow new paths, but will they finally find happiness?

Cathedral in Moscow, the city at the hub of the novel

"War and Peace is about everything that counts: love and battle, terror and desire, life and death. It's a book that you don't just read, you live." Simon Schama

"IN HISTORICAL EVENTS GREAT MEN – SO-CALLED – ARE BUT LABELS SERVING TO GIVE A NAME TO THE EVENT, AND LIKE LABELS THEY HAVE THE LEAST POSSIBLE CONNEXION WITH THE EVENT ITSELF."

Did you know?
Tolstoy had a thirst for knowledge and great energy. He had 22,000 books, the largest collection in Russia at the time. He studied 13 languages, including ancient Greek and Hebrew, and learned Japanese aged 80. Believing everyone needed a manual skill, he mastered bootmaking.

THE WIND IN THE WILLOWS
KENNETH GRAHAME

Publication date 1908

KENNETH GRAHAME
1859–1932

Grahame was born in Edinburgh, the son of an alcoholic father. When he was four years old his mother died, and he was sent with his siblings to live with their grandmother in Berkshire. The house, set in a large garden by the River Thames, would provide the inspiration for *The Wind in the Willows*. When Grahame left school, he wanted to go to Oxford University, but as there was no money he went to work at the Bank of England. He was very successful and became Secretary of the bank at the age of 38. He began writing in his spare time and *The Wind in the Willows* grew out of bedtime stories and, later, letters to his only son Alastair, whom he affectionately nicknamed Mouse. Tragically, Alastair committed suicide two days before his 20th birthday. After this Grahame became virtually a recluse, living quietly by the Thames until his death.

Other books by Kenneth Grahame:

Pagan Papers
The Golden Age
Dream Days

With its huge appeal to adults as well as children, *The Wind in the Willows* is a lyrical celebration of the simple joys of life – home, good food, friendship, the beauties of nature – set in a timeless pastoral landscape. And, like all the best fairy tales, it has hints of darkness amid the dappled sunlight.

▲ **First edition**
Arnold Bennett reviewed the book in *Punch* as "an urbane exercise in irony at the expense of the English character."

THE CHARM OF ECCENTRICITY

Toad

Grahame's talking animals are endearingly eccentric Edwardian gentlemen in Savile Row suits whose conversations are peppered with "complete ass!" and "you fellows". But while timid Mole, convivial Rat and haughty Toad set off on their jolly adventures, the tale explores a deeper dimension: the fear of change and social upheaval. Toad might have the trappings of the upper classes, but he really represents the aspirational middle class as he shows off his wealth only to find Toad Hall overrun by interlopers. Then there is the danger from another new-fangled, noisy invention: the motor car. The characters yearn for a quiet life that continues unchanged forever, like the wind through the willows.

"THEY RECALLED THE LANGUOROUS SIESTA OF HOT MID DAY, DEEP IN GREEN UNDERGROWTH, THE SUN STRIKING THROUGH IN TINY GOLDEN SHAFTS AND SPOTS; THE BOATING AND BATHING OF THE AFTERNOON, THE RAMBLES ALONG DUSTY LANES AND THROUGH YELLOW CORNFIELDS; AND THE LONG COOL EVENING AT LAST, WHEN SO MANY THREADS WERE GATHERED UP, SO MANY FRIENDSHIPS ROUNDED, AND SO MANY ADVENTURES PLANNED FOR THE MORROW."

Messing about in a boat

▲ The illustrations
E. H. Shepard was asked to illustrate a new edition of *The Wind in the Willows* in 1930. His map shows the divide: Toad Hall on one side, Wild Wood on the other.

Did you know?

A. A. Milne adapted *The Wind in the Willows* for the stage, under the title *Toad of Toad Hall*. It was first performed at the Lyric Theatre in London in 1929 and included songs by H. Fraser-Simpson. For many years it was performed on the London stage every Christmas

THE STORY IN A NUTSHELL

Mole ventures out of his underground home on a beautiful spring day and discovers the River for the first time. He meets **Rat**, who introduces him to the pleasures of "messing about in boats". Some time later he meets **Toad**, who lives in the splendid Toad Hall, and is renovating a gypsy caravan to take on the open road. But as soon as he sees a motor-car, Toad is smitten. While Toad is occupied with acquiring – and crashing – cars, winter comes and Mole ventures into the Wild Wood. Rat goes to find him and they both get lost in the snow. They find **Badger**'s house and stay with him overnight. On the way back to the River Bank they stop off at Mole's old home. They are serenaded by some field mice singing Yuletide carols and all have a jolly meal together. When summer comes again, Rat, Mole and Badger decide that something must be done about Toad's wild ways. They try to keep him under surveillance, but he escapes and steals a car. He is arrested and jailed in a dungeon, eventually escaping dressed as a washerwoman. He makes his way back to Toad Hall to find it has been taken over by an army of stoats, weasels and ferrets from the Wild Wood. Badger, Toad, Rat and Mole use an underground passage in an attempt to surprise the Wild Wooders and win back Toad Hall.

Toad descends the steps of Toad Hall

"A book that manages to incorporate some of the best set comedic pieces of the 20th century."
Bill Oddie

A. A. MILNE
1882 – 1956

Alan Alexander Milne was born in London, the third son of two schoolteachers. After an idyllic childhood, he read mathematics at Cambridge, and then worked for *Punch*, writing verses and sketches. He married Dorothy de Selincourt in 1913, and in 1920 his only child, Christopher Robin, was born. The boy became an inspiration, and Milne began to write for children. In 1924 he published a book of verse, *When We Were Very Young*, illustrated by E. H. Shepard, who had been an illustrator for *Punch*. This was followed by *Winnie the Pooh*. He also wrote a number of plays and in fact was a very successful writer of plays and novels in the 1920s and 1930s. He wished that he could have been remembered for these. But *Winnie the Pooh* took over both his life and his reputation.

Other books by A. A. Milne include:

When We Were Very Young

The House at Pooh Corner

Now We Are Six

WINNIE THE POOH
A. A. MILNE
Publication date 1926

The enduring popularity of *Winnie the Pooh* must be at least partly due to the fact that the lovable bear's fans do not desert him when they reach adulthood. While younger readers laugh at the nonsense verse and comical antics, the poignancy of Milne's narrative endures for much older devotees.

THE WISDOM OF POOH

Generations of readers have been charmed by the stout little bear and his adventures. Milne introduced a cast of characters with very human traits that were instantly recognisable and utterly appealing. Pooh is greedy (though always well meaning), while Eeyore is gloomy and self-pitying. Owl is pompous, Piglet is anxious (but tries hard to be brave), Rabbit is clever and organized. Kanga is gentle and motherly, and little Roo is a mischievous baby. Several books have been written about the "wisdom of Pooh", from *The Tao of Pooh* to *Pooh and the Philosophers*.

> "You have Winnie the Pooh days where you're happy being a bit stupid."
> Phill Jupitus

▲ **First edition**
Not everyone was totally enchanted with *Winnie the Pooh*. Dorothy Parker called the author "Mr. A. A. ('Whimsy-the-Pooh') Milne". Milne replied that no children's author would ever say to his publisher, "Don't bother about the children, Mrs Parker will love it."

▲ **The real Hundred Aker Wood**
Ashdown Forest in East Sussex was the setting for Pooh's adventures (Milne and his family lived nearby). There is a memorial in the forest to both Milne and the book's illustrator E. H. Shepard.

THE STORY IN A NUTSHELL

"Here is Edward Bear, coming downstairs now, bump, bump, bump, on the back of his head behind **Christopher Robin.**" By the time he gets to the bottom of the stairs, Edward Bear is introduced to the reader as "**Winnie the Pooh**". There are ten stories in all, each with its own heading that summarises what is going to happen. "We are introduced to Winnie the Pooh and some Bees, and the stories begin". We follow the little bear on his journeys around the Hundred Aker Wood as he gets into all sorts of scrapes. Pooh gets stuck in **Rabbit's** doorway (because he's eaten too much), and then goes off on an adventure with his friend, **Piglet**. On the way Pooh meets all his other friends, **Eeyore, Owl, Kanga** and her baby **Roo** and, of course, **Christopher Robin.** They attempt to climb some trees, search for a tail for Eeyore, try to trap a heffalump, celebrate Eeyore's birthday, sing some songs and even go on an "exposition" to the North Pole – and all this before bedtime!

▲ **Original illustrations**
The characters are brought to life by the line and wash illustrations by E. H. Shepard. Winnie himself is based on Shepard's son's own bear.

Did you know?

Although E. H. Shephard is best-known as "the man who drew Pooh", he illustrated many books and magazines – including *The Wind in the Willows* and *Punch*. He also painted Pooh and his honeypot in oils, a work now housed in a museum in Canada.

▶ **Winnie the Pooh's best friend**
Throughout his life Christopher Robin Milne, shown here with his father, was associated with the character in his father's books. Christopher, who had mixed feelings about his fame, died in 1996.

◀ **Winnie's wood**
The endpapers to the classic Winnie the Pooh books show a map, by E. H. Shepard, to help readers find their way around the Hundred Aker Wood.

▼ **Christopher Robin's toys**
The real Pooh bear, Kanga, Tigger, Piglet and Eeyore have long since left Hundred Aker Wood. They now live in the New York Public Library.

EMILY BRONTE
1818–48

The fourth daughter of a clergyman, Emily lived with her brother and sisters in the parsonage at Haworth, a remote Yorkshire village. Their mother died young and the children were reared by their father and an aunt. After the two eldest girls died and the next eldest, Charlotte, went away to school Emily became very close to her younger sister, Anne. They invented a fantastic world, Gondal, which they wrote about in poetry and prose.

Emily trained as a teacher, but later chose to stay at home, roaming the moors and writing poetry. Charlotte discovered Emily's poems and persuaded her to publish them jointly with some by Anne and herself, in 1846 (using the pseudonyms Acton, Currer and Ellis Bell). Reviews were good, and Emily was spurred to write *Wuthering Heights*. Tragically, her health deteriorated. Just one year and five days after her book was published, she died of tuberculosis at the age of 30.

WUTHERING HEIGHTS
EMILY BRONTE

Publication date 1847

From the pen of a reclusive, intensely private and unworldly woman came a complex tale of wild passion, unnatural obsession, enduring love and bitter hatred. *Wuthering Heights* is the ultimate romance – but one that is dark, troubling and deeply tragic, that draws the reader into a strange and compelling world.

A WILD AND RESTLESS SPIRIT

Emily Brontë's only novel seems born of a fevered and poetic imagination. She creates characters that fit no literary pattern and observe no convention. The book centres on the passion between the wayward Catherine and the dark, primal figure of Heathcliff – an intensity that lingers even after Catherine's death. It was this that shocked contemporary critics who, while acknowledging the power of Brontë's writing, deemed it

The Haworth Parsonage where the Brontës lived

strange, wild and, at worst, immoral. Some readers claimed that certain scenes in the book caused them to have sleepless nights. Emily's own sister, Charlotte, tried to account for such an unsettling work; in her preface to the 1850 edition she claimed that Emily's enormous creative gift controlled her, and that her writing took on a will of its own. Whatever the truth of Emily's inspiration, she has left a classic that is unique in English literature.

◄ **The literary sisters**
This famous portrait of the Brontë sisters, believed to date from 1834, was painted by their brother Branwell. Emily is in the centre, with Anne on the left and Charlotte on the right.

Did you know?
The publisher of *Wuthering Heights* and Anne Brontë's novel *Agnes Grey*, Thomas Cautley Newby, insisted that Emily and Anne help pay towards the costs, and then delayed publication. When Charlotte's *Jane Eyre* became a bestseller for another publisher, he rushed out the two novels – trying, in some editions, to pretend they were written by "the author of *Jane Eyre*".

▲ **Current edition**
In 1848 one newspaper critic wrote, "The women in the book are of a strange, fiendish, angelic, nature, tantalizing and terrible."

"This is a book about the passion we dream of feeling ripped apart by and the madness we're frightened we'd get."
Alistair McGowan

"I should be myself again were I once

"BE WITH ME ALWAYS – TAKE ANY FORM – DRIVE ME MAD! ONLY DO NOT LEAVE ME IN THE ABYSS, WHERE I CANNOT FIND YOU! OH GOD! IT IS UNUTTERABLE! I CANNOT LIVE WITHOUT MY LIFE! I CANNOT LIVE WITHOUT MY SOUL!"

▼ On the big screen
Wuthering Heights is famously difficult to adapt for the silver screen because, without the mediating voices of the narrators Ellen and Lockwood, the plot appears impossibly melodramatic. The first known dramatisation was a 1920 silent movie, but the most famous version is the 1939 film (shown here) starring Laurence Olivier as Heathcliff and Merle Oberon as the tragic, haunted Catherine.

THE STORY IN A NUTSHELL
Twenty years before the novel opens, **Mr Earnshaw** of Wuthering Heights, a farmhouse set high on the wild Yorkshire moors, brings home a young ragamuffin named **Heathcliff**. Earnshaw's young daughter **Catherine** instinctively loves him, and he her, but her brother **Hindley** hates him. When old Earnshaw dies, Hindley's resentment of Heathcliff grows, while Catherine's passionate attachment to the foundling deepens. On a trip across the moor, Heathcliff and Catherine meet **Edgar** and **Isabella Linton** of Thrushcross Grange, the grand neighbouring house, and are introduced to a world of society and riches. Catherine's subsequent betrayal of Heathcliff sets off a chain of events that seals the fate of all the protagonists, as Heathcliff's desperation and bitterness leads him to visit a terrible vengeance on both families. His brooding presence hangs over the houses for more than 20 years as the next generation struggle to escape the legacy of the past. We learn of this history though the narration of **Ellen**, the Earnshaw's servant, and **Lockwood**, the new tenant of the Grange, as the action moves towards the present. Will nothing stop the tragic cycle of events?

I am torn with *Desire* – tortured by hate!

SAMUEL GOLDWYN presents

WUTHERING HEIGHTS

starring
MERLE OBERON · LAURENCE OLIVIER · DAVID NIVEN
with FLORA ROBSON · DONALD CRISP · GERALDINE FITZGERALD · Released thru UNITED ARTISTS
Directed by WILLIAM WYLER

Film poster, 1939

among the heather on those hills."

HARRY POTTER AND THE PHI...
THE CHAMBER OF SECRETS HARRY P...
THE HOBBIT TESS OF THE D'URBERVI...
OWEN MEANY THE GRAPES OF W...
THE STORY OF TRACY BEAKER ON...
PILLARS OF THE EARTH DAVID COPP...
FACTORY TREASURE ISLAND A TOW...
ANNE OF GREEN GABLES WATERSHIP...
OF MONTE CRISTO BRIDESHEAD R...
CAROL FAR FROM THE MADDING C...
SHELL SEEKERS THE SECRET GARDEN
KARENINA A SUITABLE BOY THE B...
BEAUTY ARTEMIS FOWL CRIME AND...
MEMOIRS OF A GEISHA A TALE OF TW...
MAGIC FARAWAY TREE THE MAGUS
THE FLIES PERFUME THE RAGGED TR...
WATCH MATILDA BRIDGET JONES'S...
N WHITE ULYSSES BLEAK HOUSE...
CASTLE HOLES GORMENGHAST TH...
BRAVE NEW WORLD COLD COMFO...
GODFATHER THE CLAN OF THE CA...
ALCHEMIST KATHERINE KANE AND A...
LIES IN LOVE THE PRINCESS DIAR...

SOPHER'S STONE HARRY POTTER AND
TER AND THE PRISONER OF AZKABAN
S MIDDLEMARCH A PRAYER FOR
LICE'S ADVENTURES IN WONDERLAND
DRED YEARS OF SOLITUDE THE
IELD CHARLIE AND THE CHOCOLATE
KE ALICE PERSUASION DUNE EMMA
WN THE GREAT GATSBY THE COUNT
TED ANIMAL FARM A CHRISTMAS
D GOODNIGHT MISTER TOM THE
F MICE AND MEN THE STAND ANNA
VALLOWS AND AMAZONS BLACK
NISHMENT NOUGHTS AND CROSSES
CITIES THE THORN BIRDS MORT THE
D OMENS GUARDS! GUARDS! LORD OF
SERED PHILANTHROPISTS NIGHT
RY THE SECRET HISTORY THE WOMAN
E ACT THE TWITS I CAPTURE THE
OF SMALL THINGS VICKY ANGEL
RM MAGICIAN ON THE ROAD THE
THE COLOUR OF MAGIC THE
LOVE IN THE TIME OF CHOLERA
MIDNIGHT'S CHILDREN

22 HARRY POTTER AND THE PHILOSOPHER'S STONE
J. K. ROWLING

Publication date 1997

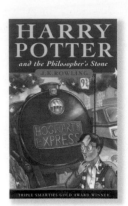

Current edition

Who but a wizard could have predicted the mega success of Harry Potter? The first meeting with Harry skilfully combines favourite elements from classic tales – an outcast hero, evil conquered by goodness, a fantastically imagined world – all infused with humour and, of course, magic.

J. K. ROWLING
See page 26

THE BIRTH OF A PHENOMENON

This first novel by the unknown J. K. Rowling (she was advised to use her initials rather than her first name in order to attract boy readers) was published quietly in June 1997 with a hardback print-run of only 500 copies. But the blend of fantasy, school story and thriller with modern humour and old-fashioned morality soon cast its spell over millions. That October it won the Smarties Prize – chosen by children – and the book took off. The single parent who wrote in a cafe found her fortunes magically changed.

▼▲ Cat and mouse
"Transfiguration" plays a key role in Rowling's magic world. The tabby cat turns out to be Professor McGonagall, while a mouse is turned into a snuffbox.

"DEAR MR POTTER, WE ARE PLEASED TO INFORM YOU THAT YOU HAVE A PLACE AT HOGWARTS SCHOOL OF WITCHCRAFT AND WIZARDRY. TERM BEGINS ON 1 SEPTEMBER. WE AWAIT YOUR OWL BY NO LATER THAN 31 JULY. YOURS SINCERELY, MINERVA MCGONAGALL DEPUTY HEADMISTRESS."

9¾
HOGWARTS EXPRESS
London King's Cross

▶ King's Cross
The Hogwarts Express leaves from Platform 9¾ at King's Cross station in London, which is reached through an apparently solid barrier.

THE STORY IN A NUTSHELL

Orphaned **Harry** lives a horrible life with his odious uncle and aunt and spoilt cousin. But on his 11th birthday a letter arrives offering a place at Hogwarts School of Witchcraft and Wizardry. To his amazement, Harry finds he has wizard blood and is already a hero of the wizarding world, having survived an attack that killed his parents and left a lightning-shaped scar on his forehead. At Hogwarts, he makes friends with **Ron Weasley** and **Hermione Granger** and studies magic under wise headmaster **Albus Dumbledore** – skills that can easily go awry when you're learning. Then there is Quidditch, a sport played on flying brooms, at which Harry excels. But strange events threaten the school and, with Ron and Hermione's help, Harry investigates, and begins to discover his own powers.

Parchment was used during Harry's exams

"This is a story full of surprises and jokes; comparisons with Dahl are, this time, justified.**"**

The Sunday Times

Did you know?

J. K. Rowling was warned by her publishers that: "You never make any money out of children's books, Jo." She proved them wrong by swiftly becoming one of the UK's richest women. And she is not alone in making money out of Harry: a signed first edition of *Harry Potter and the Philosopher's Stone* has sold for £13,500. Even a dog-eared, unsigned first edition copy fetched an impressive £1,250 at auction.

34027

THE HOGWARTS EXPRESS

23 HARRY POTTER AND THE CHAMBER OF SECRETS
J. K. ROWLING

J. K. ROWLING
See page 26

Publication date 1998

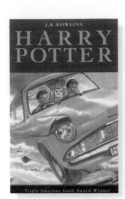

Current edition

Harry Potter was already a star when this second story was published – readers all over the world were dying to know what the boy wizard would do next. This adventure picks up where the last left off, and triumphantly keeps up the pace of thrills and spells.

THINGS CAN ONLY GET BETTER

J. K. Rowling had already written this book by the time the first was published. Even so, like many other authors, she found the second novel very hard to write – and was worried that it wouldn't live up to readers' expectations. Had she already experienced the accolades for the first book, and known just how many readers there were and how much they expected, she might never have done it! In fact, the second book delighted readers with more insights into the wizarding world, revealing both the lighter side of life and the dark forces facing Harry and his friends.

Revising for exams, Harry turns a pair of rabbits into slippers

▲ **Mythical characters**
Throughout the books, Rowling bases some of her characters on mythical creatures. In *Harry Potter and the Chamber of Secrets*, the basilisk appears. In *Harry Potter and the Philosopher's Stone*, Fluffy, the three-headed dog, is based upon Cerberus, depicted here by William Blake.

THE STORY IN A NUTSHELL

Harry Potter has spent the summer holidays with the awful **Dursley**s and can't wait to return to Hogwarts School, but something, or someone, is trying to stop him. He and **Ron** have to hurry back to school in a flying car. They are soon back to lessons and Quidditch, but something horrible and dangerous is happening, as a petrifying curse strikes first the school cat and then some pupils, including Ron's sister **Ginny**. Harry has to find out who is practising such terrifying magic and stop them. He enters the Chamber of Secrets and confronts the terrible presence within. Only his great magic and **Professor Dumbledore** can protect him.

"Harry Potter and the Chamber of Secrets, unlike many sequels, is as good as its predecessor... Hogwarts is a creation of genius."

The Times Literary Supplement

▶ **Harry's gift**
Harry is discovered to be a "parselmouth" – he can talk to snakes. He had spoken to a boa constrictor in *The Philosopher's Stone*, when he was visiting London Zoo with the Dursleys, but no one saw him. In this book, the experience is a much more public affair.

HARRY POTTER AND THE PRISONER OF AZKABAN

J. K. ROWLING

24

Publication date 1999

With the confidence of having created a literary legend, J. K. Rowling showed true magic with this darker, more adult and more terrifying tale. In it Harry rejoins the battle against Voldemort to prove that love can conquer death. But who is friend and who is foe?

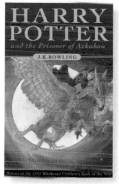

Current edition

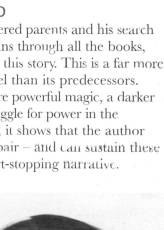

J. K. ROWLING
See page 26

ENTERING A DARKER WORLD

Harry's longing for his murdered parents and his search for truth is a theme that runs through all the books, but it reaches a new intensity in this story. This is a far more sophisticated and complex novel than its predecessors. Rowling introduces new and more powerful magic, a darker world of Dementors and the struggle for power in the wizarding world. But most of all, it shows that the author understands grief, rage and despair – and can sustain these emotions within a typically heart-stopping narrative.

◀ A dark threat
When Harry runs away in the middle of the night, he thinks he sees a large black creature in the shadows of Magnolia Crescent. Malevolent or benign, it is watching his every move

THE STORY IN A NUTSHELL

Harry has had enough of the ghastly **Dursley**s. He runs away and is picked up by a magical bus that transports him to Diagon Alley, the shopping centre of the wizarding world. Here, he has two exciting weeks of freedom before school begins. But the Dark Forces are closing in, and on the school train he has his first encounter with the fearsome Dementors. Even school isn't safe: there is a mass murderer on the loose and the Dementors have been brought in to find him. **Dumbledore** has to use all his powers to protect his pupils. Meanwhile, Harry meets **Sirius Black**, his mysterious godfather.

"AT LEAST A HUNDRED DEMENTORS, THEIR HIDDEN FACES POINTING UP AT HIM, WERE STANDING BELOW. IT WAS AS THOUGH FREEZING WATER WAS RISING IN HIS CHEST, CUTTING AT HIS INSIDES. AND THEN HE HEARD IT AGAIN... SOMEONE WAS SCREAMING, SCREAMING INSIDE HIS HEAD."

▲ Teaching aids
Professor Sybill Trelawney is teacher of Divination at Hogwarts, and uses a map of the hand, a crystal ball and tea leaves, among other props, in her lessons. She is very dramatic, prone to making dark predictions, and tells Harry that he has the shortest lifeline she has ever seen.

Did you know?
After *The Prisoner of Azkaban* won Rowling the Smarties Book Prize for children's fiction for the third year running, she asked for future Harry Potter books not to be considered for the award.

THE HOBBIT
J. R. R. TOLKIEN

Publication date 1937

J. R. R. TOLKIEN
See page 38

This is the story that gave birth to a legend. In it, Bilbo Baggins is forced to escape his cosy world and enter another – wilder, stranger and darker than he could imagine. *The Hobbit* is a stirring tale of a little person's journey from comfort to a grander, more heroic destiny, and it sets the scene for *The Lord of the Rings*.

▲ **First edition**
Tolkien designed the original dust jacket of *The Hobbit*, published by George Allen and Unwin in 1937, and was meticulous about its colour scheme. The runes around the border read: "The Hobbit or There and Back Again, being the record of a year's journey made by Bilbo Baggins; compiled from his memoirs by J. R. R. Tolkien and published by George Allen & Unwin."

◄ **A terrible foe**
Bilbo encounters Smaug when he creeps terrified into the dragon's lair. Smaug has become complacent, believing himself invulnerable. The little hobbit talks to the dragon, learns his secret and escapes with his life.

If you like this you may also enjoy books by:

Terry Brooks
David Eddings
Robert Jordan
Guy Gavriel Kay
Katharine Kerr
C. S. Lewis
Philip Pullman

THE FIRST GLIMPSE OF AN IMAGINARY REALM

Marking English exam papers at Oxford one day, Professor J. R. R. Tolkien came across a blank page. An impulse inspired him to write on it, "In a hole in the ground there lived a hobbit." His impulse grew into a story that he told his children, called "The Hobbit". When a publisher saw a typescript, she asked Tolkien to finish the story. The chairman of the publishers, Stanley Unwin, showed the book to his ten-year-old son, Rayner, who gave it his enthusiastic approval. Millions of other children and adults are grateful. With *The Hobbit* and *The Lord of the Rings* trilogy, Tolkien created not just classics, but a magical, fully realised and populated realm, Middle Earth – one of English literature's finest achievements. *The Hobbit* was our first glimpse into this world – and we liked what we saw.

Lord Snowdon photographed J. R. R. Tolkien amid the nature that inspired him

THE STORY IN A NUTSHELL

Bilbo Baggins, an unadventurous hobbit by nature, is instructed by the wizard **Gandalf** to join an expedition. The reluctant hobbit sets out with 13 dwarves, and Gandalf as guide, to reclaim the dwarves' treasure. It was stolen from them by the dragon **Smaug**, who long ago drove all the dwarves from their home, the Lonely Mountain. A perilous journey follows, in which the group are captured by trolls and goblins, must answer riddles and flee from giant wolves. Along the way, Bilbo finds a ring that a creature called **Gollum** has lost; when he puts it on, he becomes invisible. The travellers continue their odyssey, but the dangers never end. Finally they reach Lake-Town, close to the Lonely Mountain. Bilbo sneaks into the dragon's lair, escaping with a cup. On a second attempt, the hobbit discovers Smaug's weak spot. The dragon takes its revenge by burning up Lake-Town, but the discovery of his secret is his ruin. The treasure lures armies of rival claimants, and the scene is set for a terrible battle.

> "A dragon is no idle fancy. Even today you may find men not ignorant of tragic legend and history, who have heard of heroes and indeed seen them, who have yet been caught by the fascination of the worm."
>
> J. R. R. Tolkien

▲ **Gollum comes out of the dark**
We first meet the character of Gollum in *The Hobbit*. In the films of *The Lord of the Rings*, Gollum (above) is computer generated, although the voice and original movements were provided by actor Andy Serkis.

"ALL ALONE IT ROSE AND LOOKED ACROSS THE MARSHES TO THE FOREST. THE LONELY MOUNTAIN! BILBO HAD COME FAR AND THROUGH MANY ADVENTURES TO SEE IT, AND NOW HE DID NOT LIKE THE LOOK OF IT IN THE LEAST."

Did you know?
On 3 January 2003, thousands of Tolkien fans threw parties to celebrate what would have been the writer's "eleventy-first" birthday. The final chapter of *The Hobbit* describes Bilbo Baggins' party as he turns "eleventy-one", "a very respectable age for a hobbit." One hundred and forty four guests turned up to Bilbo's party. Rather more celebrated Tolkien's anniversary.

26

TESS OF THE D'URBERVILLES
THOMAS HARDY
Publication date 1891

Critics were outraged when *Tess of the D'Urbervilles* was published. They found it deplorable that a fallen woman should be glorified rather than vilified. With the passage of time, however, readers have come to agree with Hardy's assessment of Tess, and to love this powerful story and the irresistible draw of her tragic destiny.

THOMAS HARDY
1840–1928

Thomas Hardy was born in Stinsford in Dorset. A frail child, he did not start school until he was eight, by which time he could read. At 16, Hardy became an architect's apprentice. Moving to London at the age of 22 to work for an architect, he began writing poems. Poor health sent him back to Dorset, where he restored churches and published articles and books. From 1873 he wrote full time. The success of *Far from the Madding Crowd* (1874) gave him the means to marry his sweetheart Emma Lavinia Gifford. His later novels, which attempted to reconcile religion and nature, caused public outcry, so he returned to the quiet world of poetry. On Hardy's death, his ashes were placed in Poets' Corner at Westminster Abbey in London.

VIRTUE UNREWARDED

Hardy was an established, respected writer by the time *Tess* was published (this was his 12th book), but that did not protect him from criticism. He made clear his controversial view of her character, subtitling the book "A Pure Woman". Tess is seduced by one man – and falls pregnant by him – and is betrayed by another, whom she thought she could trust. Hardy's novel pours scorn on sexual hypocrisy, and sympathises with victims of a repressive society and an indifferent fate. This is a heartfelt book, revealing how people can be unwitting victims of others' passions.

▲ **First edition**
Tess of the D'Urbervilles was first published in newspaper instalments, with chapters "more especially addressed to adult readers" in the *Fortnightly Review*. Hardy "pieced the trunk and limbs of the novel together" in the three-volume first edition.

◄ **Author's manuscript**
The opening page of an autographed manuscript dating from 1891 shows that the novel was initially titled *A Daughter of the D'Urbervilles*.

Other books by Thomas Hardy include:

Far from the Madding Crowd (Big Read no. 48)

Jude the Obscure

The Mayor of Casterbridge

The Return of the Native

THE STORY IN A NUTSHELL

When **Tess Durbeyfield**'s impoverished father discovers he may be related to the esteemed D'Urberville family, Tess is sent to the estate to claim kinship. There she encounters the amorous **Alec D'Urberville** and is offered work. Alec takes advantage of her and, finding she is pregnant, she returns home to have his baby, which dies. Tess finds work on a dairy farm, where she meets and falls in love with **Angel Clare**. Aware that her virtue has been compromised, she at first resists, but eventually agrees to marry him, not relating her past until their wedding night. Angel cannot forgive Tess and they separate, Angel going to Brazil and Tess to work in harsh conditions on another farm. Tess learns that Alec is nearby, now a noted preacher and supposedly reformed, but again, he pursues her. Angel returns, keen to start life with Tess again, only to find her living with Alec. The final tragedy is about to unfold.

◀ **Down on the farm**
La Moisson de Colza, la Recolte du Colza was painted by the French artist Jules Adolphe Breton in 1860. Although the artist was born in northern France and trained under a Flemish painter, this haymaking scene is typical of English farm life in the late 19th century, of the kind that features in many of Hardy's novels.

"I would ask any too genteel reader... to remember a well-worn sentence of St. Jerome's: 'If an offence come out of the truth, better is it that the offence come than the truth be concealed'."

Thomas Hardy

◀ **Hardy country**
Hardy's prose shows his affinity with nature and his beloved county of Dorset. He used the name "Wessex" in his writing: this was the name of the ancient English kingdom in the region. "Hardy country" is now a popular attraction, with visitors making pilgrimages to landmarks such as the author's home.

◀ **On the big screen**
The film of *Tess of the D'Urbervilles*, made in 1979, was called simply *Tess*. Directed by Roman Polanski, it starred Nastassja Kinski, Leigh Lawson and Peter Firth. Much of the film was shot in northern France, where the countryside still bears a striking resemblance to Thomas Hardy's Wessex.

MIDDLEMARCH
GEORGE ELIOT

Publication date 1871-72

GEORGE ELIOT
1819–80

Born Mary Ann Evans, George Eliot was the daughter of a land-agent in Warwickshire. To the horror of her strict Protestant family, she abandoned her religion in her early 20s, and joined a group of free-thinking intellectuals. Eliot edited and wrote for the *Westminster Review* in London where, in 1853, she met the author and philosopher George Henry Lewes – a married man but separated. Eliot set up house with him, and was ostracised by much of society. Their happy "moral marriage" lasted 24 years until Lewes' death. In 1856, Eliot turned to writing fiction and poetry and became one of the foremost novelists of the day – though her true identity remained a secret. In 1880, she caused another scandal by marrying a man 20 years her junior. She died later the same year.

Eliot's novel is no middling book: full of wit, wisdom and insight, this brilliant story of a provincial community is also a masterly evocation of 19th-century society. The stories of a scholar, a doctor and a religious hypocrite mingle with those of rural people in a plot that is as lively as any of Dickens', yet also remarkably modern.

A STUDY OF PROVINCIAL LIFE

The story brims with events and characters inspired by Eliot's own experience, and is set in a bustling market town reminiscent of Coventry, where she spent some of her early years. One of its most stunning qualities is its sheer scale and complexity – the town seems to be a microcosm of the whole of English society. When asked how Eliot managed to achieve such a monumental yet cohesive work, her partner Lewes explained, "She never forgets anything that comes within a curl of her eyelash." Eliot anticpated the direction of the 20th-century novel by portraying her characters' inner lives, from the local squire to the lowliest stable hand. Fans of the book included the novelist Henry James, who praised its representation of the "vastness and variety of human life".

▲ **First edition**
Another great writer, the American poet Emily Dickinson said of Eliot's book, "What do I think of *Middlemarch*? What do I think of glory?"

▲ **Model for Middlemarch**
The landscape of the Midlands was George Eliot's inspiration for *Middlemarch*.

George Eliot

Other books by George Eliot:

Scenes of Clerical Life
Adam Bede
The Mill on the Floss
Silas Marner
Daniel Deronda

"Miss Brooke had that kind of beauty which

"WOMEN WERE EXPECTED TO HAVE WEAK OPINIONS; BUT THE GREAT SAFEGUARD OF SOCIETY AND OF DOMESTIC LIFE WAS, THAT OPINIONS WERE NOT ACTED ON. SANE PEOPLE DID WHAT THEIR NEIGHBOURS DID, SO THAT IF ANY LUNATICS WERE AT LARGE, ONE MIGHT KNOW AND AVOID THEM."

THE STORY IN A NUTSHELL

Dorothea Brooke, an idealistic, wealthy would-be philanthropist, marries a crusty, pedantic old scholar, **Edward Casaubon**, hoping to be of service to him in his work. Meanwhile, a flighty local beauty, **Rosamond Vincy**, marries the new doctor in town, **Lydgate**, planning to elevate herself socially. Both marriages are unhappy: Casaubon rejects Dorothea's assistance and becomes jealous of her innocent relationship with his cousin, the artistic outsider **Will Ladislaw**. Lydgate falls into debt by trying to give his wife what she craves, and subsequently is disgraced. The many sub-plots developed around these two central relationships touch on various themes, including national politics, religious hypocrisy, medical reform and class snobbery – but at the heart of the book is the question of how to make the right choices and live a truly fulfilling life.

▲ **On the small screen**
Unlike the work of other Victorian female novelists, *Middlemarch* had not been endlessly adapted for cinema and TV. Then in 1994 came an acclaimed TV serialisation, set in Stamford and starring Rufus Sewell, Robert Hardy and Juliet Aubrey.

"One of the few English novels written for grown-up people."
Virginia Woolf

seems to be thrown into relief by poor dress."

28 A PRAYER FOR OWEN MEANY
JOHN IRVING

Publication date 1989

Big themes dominate this moving novel: faith and doubt; the death of family and close friends; the rights and wrongs of American foreign policy from the 1950s to the late 1980s. Yet it will always be remembered first and foremost for its eponymous hero, one of the most extraordinary characters in modern American literature.

JOHN IRVING
1942–

John Irving was born in Exeter, New Hampshire, US. He is dyslexic, but was determined to write. After attending the University of Pittsburgh he studied in Vienna under Günter Grass. Back in the US, he graduated from the University of New Hampshire and joined the University of Iowa writers' workshop, where he was influenced by the writing of Kurt Vonnegut. Irving's first novel *Setting Free the Bears* was published in 1968, but it was *The World According to Garp* (1978) that brought him recognition and mass sales. He wrote the screenplay of his *The Cider House Rules,* the 1999 Oscar-winning film. Irving now sees his dyslexia as beneficial: it taught him "to pay more particular attention to the way a sentence works and the way a word is sounded".

Other books by John Irving include:

Setting Free the Bears

The Water-Method Man

The World According to Garp

The Hotel New Hampshire

The Cider House Rules

▲ **First edition**
Contrary to popular belief, *A Prayer for Owen Meany* is John Irving's most successful book. It has been translated into 25 languages.

THE MAKING OF A HERO

Owen Meany is an unlikely hero, remarkable most obviously for his tiny stature and squeaky voice. His classmates can't resist picking him up, their mothers can't resist touching him and his friend John can't resist idolising him. Then, as he grows older if not taller, people start listening to Owen. He speaks with a wisdom beyond his years and a conviction that his physical abnormalities must mean he is God's instrument on Earth. The singularity of this American hero struck chords with readers worldwide, although the novel's success was due also to beguiling echoes of its literary predecessors: the warmth of Owen and John's adolescent friendship recalls that of Huck Finn and Tom Sawyer; the bemusement at the conduct of war is redolent of *Catch-22*; while the sprawling, boisterous storytelling calls to mind Dickens, whose novels inspired Irving as a child.

> "A Prayer for Owen Meany is a rare creation in the somehow exhausted world of late-20th-century fiction – it is an amazingly brave piece of work, so extraordinary, so original, and so enriching."
> Stephen King

Did you know?
Irving is a lifelong wrestling enthusiast. In 1992 he was inducted into the National Wrestling Hall of Fame in Stillwater, Oklahoma.

◄ **The Shot**
A key element of the book is "The Shot", a move whereby John lifts Owen to throw the ball.

THE STORY IN A NUTSHELL

When he is 11 years old, **Owen Meany** inadvertently kills his best friend **John**'s mother during a Little League baseball game. In Owen's mind, however, her death was no accident: it was providence and implies that he has been chosen as a divine spokesman. As he and John grow older, it becomes clear that, despite his diminutive stature and strange voice, Owen does have an inexplicable influence and authority. He also experiences a recurrent dream that convinces him of his higher purpose on earth. He has seen the date and manner of his death, but cannot be sure exactly how it will come about. All he knows is that he will die a hero and fulfil God's will. As the destined time grows nearer, apparently random events from Owen and John's past slot into place, and Owen's true purpose becomes clear. *A Prayer for Owen Meany* is narrated by John, nearly 20 years after Owen's death. He is extremely bitter. He rants at the ignorance of Americans and the improbity of their leaders, he questions the nature of religious faith and doubt and he mourns the loss of his great friend, whose death left a great hole in his life.

Children taking part in Little League baseball games

"I AM DOOMED TO REMEMBER A BOY WITH A WRECKED VOICE – NOT BECAUSE OF HIS VOICE, OR BECAUSE HE WAS THE SMALLEST PERSON I EVER KNEW, OR EVEN BECAUSE HE WAS THE INSTRUMENT OF MY MOTHER'S DEATH, BUT BECAUSE HE IS THE REASON I BELIEVE IN GOD. I AM A CHRISTIAN BECAUSE OF OWEN MEANY."

29

THE GRAPES OF WRATH
JOHN STEINBECK

Publication date 1939

JOHN STEINBECK
1902–68

John Steinbeck was born in Salinas, California, to an educated middle-class family. His mother encouraged him to read widely – writers such as Eliot, Dostoyevsky, Hardy and Malory. The rhythms and scope of the King James Bible in particular made an impression. He attended Stanford University, but did not finish his degree. Next came a variety of outdoor labouring jobs, before work as a reporter in New York. His first novel, *Cup of Gold*, was published in 1929. During the Second World War, Steinbeck was a war correspondent, but afterwards returned to fiction. He won the Nobel Prize for Literature in 1962.

This near-mythical portrait of labourers' struggle to survive in Depression-hit dust-bowl America is a celebration of the working man and the indomitable human spirit. For Steinbeck, these people were "stronger and purer and braver" than him. This is the book that inspired a generation of writers, film-makers and singers.

Steinbeck's home in Salinas, California

THE LONG AND ROCKY ROAD

After the 1929 stock-market crash, many sharecroppers lost their farms, which were merged into large units. Uneducated and inexperienced outside agriculture, they were lured west. More than 450,000 took to the road, creating a vast underclass of unwanted labour that had to find new ways to survive. Thus the myth of the American road was born. Steinbeck's faithful picture of blue-collar heroism in all its raw and ragged glory was denounced at the time as inaccurate and even obscene, but it was based on the lives of the real men he befriended – and immortalised.

▲ **First edition**
The book received largely positive reviews, although it was denounced by the hard right for questioning the American dream. But by May 1939 it was selling more than 10,000 copies a week. It became the year's top-selling novel, and won the Pulitzer Prize. Translated into nearly 30 languages, *The Grapes of Wrath* has now sold more than 14 million copies.

"They were not farm men anymore but migrant men."

Other books by John Steinbeck include:

Of Mice and Men (Big Read no. 52)
Tortilla Flat
In Dubious Battle
The Long Valley
Cannery Row

"YOU'RE NOT BUYING ONLY JUNK, YOU'RE BUYING JUNKED LIVES. AND MORE – YOU'LL SEE – YOU'RE BUYING BITTERNESS. BUYING A PLOW TO PLOW YOUR OWN CHILDREN UNDER, BUYING THE ARMS AND SPIRITS THAT MIGHT HAVE SAVED YOU."

A migrant family walking from Arizona to California in 1939; here they are on US Highway 99 near Brawley, Imperial Valley, California

▲ "Tom Joad"
In 1938, in collaboration with Steinbeck, Horace Bristol photographed migrant farm workers in California's Central Valley, some of the subjects inspiring his characters.

THE STORY IN A NUTSHELL

The **Joad family** have been cleared off their land by the bank, and are forced to hit the long hard road from the dust bowl of Oklahoma to California in search of a new life. Lapsed preacher **Jim Casy** meets **Tom Joad** and joins them. But the road is as harsh as the land they have left behind: **Grampa Joad** dies, and **Granma** falls ill, later to die as well. Cut off now from their roots and the previous generation, Tom suggests splitting up, but Ma, the family bedrock, refuses. Tom and Casy find trouble with the law; Casy gives himself up and the Joads travel on. Failing to find work, they move to Tulare to pick peaches. Tom again meets Casy, who by now is leading a strike against the orchard owners; Tom learns that his family are being paid as strikebreakers. Depite their trials and labours, the Joad family strive to keep their spirit alive. They continue their journey ever westwards towards a promised land.

> "The writer must believe that what he is doing is the most important thing in the world. And he must hold to this illusion even when he knows it is not true."
>
> John Steinbeck

Did you know?

Steinbeck angered many with his stark portrait. Oklahoma's Democrat Congressman, Lyle Boren, claimed that the work was insulting to the farmers of the Midwest and was "a lie, a black, infernal creation of a twisted, distorted mind". He famously described the book as a "dirty, lying, filthy manuscript". A Jesuit priest called it "an embodiment of the Marxist Soviet propaganda".

▼ **On the big screen**
The 1940 film adaptation was directed by John Ford and starred Henry Fonda. Steinbeck described it as a "hard, straight picture... that looks and feels like a documentary film and... has a hard, truthful ring".

30

ALICE'S ADVENTURES IN WONDERLAND
LEWIS CARROLL

Publication date 1865

LEWIS CARROLL
1832–98

"Lewis Carroll" was the pseudonym of Charles Lutwidge Dodgson. Born in Cheshire, the son of a clergyman, he became a mathematics lecturer at Christ Church College, Oxford. It was on a boating trip with the young Alice Liddell and her sisters that he began to tell the strange tale that became *Alice's Adventures in Wonderland.* His mathematical brain delighted in the limits of logic and the paradoxes of thought and language. He was also an accomplished photographer and often used the Liddell children as his subjects. Alice was his favourite.

The three gardeners

Other books by Lewis Carroll include:

Through the Looking Glass, and What Alice Found There

The Hunting of the Snark

If you've yet to discover this surreal fantasy, it is never too late to follow Alice down the rabbit hole. From disappearing cats to the Mad Hatter's tea party, Carroll's wonderland of characters has passed into the national subconscious. Open its pages and tumble into a world where the only limits are imaginary ones.

OFF WITH YOUR HEAD!

To follow Alice is to enter a world where anything can happen. Children will be excited and scared by *Alice* – especially by the furious Queen of Hearts. Adults will be intrigued as well, just as they always have been by the very best children's fantasies. The book poses many questions, a lot of which are asked by Alice herself as she struggles to comprehend what is happening to her, and around her. But for girls and boys who grow almost as fast as she does, the more important questions are the ones asked of her: "Who are you?" and "What are you?" and "What do you mean by that?" The riddles and debates will delight both young and old, such as the one about whether you can have less or more than nothing, and whether there is a difference between "important" and "unimportant". In Wonderland, logic is stood on its head and paradoxes come to life, baffling, challenging and entrancing all of us.

▲ **First edition**
The first edition met mixed reviews. *The Times* praised it as "an excellent piece of nonsense", but the *Athenaeum* called it an "over-wrought story".

▲ **On the big screen**
There have been many film and TV versions of *Wonderland* – and *Through the Looking Glass* – some animated and others using actors. The 1972 film (above) starred Dame Flora Robson as the Queen of Hearts and Dennis Price as the King.

Did you know?
The character of the Mad Hatter has been recreated as one of Batman's foes. The drawings of the Mad Hatter in the Batman comics closely resemble Tenniel's drawings.

◄ **Author's original**
Alice's Adventures Under Ground was the manuscript that later became *Alice's Adventures in Wonderland.* The author added his own illustrations, then bound it in green morocco and presented it to Alice Liddell in 1864.

▲ **The real Alice**
Alice Liddell was the real life inspiration, but her three sisters also appear – in the Dormouse's tale about the sisters who lived at the bottom of a well.

"Curiouser and curiouser..."

THE STORY IN A NUTSHELL
One day, a young girl called **Alice** follows a talking **White Rabbit** down a rabbit hole, and finds herself in a fantastical land. As she endeavours to make sense of her new surroundings Alice encounters a number of bizarre characters, including the hookah-smoking **Caterpillar** with his cryptic questions, the ugly **Duchess** nursing a baby who changes into a pig and the mysterious **Cheshire Cat** who can vanish at will. The **March Hare** and the **Mad Hatter** introduce Alice to their endless crazy tea party. She meets the **King** and **Queen of Hearts**, becomes involved in an unusual game of croquet and learns to dance the Lobster Quadrille with the **Gryphon** and the **Mock Turtle**. Can Alice survive the madness without losing her head to the angry Queen of Hearts?

The White Rabbit

◀ ▶ **The artist**
John Tenniel, a political cartoonist whose work appeared in *Punch*, was the author's choice to illustrate the first edition of the book.

" 'BUT I DON'T WANT TO GO AMONG MAD PEOPLE', ALICE REMARKED. 'OH YOU CAN'T HELP THAT,' SAID THE CAT: 'WE'RE ALL MAD HERE. I'M MAD. YOU'RE MAD.' 'HOW DO YOU KNOW I'M MAD?' SAID ALICE. 'YOU MUST BE,' SAID THE CAT, 'OR YOU WOULDN'T HAVE COME HERE.' "

31

THE STORY OF TRACY BEAKER
JACQUELINE WILSON

Publication date 1991

▲ **First edition**
The book was shortlisted for the Smarties Prize and the Carnegie Medal, and won the Blue Peter Best Story Book award in 2002.

This is not just one of the best children's books, but a great book for all. Smart, sassy and fierce, this fictional biography of a ten-year-old orphan is witty, sad, uproarious and crammed to the covers with insight and telling comments about the adult world. As Tracy herself says, "This is a book about me. I'd read it if I were you."

JACQUELINE WILSON
1945–

Jacqueline Wilson was born in Bath, but has spent most of her life in Kingston, Surrey. An only child, she was always writing stories, and knew she wanted to be a writer. She worked for Scottish publisher D.C. Thomson & Co, and then helped found *Jackie* magazine (some say it was named after her). She has written crime novels and several radio plays, but her real reputation is as a children's author. Her fresh and friendly approach to social realism has won her a worldwide audience, and many awards. In 2002 she was given an OBE for services to literacy. She has run creative writing classes for children, and has a web-based fan club. With her short silver hair and silver jewellery, she has a unique personal style, which – like her writing – makes her instantly recognisable.

CUTTING-EDGE COMEDY

Jacqueline Wilson has a way of writing books for children in the first person that lets us read between the lines to find the real story. In this one, ten-year-old Tracy fills the page with everyday facts, feuds, friendships and quips, revealing far more about herself, her hopes and dreams than she realises. This adds immeasurably to the power of her story – and in all of Wilson's work there's a lot of emotion tangled up in her characters' one-liners. Here, Tracy is in care, her mother out of touch; she writes confidently that she expects her back any minute, but the reader can feel her desperation. She writes with a child's bravado, but can't conceal her need to be loved – and her fear of seeming vulnerable.

▶ ▼ **Looking for home**
"I was Child of the Week in the local paper. If she'd only let me write it."
Jacqueline Wilson got the idea for the book from newspaper adverts featuring photographs of children who were up for adoption. Nick Sharratt, who illustrated the book, also illustrates Tracy's wild imaginings in the television series.

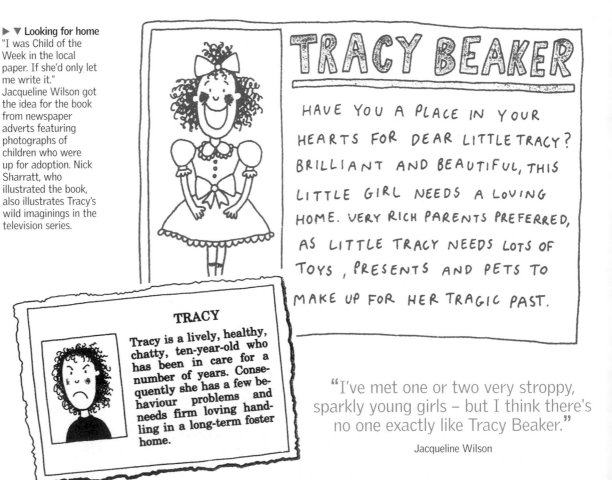

TRACY BEAKER

HAVE YOU A PLACE IN YOUR HEARTS FOR DEAR LITTLE TRACY? BRILLIANT AND BEAUTIFUL, THIS LITTLE GIRL NEEDS A LOVING HOME. VERY RICH PARENTS PREFERRED, AS LITTLE TRACY NEEDS LOTS OF TOYS, PRESENTS AND PETS TO MAKE UP FOR HER TRAGIC PAST.

TRACY

Tracy is a lively, healthy, chatty, ten-year-old who has been in care for a number of years. Consequently she has a few behaviour problems and needs firm loving handling in a long-term foster home.

Other books by Jacqueline Wilson include:

Double Act
(Big Read no. 80)

Vicky Angel
(Big Read no. 86)

Girls in Love
(Big Read no. 98)

Bad Girls

"I've met one or two very stroppy, sparkly young girls – but I think there's no one exactly like Tracy Beaker."

Jacqueline Wilson

THE STORY IN A NUTSHELL

Ten-year-old **Tracy Beaker** is writing her autobiography. She tells us she's been in and out of care all her life, and now she's back in the children's home. We hear all about the wild and wacky characters she's encountered. Tracy doesn't know where her mother is – except it will be somewhere glamorous – but she expects her to come and take her away soon. One day a writer named **Cam Lawson** comes to the home; she's doing a magazine article about children in care. She and Tracy hit it off, and they write to each other. Cam reads some of Tracy's autobiography and thinks Tracy could do a better job of the article than she could. They get on so well that Tracy begins to hope she could live with Cam... The story continues in the sequel, *The Dare Game*.

"I'VE GONE PAST MY SELL-BY DATE ALREADY. IT GETS HOPELESS WHEN YOU GET OLDER THAN FIVE OR SIX. YOU'VE STOPPED BEING A CUTE LITTLE TODDLER AND STARTED TO BE DIFFICULT. AND I'M NOT PRETTY EITHER."

If you like this you may also enjoy books by:

Judy Blume
Paula Danzinger
Anne Fine
Sandra Glover
Rosie Rushton
Sue Townsend

Cam and Tracy

Did you know?

Jacqueline Wilson got the idea for Tracy Beaker's surname when she was in the bathroom. "I wanted her first name to sound sharp and modern and bouncy. 'Tracy' seemed spot on straight away". She found the surname more difficult, but one day when she was rinsing her hair with a Snoopy beaker, inspiration hit. "I held it in my hand – and then grinned. I'd found the perfect name. Tracy Beaker!"

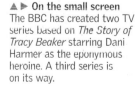

▲ ▶ On the small screen
The BBC has created two TV series based on *The Story of Tracy Beaker* starring Dani Harmer as the eponymous heroine. A third series is on its way.

32 ONE HUNDRED YEARS OF SOLITUDE
GABRIEL GARCIA MARQUEZ

Publication date 1967

GABRIEL GARCIA MARQUEZ
1928–

Born in Aracataca, a small town in Colombia, Gabriel García Márquez was raised largely by his grandparents. He first met his future wife when he was 18 and she was 13. Although he proposed to her almost at once, they did not marry for another 14 years. Meanwhile, he studied at the University of Bogotá then became a journalist. During the 1950s he was a foreign correspondent in Paris, Rome, Barcelona and New York. In 1961, García Márquez and his family settled in Mexico City. He had begun publishing short stories while a student, but his breakthrough novel, *One Hundred Years of Solitude*, was not published until 1967. Many distinguished works followed, and in 1982 he was awarded the Nobel Prize for Literature.

Other books by Gabriel García Márquez include:

Love in the Time of Cholera (Big Read No. 97)

The Autumn of the Patriarch

Chronicle of a Death Foretold

The General in His Labyrinth

Of Love and Other Demons

This is the book that introduced "magical realism" to the world. The fantastical and the everyday are woven together, the extraordinary – magic carpets, ghosts, mysterious prophecies, alchemy and levitation (powered by chocolate) – is described in matter-of-fact style: a masterly fusion that continues to dazzle readers.

▲ **First US edition**
Initially published in Argentina in Spanish, the novel was translated and published in the UK and the US in 1970.

▼ **Exploitation**
The lifeblood of many Colombian towns, banana plantations often exploited their workers.

SURREAL LIFE STORIES

Time is elastic in this novel. Events runs in cycles, and past, present and future merge into one another, linking the history of much of Latin America, the story of the small town of Macondo and the chronology of the Buendías family. The novel draws heavily on the lives of García Márquez's grandparents. Later in life, he wrote, "All my writing has been about the experiences of the time I spent with my grandparents." His grandfather was Colonel Nicolás Ricardo Márquez Mejía, a Liberal who fought in the War of a Thousand Days and co-founded the banana-producing town of Aracataca, on which Macondo is based. His grandmother was the role model for Ursula and the source of the family legends, stories, folk tales, superstitions and supernatural beliefs that are the ingredients of "magical realism".

Did you know?
In 1959 Gabriel García Márquez went to Cuba where he met and became friends with Fidel Castro, whom he lists among his cultural heroes. He also worked for a Cuban news agency. As a result of these connections and his interest in communist politics he was refused a visa for entry to the US.

◀ **Gold doubloons**
The villagers of Macondo use doubloons to buy alchemical equipment and compasses.

MAGICAL REALISM

García Márquez said that the tone of *One Hundred Years of Solitude* was based on the way his grandmother told stories: "She told things that sounded supernatural and fantastic, but she told them with complete naturalness." Magical realism is usually thought of as a literary mode, but the term was originally applied to a school of painters in the 1920s. Magical realist writing interweaves ordinary events with fantasy, myth and dreamlike imagery, and the carnival is a recurring theme. Unlike the made-up worlds of writers such as Tolkien or Pratchett, the realm of the magical realist is the normal world. It is a style particularly associated with Latin American writers.

THE STORY IN A NUTSHELL

In the early 1800s Macondo is a small settlement, cut off from the modern world. Visiting gypsies, led by the enigmatic **Melquíades**, introduce exotic technologies such as magnets, compasses and telescopes, which are seized upon by **José Arcadio Buendía**, founder of the village, who becomes obsessed with alchemy. His wife, **Ursula Iguarán**, is the matriarch of the family, the emotional constant who binds the generations. As Macondo grows, Colombia's violent civil wars impinge; government officials arrive; there are insurrections, killings and reprisals. **Aurellano Buendía**, youngest son of José Arcadio and Ursula, joins the Liberal cause and becomes a national hero. An American company establishes a banana plantation in Macondo, but its exploited workers revolt and thousands are killed. The town sinks into decline, once more isolated, until **Aureliano**, great-great-great-grandson of José Arcadio and Ursula, deciphers the gypsy writings of Melquíades.

"MANY YEARS LATER, AS HE FACED THE FIRING SQUAD, COLONEL AURELIANO BUENDIA WAS TO REMEMBER THAT DISTANT AFTERNOON WHEN HIS FATHER TOOK HIM TO DISCOVER ICE."

◀ **The railway arrives**
Macondo's seclusion is destroyed by the arrival of the railway. It opens the way for outsiders to introduce commerce and politics, and initiates the growth of the town. Later in the book, when Macondo reverts to its original state, the trains no longer run.

33

THE PILLARS OF THE EARTH
KEN FOLLETT

First edition

Publication date 1989

In this extraordinary story, Follett whisks us back in time to medieval England in a spirited tale of love and revenge at a time of great religious and political tension. At the heart of the novel is the cathedral that rises majestically as the plot unfolds.

KEN FOLLETT
1949–

Born in Cardiff, to parents who belonged to the austere Plymouth Brethren, Ken Follett was not allowed to watch television or films or listen to the radio, but his mother's stories and, later, books fed his imagination. He moved to London when he was ten, and later studied philosophy at University College London, where he was involved in politics. In 1970 he became a pop music journalist in Cardiff, then moved to the *Evening News* in London and joined the Labour Party. He began to write fiction and pursued an interest in medieval cathedrals. Follett hit the big time with *The Eye of the Needle*, followed by other number-one thrillers. He is President of the Dyslexia Institute and also a council member of the National Literacy Trust.

Other books by Ken Follett include:

The Eye of the Needle
On Wings of Eagles
The Key to Rebecca
Lie Down with Lions
The Third Twin
The Hammer of Eden
Jackdaws
Hornet Flight

INSPIRATION IN STONE

Best known as a writer of contemporary thrillers, populist Follett radically changes course with *The Pillars of the Earth*. Maintaining the strong female personalities and intrigue of his suspense novels, he weaves a story of power, revenge, betrayal and ultimate goodness as a cathedral is built. The book follows a prior, his master builder and their community as they struggle to create something perfect that will enhance civilisation while protecting themselves during the violent power struggles that beset 12th-century England.

"TOM HAD BEEN OFFERED THE POST OF BUILDER TO THE EXETER CASTELLAN, REPAIRING AND IMPROVING THE CITY'S FORTIFICATIONS. IT WOULD HAVE BEEN A LIFETIME JOB, BARRING ACCIDENTS. BUT TOM HAD TURNED IT DOWN, FOR HE WANTED TO BUILD ANOTHER CATHEDRAL... ONCE HE HAD TASTED THAT WINE, TOM WAS NEVER SATISFIED WITH ANYTHING ELSE."

▲ **Medieval farm life**
Medieval times are the backdrop against which a cathedral is built. A simple but tough way of life is the harsher for the oppression and violence as England's noblemen fight over the crown, and the Church too vies for greater power.

THE STORY IN A NUTSHELL

In the 12th century, the violence of war in England is worsened by the threat of famine and oppression, and the Church is in conflict with the State. Amid all this, a magnificent new cathedral is rising. Its building is the focus of 40 years for idealistic master builder **Tom**, whose drive to build a great cathedral is stronger than his desire to raise his family from poverty. It is also a passion for determined but compassionate prior **Philip**, who struggles under his ruthless bishop and a tyrannical earl. These men, ambitious in different ways, are offset by a courageous, resourceful noblewoman, **Aliena**, who has lost her wealth but is determined to regain it, and a mysterious, forest-dwelling curse-caster, **Ellen**. Their lives intertwine through two generations.

DAVID COPPERFIELD
CHARLES DICKENS

Publication date 1849–50

Readers love this story's combination of autobiography and fiction, its feeling of suspense and its cast of vivid characters. These include one of literature's greatest comic figures, Mr Micawber, and one of its creepiest villains, 'umble Uriah Heep.

First edition

CHARLES DICKENS
See page 24

◄ **Wilkins Micawber**
This 1911 illustration by Frank Reynolds shows the ever-optimistic, debt-ridden Micawber, a character based on the author's father. John Dickens' ineptitude drove his family to the brink of ruin; in 1824 he was sent to debtor's prison.

A SLOW STARTER

Like most of Dickens' work, *David Copperfield* first appeared in monthly instalments, followed by publication as a single volume in 1850. It was well received by such luminaries as W. M. Thackeray and John Ruskin, but commercially it was a disappointment. Initial sales were so much slower than for the previous book, *Dombey and Son*, that the publisher reduced the print run. Today the novel is among literature's most loved works.

THE STORY IN A NUTSHELL

David Copperfield's idyllic childhood ends when his mother marries cruel **Mr Murdstone**. David is sent away to school, his mother dies and Murdstone forces the boy to work in a London warehouse. His only friend is **Mr Micawber**. When Micawber has to flee London, David also runs away – to eccentric **Aunt Betsey**. She sends him to a decent school; he stays with kindly **Mr Wickfield**, who has a daughter, **Agnes**, and a sinister clerk, **Uriah Heep**. Years pass and David goes to work as a clerk. He marries his employer's beautiful but empty-headed daughter, **Dora**, and becomes a writer. Then he hears that Heep has designs on Agnes and plans to ruin Wickfield. With Mr Micawber, David sets about discrediting Heep and rescuing Agnes and the Micawbers.

▲ **On the small screen**
The BBC adaptation of David Copperfield (1999) featured Maggie Smith, Ian McKellan, Bob Hoskins and a young Daniel Radcliffe in the title role. Daniel was soon to be world famous for playing Harry Potter in the film adaptations of the novels.

Did you know?

When his father was imprisoned Dickens went to work, aged 12, in a blacking (shoe polish) factory. According to the writer G. K. Chesterton, it was a traumatic time. "He never spoke of the whole experience except once or twice, and he never spoke of it otherwise than as a man might speak of hell." These traumas formed useful raw material, however, to be put to good use in his fiction.

► **Child labourers cleaning coal**
The shameful practice of child labour played an important role in the Industrial Revolution from its outset. The working classes took it for granted that a family would not be able to support itself if the children were not employed.

"It will be easily believed that I am a fond parent to every child of my fancy, and that no one can ever love that family as dearly as I love them. But, like many fond parents, I have in my heart of hearts a favourite child. And his name is David Copperfield."

Charles Dickens

CHARLIE AND THE CHOCOLATE FACTORY
ROALD DAHL

Publication date 1964

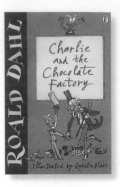

Current edition

The ultimate rags-to-riches wish-fulfilment fantasy for children, *Charlie and the Chocolate Factory* has a sweet coating but, like many of Dahl's books, a hard centre. The story is a wickedly funny twist on traditional fairy tales, where the good are really good, the bad are really bad and virtue wins through in the end.

ROALD DAHL
1916–90

Roald Dahl was born of Norwegian parents, in Llandaff, South Wales, and went to Repton School. When he was 22 he went to work for the Shell oil company in East Africa, and during the Second World War he became a fighter-pilot. He began to write while working in Washington DC as Assistant Air Attaché. His work was initially published in American magazines. His fondness for telling his children stories led to him writing his first children's book, *James and the Giant Peach*, published in 1961. This was followed by *Charlie and the Chocolate Factory*. Dahl won the Whitbread Children's Novel Award in 1983 for *The Witches*. In 2000 he was voted the nation's favourite author in a survey to celebrate World Book Day.

Other books by Roald Dahl include:

Charlie and the Great Glass Elevator

The BFG
(Big Read no. 56)

Matilda
(Big Read no. 74)

The Twits
(Big Read no. 81)

James and the Giant Peach

Revolting Rhymes

The Witches

BREAKING THE (CHOCOLATE) MOULD

In his books for children, Roald Dahl saw the world through their eyes – and in the process often got up adults' noses. He didn't like authority figures and his ruthless treatment of adults who don't mean well is hugely appealing for young readers. Dahl knew that a child's anarchic spirit is delighted by upsets in the usual order, and their sense of justice satisfied when the good are rewarded and the bad – adults as well as children – punished. Until *Charlie and the Chocolate Factory*, Dahl was best known as a writer of adult "sting-in-the-tail" stories and a James Bond script; after Charlie, his new career took off, and from then on children were as hungry for his books as Charlie was for chocolate.

▲ **Dahl's manuscript**
In the original manuscript for *Charlie and the Chocolate Factory* Roald Dahl drew little stick-men to represent the book's main characters.

▲ **Charlie Bucket**
Charlie finds a coveted golden ticket to visit the world-famous Wonka factory.

▶ **The "hut"**
Roald Dahl wrote many of his most famous books in this shed, which he referred to as his "hut". It was in the garden of his home in Great Missenden in Buckinghamshire. Dahl wrote several drafts of his books "because I never get anything right first time".

THE STORY IN A NUTSHELL

Charlie Bucket is incredibly poor and incredibly hungry. He lives with his parents and four grandparents in a tiny house, and there is never enough to eat. Charlie dreams of chocolate, but he gets only one chocolate bar a year – on his birthday. The confectionery genius **Willie Wonka** decides to open his factory to five lucky children; the winners will find one of five golden tickets hidden under the wrappers of five bars of chocolate. Four tickets are found by four horrible children who don't deserve to win anything. Meanwhile Charlie's father loses his job and the family has nothing to eat. Charlie finds some money and buys a bar of chocolate, just because he is hungry. Then he buys a second bar – and there's the last ticket! He and the other winners visit the chocolate factory, which turns out to be a delicious adventure.

QUENTIN BLAKE

Illustrator and Children's Laureate Quentin Blake (seen above with Dahl's granddaughter Sophie) has produced hundreds of whimsical illustrations that have become as much a part of Roald Dahl's books as the eccentric characters and outrageous rhymes. He has described his style as "a kind of hand-writing". He said "What was so nice about Roald was that he actually wanted the pictures – he didn't like it if there weren't enough." Blake has illustrated more than 300 books for many writers and is a respected writer himself.

▶ **Augustus Gloop**
(who fell into a river of chocolate) "This boy, who only just before Was loathed by men from shore to shore, This greedy brute, this louse's ear, Is loved by people everywhere! For who could hate or bear a grudge Against a luscious bit of fudge?"

> "The rude idea is very interesting because children are terribly rude compared to us snotty grown-ups... they are coarse and crude and rude."
>
> Roald Dahl

◀ **Charlie and Mr Wonka**
Before opening his factory to the lucky winners Mr Wonka had not been seen for many years.

◀ **Veruca Salt**
(who has been spoiled by her parents)
"Veruca Salt, the little brute, Has just gone down the rubbish chute, (And as we very rightly thought That in a case like this we ought To see the thing completely through, We've polished off her parents, too)."

▶ **Mike Teavee**
(a television addict) "The most important thing we've learned, So far as children are concerned, Is never, NEVER, NEVER let Them near your television set – Or better still, just don't install The idiotic thing at all."

◀ **Violet Beauregarde**
(who always chews gum) "Dear friends, we surely all agree There's almost nothing worse to see Than some repulsive little bum Who's always chewing chewing-gum. (It's very near as bad as those Who sit around and pick the nose.)"

36 TREASURE ISLAND
ROBERT LOUIS STEVENSON
Publication date 1883

A gripping yarn packed with swashbuckling action, humour, murder and treachery, and a vibrant cast of characters, *Treasure Island* is the definitive tale of adventure and piracy on the high seas. With honour and courage set against evil and cruelty, the story appeals to the adventure-loving child in all of us.

ROBERT LOUIS STEVENSON
1850–94

Robert Lewis Stevenson (he later changed Lewis to Louis, keeping its original pronunciation) was born in Edinburgh. A sickly boy, his imagination was sparked by children's bedtime stories. The only child in a family of famous lighthouse engineers, he dismayed his father by giving up an engineering degree to write. He agreed to study law so that he would have a profession to fall back on, but he never needed to. He met and married an American divorcée more than ten years his senior with two children, to the alarm of his middle-class family. A life of travel followed, with Stevenson always looking for a climate that suited his sickly constitution. In 1889, he moved to Western Samoa, where he died five years later of a stroke, aged just 44.

Other books by Robert Louis Stevenson include:

The Strange Case of Dr Jekyll and Mr Hyde

Kidnapped

Catriona

A Child's Garden of Verses

The pirate's flag

A BOYS' OWN CLASSIC

On a rainy holiday in Scotland, Stevenson and his 12-year-old stepson, Lloyd, sketched out a map of an imaginary island. The drawing caught Stevenson's imagination. The book was originally called *The Sea Cook: A Story for Boys*. Long John Silver and his crew of rum-sodden rogues ("Shiver my timbers!", "Yo-ho-ho and a bottle of rum!") were so brilliantly conceived that they became everyone's idea of what pirates are all about. Stevenson was following a well-established tradition of sea-borne adventures after such heavyweights as Defoe, Ballantyne, Scott and Poe. It is Stevenson's expert handling of pace and style that has allowed his novel to endure where others have been forgotten.

▲ **First edition**
This was Stevenson's first full-length novel, for which he was paid £100 by his publisher, Cassell.

▲ **Map of the island**
This is the map that appears in *Treasure Island*. Based on one Stevenson devised with his stepson, the location is believed to have been off the coast of South America.

◀ **On the big screen**
Disney's 1950 film adaptation of *Treasure Island* was directed by Byron Haskin and starred Robert Newton as Long John Silver. It was Walt Disney's first completely live-action feature film.

"Fifteen men on the dead man's chest

THE STORY IN A NUTSHELL

When **Billy Bones**, an irascible old seaman, falls dead in the Inn owned by young **Jim Hawkins'** father, Jim comes upon Bones' map showing where **Captain Flint**, a famous pirate, buried his treasure before he died. He shows the map to his father's doctor, **Livesey**, and to the local squire, **Mr Trelawney**, and the three of them resolve to find the treasure. Trelawney buys a ship, the *Hispaniola*, and hires a crew, including the charming, but dangerous, one-legged **Long John Silver** as the ship's cook, and they all set sail in search of the treasure. It soon transpires that not everyone on board is loyal to the treasure seekers. Jim discovers that all is not well on the *Hispaniola*, and he will need to use all his cunning and bravery if he is to escape with the treasure, or even his life.

A 1946 illustration for *Treasure Island* by Roland Hilder

Did you know?
Stevenson borrowed the parrot from *Robinson Crusoe*, the skeleton from Edgar Allan Poe, the stockade from Captain Marryat's *Masterman Ready* and "a good deal of the material of the first chapters" from Irving's *Tales of a Traveller*.

"If this don't fetch the kids, why, they have gone rotten since my day"

Robert Louis Stevenson

"AND I WAS GOING TO SEA MYSELF, TO SEA IN A SCHOONER, WITH A PIPING BOATSWAIN AND PIG-TAILED SINGING SEAMEN, TO SEA, BOUND FOR AN UNKNOWN ISLAND, AND TO SEEK FOR BURIED TREASURE!"

– Yo-ho-ho and a bottle of rum!"

37 A TOWN LIKE ALICE
NEVIL SHUTE

Publication date 1950

NEVIL SHUTE
1899–1960

Nevil Shute Norway was born in Ealing, Middlesex. His life was shaped by a fascination for aircraft. Rejected from the Royal Flying Corps because of a stammer, he spent the end of the First World War as a private in the Suffolk Regiment. He studied engineering at Balliol College, Oxford, and on graduating worked as an aeronautical engineer. While working, he learned to fly a plane. His first novel, *Marazan*, was published in 1926 under the pen name Nevil Shute. When the Second World War broke out he joined the Royal Naval Volunteer Reserve and was involved in experiments with secret weapons. In 1945 Shute and his family emigrated to Australia. He continued to write, producing more than 20 novels.

Shute's tale of survival, post-war fortune and the remembrance of youth has old-fashioned grit and excitement, but also a heroine and hero of equal zest and strength. This is a book for everyone – from those in search of action-packed adventure to fans of high romance. It might be a product of the 1950s, but its appeal never seems to fade.

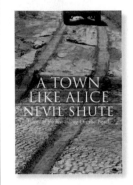

▲ **Current edition**
This was published half a century after the original, and is also available "published on demand" via the Internet.

AN AGELESS TALE OF LOVE AND LOSS

Nevil Shute spins a rattling good yarn – in this instance about the fortunes of a young Englishwoman taken prisoner by the Japanese during the Second World War. Bringing wartime Malaya and the Australian outback to colourful life, Shute's narrative is in the bold and worldly post-war style that he pioneered. Indeed, *A Town Like Alice* is a work that is very much of the 1950s, when the West was still telling tales of wartime heroism, but also witnessing the Atomic age, feminism and the birth of youth culture. As a result, its characters can seem at once curiously old-fashioned, yet also hopeful, identifiably modern, very human and subtly drawn. The book's coda nearly brings us to up the present, as the ageing narrator looks back on the girl he met "forty years too late".

Released prisoners at a camp in Manila in 1945

"I expect to be accused of falsifying history, especially in regard to the march and death of the homeless women prisoners. I shall be told that nothing of the sort ever happened in Malaya, and this is true. It happened in Sumatra."

Nevil Shute

▼ **On the small screen**
A mini-series for Australian TV was made in 1980, starring Bryan Brown, Helen Morse and Gordon Jackson.

Did you know?
In 1948 Shute decided he needed fresh inspiration and, with a friend, flew his light aircraft from Europe to Australia and back. His experiences provided material for several novels, including *A Town Like Alice*.

Other books by Nevil Shute include:

Trustee from the Toolroom

Round the Bend

On the Beach

Requiem for a Wren

Ruined City

Pied Piper

"IT'S A GRAND COUNTRY FOR A MAN TO LIVE AND WORK IN, AND GOOD MONEY, TOO. BUT IT'S A CROOK PLACE FOR A WOMAN."

THE STORY IN A NUTSHELL

When the Japanese invade Malaya in 1941, 19-year-old **Jean Paget** finds herself among a group of captive women and children who are marched around the country in search of a prison camp. Conditions are harsh, and it is largely thanks to Jean's leadership that a number of them survive. It is also down to

the assistance of **Joe Harman**, a brave Australian stockman and fellow prisoner. Joe tells Jean about his hometown of Alice Springs, an oasis in the Australian outback. When he steals a chicken to feed Jean and the others, Joe is caught. The Japanese put him on a crucifix and leave him to die, and the women survive only by lying low in a Malay village. After the war Jean inherits a large sum of money, and decides to spend some of it on building a well for the villagers who helped her. While doing so, she discovers that Joe survived after all, and she travels to Australia to find him. Meanwhile, Joe has learned that Jean is not married, as he had thought, so he goes to England to look for her. Will their paths cross again?

▲ **On the big screen**
Directed by Jack Lee, this screen version of *A Town Like Alice* starred Peter Finch as Joe Harman and Virginia McKenna as Jean Paget. The stars ably embodied the grit, courage and indomitability of the characters. It was the most successful British film of 1956 and made a star of the young Virginia McKenna.

38 PERSUASION
JANE AUSTEN

Publication date 1818

Full of Jane Austen's customary precision and wit, *Persuasion* is a brilliant satire and a beautiful portrait of love and missed opportunities. Anne Elliot is a complex and appealing heroine: mature and magnanimous, unembittered by heartache and, some say, not unlike Jane Austen herself.

JANE AUSTEN
See page 42

▲ **First edition**
After Jane Austen's death, her brother oversaw the publication of *Persuasion*.

A fragment of Chapter 11 of Jane Austen's manuscript

Did you know?
On July 8th 1816 Austen began what she called Chapter 10 of the second volume of *Persuasion*. She wrote "Finish July 18th 1816" on the last page of Chapter 11. On finding the ending "tame and flat" she returned to the novel some days later and rewrote the final chapters. These cancelled chapters can be found in their original form in the British Museum. The completed novel was published posthumously two years later with a preface written by her brother Henry.

▶ **19th-century Bath**
This painting of Bath was produced in 1806 by John Claude Nattes, and shows how the city would have looked around the time *Persuasion* was written.

LOVE CONQUERS ALL

In *Persuasion*, Austen's characteristic focus on the need for women of a certain standing (and age) to marry well has poignancy, because of her own declining health and our knowledge that she was never to write another novel. In Anne Elliot, Austen finds a heroine who persuades us that, in spite of social mores and passing fashions, true love holds the key to happiness. Anne is considered too old to find a husband, while her former suitor has yet to be convinced that their relationship can work again. Austen's portrayal of love conquering the social pressures she records so brilliantly is a fitting end to a brilliant career.

THE STORY IN A NUTSHELL

Eight years ago, **Anne Elliot** had been happily in love with **Frederick Wentworth**, a lieutenant in the Navy. But she was persuaded by family pressure and a friend's misjudged advice that his financial status was not high enough, and his prospects not good enough, to make him a worthy match. Anne spurned his proposal. Now they meet again. Wentworth has risen to the rank of captain and has made his fortune; Anne is living temporarily with her sister in Bath – resigned to a contemplative life of spinsterhood, sidelined and unappreciated. Obviously hurt by her previous rejection, Wentworth treats her coolly. Anne has never lost her feelings for him, and regrets that she no longer has the bloom of youth on her side. Warily, the former lovers circle each other – can their love be rekindled?

"Her power of inventing characters seems to have been intuitive, and almost unlimited. She drew from nature; but, whatever may have been surmised to the contrary, never from individuals."

Henry Austen in the preface to *Persuasion*

"IT SOMETIMES HAPPENS THAT A WOMAN IS HANDSOMER AT TWENTY-NINE THAN SHE WAS TEN YEARS BEFORE; AND, GENERALLY SPEAKING, IF THERE HAS BEEN NEITHER ILL HEALTH NOR ANXIETY, IT IS A TIME OF LIFE AT WHICH SCARCELY ANY CHARM IS LOST."

▲ ▶ **On the small screen**
With her acute and witty character observations, Jane Austen's work is regularly plundered for the screen. Before achieving success with "Notting Hill", Roger Michell directed a BBC adaptation of the novel in 1995. Amanda Root starred as Anne Eliot and Ciaran Hinds played Captain Wentworth.

39

DUNE
FRANK HERBERT
Publication date 1965

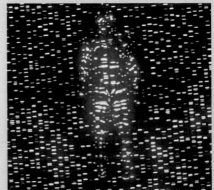

Winner of the Hugo and Nebula awards in the year of its publication, *Dune* is a story of power-hungry despots and idealistic fighters, set in a fantasy world as powerfully imagined as that of *The Lord of the Rings*. What began as a cult book now has legions of fans around the world.

FRANK HERBERT
1920–86

Born in Tacoma in the US, Frank Herbert was educated at the University of Washington, Seattle, and served in the US Navy in the Second World War. Before his success as an author, he worked as a television cameraman, political speech writer, photographer, radio commentator and journalist. His first novel, *The Dragon in the Sea*, was published in 1956. In 1972 Herbert turned to writing full-time, publishing over 20 books. He also worked as a social and ecological studies consultant in Vietnam and Pakistan, and experimented with solar collectors, wind plants and methane fuel generators.

▲ **First edition**
The story appeared in serial form as *Dune World* in the magazine *Analog* in 1963–4. It was heavily reworked before publication, to great acclaim, as the novel *Dune* in 1965.

ASTOUNDING WORLDS

Although *Dune* stands alone as a novel, it has spawned five sequels, including *Dune Messiah* and *Children of Dune*. Drawing comparisons with *Star Wars*, it features warring galactic federations, robots, hostile environments and frighteningly weird creatures. It was one of the first major works of science fiction to show the power of religion as a force in human history. Herbert explores tribe mentality and racial mistrust, exposing the dangers of a society dependent on certain commodities: themes that are as potent today as they were in the 1960s. Written at the time of Vietnam War protests, *Dune* shows how power can overturn ideals. Like all the best science fiction, Herbert's world is grounded in the characters' human machinations and failings; more than anything, *Dune* asserts the weakness of the human body and the strength of the human mind.

▲ **Sting**
This was the movie that made pop star Sting's name as an actor. He played Feyd-Rautha.

Other books by Frank Herbert include:

The Dragon in the Sea

The Green Brain

The Eyes of Heisenberg

Whipping Star

The God Makers

Soul Catcher

Hellstrom's Hive

The Priests of Psi and other stories

The White Plague

▲ **On the big screen**
Dune was made into a film in 1984, directed by David Lynch and starring Kyle MacLachlan, Francesca Annis, Patrick Stewart, Sting and, shown here, Jose Ferrer. Lynch turned down *Return of the Jedi* to direct the film.

SCIENCE-FICTION CLASSICS

Dune is a classic of sci-fi literature, but it is a genre rich with classics. Arthur C. Clark's story *The Sentinel* (the basis of *2001: A Space Odyssey*) made science fiction cerebral, while Robert Heinlein's *Starship Troopers* gave the genre a satirical edge. In *Fahrenheit 451*, Ray Bradbury depicted a future of book-burning firemen and reality TV, while Isaac Asimov's *I, Robot* remains a key study of artificial intelligence and the ethical use of technology.

THE STORY IN A NUTSHELL

In the year 10,091 Padishah Emperor Shaddam IV sends Duke Leto Atreides to rule the planet of Arrakis in order to harvest Melange, a valuable spice that is essential for space travel. It is found only in the desert sands of Arrakis. With him he takes Paul, his 15-year old son by his bound concubine, the Lady Jessica (an adept of the Bene Gesserit Sisterhood). As a result of the sisterhood's ancient breeding programme, Paul may have special powers, such as heightened sensory perception and the ability to see into the future. However, the travellers are in danger. Someone is plotting against the House of Atreides, perhaps even those they consider to be friends; meanwhile their enemies, the House of Harkonnen, are not far away. When Paul and the Lady Jessica arrive on Arrakis, its inhabitants, the Fremen, believe that their arrival is the realisation of an ancient prophecy and that Paul is their saviour. Using his sensory gifts, and aided by the Fremen, Paul battles for the survival of his own people, and the planet's inhabitants. With the odds dramatically stacked against him, he hurtles towards a terrifying confrontation with his powerful enemies.

"I was never a science fiction fan. But Herbert's book incorporates dream sequences, complex textures, different levels of meaning and symbolism; it concerns people, their emotions, their fears and goals."
David Lynch

Did you know?

Before the 1984 version, there were two previous attempts to bring *Dune* to the big screen. In 1975 director Alexandro Jodorowsky decided to make the film. Salvador Dali drew sketches and Orson Welles was cast as Baron Karkonnen. Then the money ran out. Next up was Ridley Scott. He spent months creating drawings, storyboards and special effects models. Again the money could not be found.

▶ **Desert planet**
Herbert drew inspiration for the surreal planet Arrakis from flying over "enormous, stationary waves" of sand dunes while researching a newspaper article. "Later, I realised I had found the location for my book on messianic leaders."

"ONCE MEN TURNED THEIR THINKING OVER TO MACHINES IN HOPE THAT THIS WOULD SET THEM FREE. BUT THAT ONLY PERMITTED OTHER MEN WITH MACHINES TO ENSLAVE THEM."

EMMA
JANE AUSTEN

Publication date 1816

On starting to write *Emma*, Jane Austen announced, "I am going to take a heroine whom no one but myself will much like." Generations of readers have emphatically disagreed with her, loving Emma Woodhouse as much for her failings as for her beauty and spirit.

First edition

JANE AUSTEN
See page 42

▲ **Jane Austen's house**
Austen spent the last eight years of her life at Chawton in Hampshire. *Emma* and *Persuasion* were both written here. The 17th-century house now houses a library.

A PERFECT JEWEL

Jane Austen's fourth novel is her longest and most ambitious, the crowning achievement of her genius. She finished it unusually quickly (in just over a year), and her confidence as a writer dazzles on the page.

The wit is sharper, the famous irony more exquisite, the characters more rounded. Like all Austen's novels, *Emma* concerns itself with the serious business of finding a husband. The book's incisive portrayal of social class and customs, together with its subtle exploration of relationships, still resonate with modern readers.

"EMMA WOODHOUSE, HANDSOME, CLEVER, AND RICH, WITH A COMFORTABLE HOME AND HAPPY DISPOSITION, SEEMED TO UNITE SOME OF THE BEST BLESSINGS OF EXISTENCE; AND HAD LIVED NEARLY TWENTY-ONE YEARS IN THE WORLD WITH VERY LITTLE TO DISTRESS OR VEX HER."

▲ **On the big screen**
Emma has translated well into modern period drama. The 1996 film version starred Gwynneth Paltrow.

THE STORY IN A NUTSHELL

The good-hearted but strong-willed **Emma Woodhouse** fills her time by matchmaking. Ignoring the advice of her good friend **Mr Knightley**, she takes a poor young woman, **Harriet**, under her wing. Emma discourages Harriet's relationship with a farmer, and insists that Harriet fall in love with the vicar, **Mr Elton**. Harriet complies, but the plan goes awry when Mr Elton makes a proposal to Emma herself. Shocked at his presumption, Emma next sets Harriet up with **Frank Churchill**. Again Harriet falls in love and the confusion is further compounded when it looks as if Frank, too, is in love with Emma. Emma's carefully laid plans soon begin to unravel, with unexpected consequences.

A.D.

ANNE OF GREEN GABLES
L. M. MONTGOMERY

Publication date 1908

First edition

One of the most heartwarming and captivating heroines in children's literature is introduced in *Anne of Green Gables*. Assertive, talkative, intelligent, temperamental and imaginative, the irrepressible Anne Shirley has entertained generations of young readers.

A CARROT TOP CINDERELLA

Skinny, red-headed Anne starts the book a frightened, hopeful orphan, sustained by her ability to imagine a better world. Her transformation to a secure and happy young woman who is loved by others as much as she loves them is the most satisfying of rags-to-riches tales. Lucy Montgomery's message in the book, however, is that happiness does not come from material goods. Anne's loving heart and generous spirit are her wealth, while her passionate conviction and articulate wit make her a rounded, endearing and amusing character – brought back by popular demand in several sequels.

▲ **The model for Green Gables**
Green Gables was based on a real house. Today busloads of Anne fans come to see the original Prince Edward Island off the east coast of Canada. There are several replicas of the farm in Japan.

THE STORY IN A NUTSHELL

Matthew and **Marilla Cuthbert**, an elderly brother and sister, think they've adopted a boy who will help them around the farm. But when the child arrives it is a lanky, freckled, chattering girl called **Anne Shirley**. At first Marilla wants to send her back to the orphanage, but when she discovers that Anne doesn't even know how to say her prayers she takes on the challenge of bringing her up. Anne is thrilled, but soon displays her temper. Matthew is already fond of Anne, and Marilla begins to melt too. Anne finds a "bosom friend" in **Diana**, and soon Marilla and Matthew find it hard to remember what Green Gables was like before Anne arrived.

Prince Edward Island, where the story is set, looks much as it did in Anne's day

" 'YOU'D FIND IT EASIER TO BE BAD THAN GOOD IF YOU HAD RED HAIR,' SAID ANNE REPROACHFULLY. 'PEOPLE WHO HAVEN'T RED HAIR DON'T KNOW WHAT TROUBLE IS. MRS THOMAS TOLD ME THAT GOD MADE MY RED HAIR ON PURPOSE, AND I'VE NEVER CARED ABOUT HIM SINCE.' "

L. M. MONTGOMERY
1874–1942

Lucy Maud Montgomery was born in Clifton, Prince Edward Island, Canada. Her mother died when she was two, and her father sent her to live with her maternal grandparents on their farm – a life very much re-created in *Anne of Green Gables*. She started writing at an early age; her first poem was published in a local newspaper when she was 15. She became a journalist and a teacher, but gave up work to look after her widowed grandmother. *Anne of Green Gables* was her first novel. In 1911 she married Reverend Ewan Macdonald, a Presbyterian minister, and spent the rest of her life in Ontario. She received a number of international honours, including the Fellowship of the British Royal Society of Arts, and a CBE.

◄ **On the big screen**
Anne of Green Gables has been staged and filmed many times. One of the first versions was made in 1934, starring Anne Shirley and Tom Brown and directed by George Nicholls Jnr.

Other books by L. M. Montgomery include:
Anne of Avonlea
Anne of the Island
Rainbow Valley
Chronicles of Avonlea

42 WATERSHIP DOWN
RICHARD ADAMS

Publication date 1972

An epic novel with a cast of rabbits and a hero called Hazel? Richard Adams' extraordinary tale might have seemed an unlikely publishing hit, but an atmosphere of dark foreboding and appealing characters saw it leap off the shelves. For many young people, this was the book that introduced them to adult literature.

▲ **First edition**
Only 2,500 copies of *Watership Down* were printed by the original publisher, Rex Collings. It has since sold more than 50 million copies worldwide and has never been out of print.

RICHARD ADAMS
1920–

Adams was brought up in Berkshire not far from the real Watership Down. He studied history at Oxford and served in the Second World War before joining the Civil Service in 1948. During his 25-year career in the Department of the Environment he was involved in the Clean Air Act and other projects, work that reflected his passion for the environment. This love of nature was to bring him huge commercial success when he made up a story for his daughters to ease their boredom on a long car journey. It was this story about a rabbit called Hazel that eventually became *Watership Down*. He left the Civil Service in 1974 to write full time. He has been President of the RSPCA and is a keen campaigner for animal welfare.

RABBITS WITH A PUNCH

One thing *Watership Down* is not is sentimental. Its characters are rabbits rather than bunnies, and they certainly aren't fluffy. This is a visceral book of adventure and heroism. Adams has acknowledged his debt to the theory of the monomyth, which says that all myths conform to a pattern: a hero sets out to face danger in another realm and bring back a prize to save his people. Adams brilliantly evokes a complex world within our own, creating a rabbit culture, language, proverbs and mythology. Like *Animal Farm* it is an effective vehicle for political allegory, but a rich and rewarding novel as well. Adams' wartime experiences can be detected in the sinister decadence of Cowslip's warren; the totalitarian Efrafa; and the liberal Honeycomb warren at Watership Down. It is a book that burrows deep, and stays there.

▲ **The real Watership Down**
The story was set in a real area of the Berkshire Downs near Basingstoke, close to where Richard Adams grew up. The rabbits' journey can be traced on a map at the front of the book.

"They said... older children wouldn't like it because it's about rabbits; younger children wouldn't like it because it's... too adult... But I didn't mean it to be a children's book!... It's a book!"

Richard Adams

▶ **On the big screen**
The animated film version of the book was released in 1978, directed by Martin Rosen. It featured the voices of John Hurt as Hazel and Richard Briers as Fiver, along with other famous names, such as Zero Mostell, Roy Kinnear, Hannah Gordon, Michael Horden and Denholm Elliott. Taken from the soundtrack, the song "Bright Eyes" was a hit for Art Garfunkel.

"FIVER SAT TREMBLING AND CRYING AMONG THE NETTLES AS HAZEL TRIED TO REASSURE HIM. IF HE WAS TERRIFIED, WHY DID HE NOT RUN FOR SAFETY, AS ANY SENSIBLE RABBIT WOULD? BUT FIVER COULD NOT EXPLAIN AND ONLY GREW MORE AND MORE DISTRESSED."

THE STORY IN A NUTSHELL

When a sensitive rabbit called **Fiver** feels a strong foreboding about the future of his warren, he and his brother **Hazel** resolve to leave. Gathering a group of willing rabbits, they set off to find a new home. After a hazardous journey, they stumble across a new warren where a rabbit called **Cowslip** offers a strangely carefree welcome. These new rabbits' attitude and their unfamiliar customs arouse the suspicion of their guests, but it is some time before they recognise the peril they are in. They set out once more and, having overcome many dangers, come to Watership Down where they establish a new home. They soon realise, however, that as an all-male group, their warren will not survive. A search locates a warren where they might find females, but a closer look brings alarming stories of the terrifying **General Woundwort** and his warren, Efrafa. A rabbit called **Bigwig** infiltrates Efrafa and leads a raid. Through ingenuity, the rabbits escape with a number of does and the new warren thrives. But General Woundwort has revenge in mind.

▲ **A useful ally**
Encouraged by Hazel, the rabbits befriend Kehaar, an irritable seagull.

Did you know?
The rabbits' characters were based on Richard Adams' colleagues in the army's airborne force during the Second World War. Hazel resembles Adams' commanding officer, for whose moral authority the author had enormous respect. The Sandleford Chief Rabbit (or Threarah), takes after a civil servant that Adams knew. It has been said that the rabbits talk to each other like civil servants. Adams has claimed the book was not primarily aimed at children, because "children aren't bothered about conscience and values and that's the kind of book I want to write."

43

THE GREAT GATSBY
F. SCOTT FITZGERALD
Publication date 1925

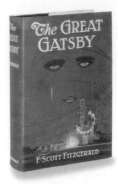

This wonderfully crafted story of love, idealism, decadence and inevitable tragedy among the super-rich elite of 1920s Jazz Age America is one of the most widely read of all 20th-century works of fiction. "The beautiful and the damned" characters are the very stuff of which the American dream was made.

▲ **First edition**
The eyes on the original dust jacket echo one of the book's recurring symbols: the all-seeing eyes that gaze out over an industrial wasteland, signifying the bleak reality of the American dream.

F. SCOTT FITZGERALD
1896–1940

Fitzgerald was born in St Paul, Minnesota. His first novel, *This Side of Paradise* – published when he was 24 – was an instant bestseller and catapulted him to stardom. Suddenly he had the wealth he'd always wanted, and his fiancée Zelda agreed to marry him at last. The high life began, the glamorous parties became legendary and the money and alcohol flowed. The Fitzgeralds moved to Long Island, then to Europe. But his drinking intensified, and Zelda's mental health deteriorated. They moved back to Hollywood, and he began writing hack film scripts – lucrative work, but bad for his self-respect. Zelda was forced into a mental hospital, and Fitzgerald died of a heart attack in his mistress' apartment – a sad testament to the shattered American dream he felt his life had come to reflect.

THE EPITOME OF AN AGE

The magic of *The Great Gatsby* lies not just in the fact that it tells a wonderful, multi-faceted story about a flawed and tragic hero, but also that it captures the spirit of a unique age in American history. Gatsby's story is set against the excitement and glamour that characterised high society during the glittering decade following the end of the First World War. In 1922, Fitzgerald wrote to his editor that he wanted to write "something new – something extraordinary and beautiful and simple and intricately patterned". He succeeded: *The Great Gatsby* is as crafted as a Fabergé egg, a concise but devastating work. But the book is more than the period piece it might appear to be: Fitzgerald explores the disillusionment and emptiness that lie at the heart of those who lead their lives solely in the careless pursuit of money and pleasure.

If you like this you may also enjoy books by:

Dominick Dunne
Ford Maddox Ford
E. M. Forster
Ernest Hemingway
John Steinbeck

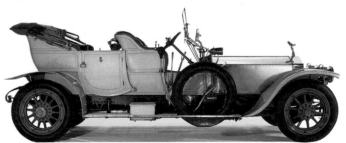
Luxury automobile design began in the 1920s

▲ ▶ **On the big screen**
The 1974 Hollywood film, which won two Oscars, is the best known of the three films that have been made of *The Great Gatsby*. It starred Robert Redford, Mia Farrow, Bruce Stern and Sam Waterson. The screenplay was written by Francis Ford Coppola – but only after the producer's first choice, Truman Capote, was fired. Watch out for a young Patsy Kensit, who appears as Daisy Buchanan's little daughter.

WHAT WAS THE JAZZ AGE?

On the surface, America in the "Roaring Twenties" had never had it so good. Prosperity was at an unprecedented level. Popular music, dance and movies were booming. It was party time and, after the constraints of the First World War, there was a sense that fortunes could be made and anything was possible if one was energetic and determined enough. Yet there was a dark side, too, and Fitzgerald was one of a number of writers who sensed a profound emptiness beneath the superficial glamour. His novels portray "a generation grown up to find all Gods dead, all wars fought, all faiths in man shaken". They point to the moral vacuum that lay beneath the headlong rush into materialism and the evaporation of society's traditional values. In *The Great Gatsby*, Fitzgerald captured both the excitement and the corruption of the Jazz Age.

Other books by F. Scott Fitzgerald include:

This Side of Paradise
The Beautiful and the Damned
Tender is the Night
The Last Tycoon

"Still in nearly perfect health at 70, this is the American novel of the century, the novel of the American century."

The Guardian
on the 70th anniversary of publication

ALAN BETTY MACDONALD
LADD · FIELD · CAREY
RUTH BARRY HOWARD
HUSSEY · SULLIVAN · DA SILVA

A Great Cast...
A Great Novel...
A Great Motion Picture

The Great Gatsby

SHELLEY WINTERS

Did you know?
The Great Gatsby inspired an opera of the same name by John Harbison. It premiered at New York's Metropolitan Opera House on the 20th December 1999 with an all-star cast.

◀ **A great poster**
The 1949 movie starred Alan Ladd as Gatsby, Betty Field as Daisy and Shelley Winters as Myrtle, Tom Buchanan's doomed mistress.

THE STORY IN A NUTSHELL

Nick Carraway narrates the story of his friend **Jay Gatsby** – handsome, well bred, successful, fabulously wealthy and a generous party-giver. He is the epitome of the American dream. Or so it appears. But we gradually begin to realise that things are not as they seem. Gatsby's past is a sham, and his wealth derives not from "old money" but from the proceeds of bootleg liquor and his shady involvement in organised crime. In truth, he represents the corruption of that dream. At the same time, we understand that everything in Gatsby's life is directed at impressing and winning back the woman he once loved, subsequently lost, but continues to idolise: **Daisy Buchanan**. Gatsby's romantic, idealised vision of her blinds him to that fact that she and her rich husband **Tom** are vacuous, mercenary and cruel. Nevertheless, Gatsby and Daisy rekindle their relationship, and begin an affair. Tom Buchanan is meanwhile carrying on an affair himself, a cynical, loveless liaison with **Myrtle Wilson**, the wife of a local garage owner. A freak, fatal motor accident is the catalyst that sets off a chain of events leading inexorably to tragedy.

"AND AS I SAT THERE BROODING ON THE OLD, UNKNOWN WORLD, I THOUGHT OF GATSBY'S WONDER WHEN HE FIRST PICKED OUT THE GREEN LIGHT AT THE END OF DAISY'S DOCK. HE HAD COME A LONG WAY TO THIS BLUE LAWN, AND HIS DREAM MUST HAVE SEEMED SO CLOSE THAT HE COULD HARDLY FAIL TO GRASP IT. HE DID NOT KNOW THAT IT WAS ALREADY BEHIND HIM, SOMEWHERE BACK IN THAT VAST OBSCURITY BEYOND THE CITY, WHERE THE DARK FIELDS OF THE REPUBLIC ROLLED ON UNDER THE NIGHT."

44

THE COUNT OF MONTE CRISTO
ALEXANDRE DUMAS

Publication date 1844–46

ALEXANDRE DUMAS
1802–70

Alexandre Dumas (or Dumas *père*) was born in Villers-Cotterêts in northern France. His father, a general, died when he was four, leaving little money for education. In 1822 his first job, with a solicitor, ended after he went hunting during office hours. He then worked in Paris as a clerk for the Duc d'Orléans, before success as a playwright with *Henri III et sa cour* (1829). Historical novels, children's stories and travelogues followed. Dumas brought French history to a popular audience, but was accused of plagiarism and altering facts. His appetite for work and life was prodigious: he published almost 300 works, and had many lovers; one illegitimate son (Dumas *fils*) was also a writer. Having made and lost several fortunes, Dumas died of a stroke at the age of 68.

Dumas' epic tale of courage in adversity, treasure hunting, wrongful imprisonment, love and intrigue is an action-packed thriller from the first page to the last. The revenge element of *The Count of Monte Cristo* is simple enough, but Dumas grips his readers for well over a thousand pages of breathtaking twists and turns.

▲ **Current edition**
This edition of *The Count of Monte Cristo*, first published in 1996, is a critically acclaimed translation into English by Robin Buss.

ACTION PAR EXCELLENCE

The book was originally published in serial form, like much of Dickens' fiction. With such an eventful plot, Dumas could make the most of these weekly cliffhangers, leaving readers so captivated that they overlooked excessive melodrama and length, or lack of characterisation. He had an unorthodox writing method, relying on collaborators to provide most of the material and adding finishing touches himself – much as an Old Master would work in his studio. But this in no way detracts from the depiction of Edmond Dantès as he is transformed from naive youth to hardened avenger against the backdrop of post-Napoleonic France. Inspiring sequels, plays, films and comic strips, this is one of the great popular novels.

▲ **A rock and a hard place**
If you ask a Marseillais about Château d'If, where Dumas' hero is imprisoned, they will tell you that "there's nothing there except an empty castle on a rock." Finished in 1529, the chateau was used from 1634 for political prisoners. Its best-known real inmate was the Comte de Mirabeau (briefly famous during the Revolution), who was imprisoned for debt.

> "History is only ever a nail on which I hang my novels."
>
> Alexander Dumas

Other books by Alexandre Dumas include:

The Three Musketeers

The Man in the Iron Mask

The Black Tulip

A poster for the 1943 film, directed by Robert Vernay

Did you know?
In 2002 Dumas was reburied in the Panthéon in Paris – with other great Frenchmen. Only two other writers, Victor Hugo and André Malraux, have been similarly honoured.

▶ **A cell at Château d'If**
Today these dungeons are open to visitors. For all the horror of incarceration, some prisoners used the time to think and study. Abbé Faria, a highly educated man, made ink from soot, recorded sunlight falling through the bars of his cell window and, using complex maths, created a kind of sundial.

▼ **On the big screen**
Few books have inspired so many adaptations (more than 30). Whether for film, television or theatre, the novel's thrilling, episodic plot has fired the imaginations of producers worldwide. The first adaptation was crafted by Dumas himself. This 2002 film version, directed by Kevin Reynolds, stars Guy Pierce and Jim Caviezel.

STORY IN A NUTSHELL

Edmond Dantès contemplates a bright future as a ship's captain and husband of his sweetheart, **Mercedes**. Falsely accused of treachery by his rivals, he is thrown into a cell in the infamous Château d'If. Trapped for 14 years, Dantès befriends the elderly **Abbé Faria**, who teaches him everything he knows and reveals the location of a priceless buried treasure. Dantès vows revenge, escapes and finds the treasure. With his newfound wealth, he transforms himself into the mysterious **Count of Monte Cristo**. He rewards his bankrupt master, **Morrel**, for his kindness, and patiently devises an intricate scheme of revenge on his four tormentors: **Caderousse**, the jealous neighbour, lured by greed to criminality; **Fernand**, now a Count, who coveted and married Dantès' fiancée; **Danglars**, now a wealthy Baron, jealous of Dantès' promotion; and **Villefort**, the ambitious prosecutor, who ordered Dantès' imprisonment to protect his career. Dantès exploits the flaws and weaknesses of each man in turn, engineering their downfall. Then comes one last act of kindness.

"An eye for an eye and a tooth for a tooth"

"I WOULD FIGHT A DUEL FOR A TRIFLE, FOR AN INSULT, FOR A BLOW; AND THE MORE SO THAT, THANKS TO MY SKILL IN ALL BODILY EXERCISES, AND THE INDIFFERENCE TO DANGER I HAVE GRADUALLY ACQUIRED, I SHOULD BE ALMOST CERTAIN TO KILL MY MAN."

BRIDESHEAD REVISITED
EVELYN WAUGH

Publication date 1945

Here is a rare glimpse into the privileged world of Oxford University during the 1920s and the complex lives of an aristocratic family. Renowned as a satirical and comic writer, Waugh presents a much more contemplative offering in this book, based on a lush and colourful way of life that most readers could barely imagine without such keen insight.

EVELYN WAUGH
1903–66

Evelyn Arthur St John Waugh was born in Hampstead, London. After graduating from Oxford University, where he read modern history, Waugh worked as a teacher and studied art. He converted to Roman Catholicism in 1930. Five years later, as a reporter, he covered the Italo-Ethiopian War, where his experiences formed the fictional basis for *Scoop* (1938). When the Second World War broke out Waugh joined the Royal Marines and later the Royal Horse Guards, serving in North Africa, Crete and Yugoslavia. He died in Somerset, where he had lived since his discharge from the army. His son, Auberon Waugh, was also a well-known author and journalist.

**Other books
by Evelyn Waugh
include:**

Scoop
Decline and Fall
A Handful of Dust
Vile Bodies

LOOK BACK IN ANGST

Evelyn Waugh is widely acknowledged as having written some of the most brilliant and satirical novels of his day. His biting wit and healthy love of black humour were evident in his earlier books, but in later works – such as *Brideshead Revisited* – the influences of Waugh's deep-seated pessimism and conservative Catholicism play an increasingly central role. He drew on his own experience at Oxford University in a somewhat elite atmosphere that had been fading into obscurity and austerity throughout the 1930s. Waugh claimed, in fact, that he wrote *Brideshead Revisited* as "a panegyric [eulogy] preached over an empty coffin"; he looks back regretfully on lost youth, lost love and what he believes to be the demise of the upper class. The writing is masterful, the language stunning and the characters unforgettable.

▲ **First edition**
Brideshead Revisited achieved great success on publication, but was also criticised because it seemed to be glorifying the upper classes.

STORY IN A NUTSHELL

As a student at Oxford, **Charles Ryder** encounters the teddy-bear-toting **Sebastian Flyte**, the louche, troubled yet charismatic younger son of **Lord Marchmain**. Marchmain himself has moved to Europe, leaving his four children to be raised by his wife, a strict Catholic. Charles and Sebastian become close friends, and Charles is taken to Brideshead, the palatial Marchmain home, where he is introduced to Sebastian's family, including his attractive, thoughtful sister **Julia**. Charles is drawn inevitably into the Marchmains' privileged and flawed embrace, but his friendship with Sebastian falters as Sebastian starts to drink heavily. Twenty years on, in the 1940s, Charles returns to Brideshead, not as a guest but as an officer with his regiment, which is to be billeted there. The memories this evokes are the starting point for Charles' account of the Marchmains' struggle to maintain their eccentric, aristocratic way of life, as well as their religious beliefs, in a fast-disappearing realm of society.

◄ **On the small screen**
Granada Television's 1981 adaptation of *Brideshead Revisited* starred Jeremy Irons, Anthony Andrews (with Aloysius the bear), Diana Quick, Laurence Olivier, John Gielgud, Claire Bloom, Stéphane Audran and Phoebe Nicholls. Scripted by John Mortimer, it was a benchmark in broadcasting history, and still stands today as a definitive recreation of a literary masterpiece for the screen.

▶ **Oxford spires**
The legendary dreaming spires of Oxford form the backdrop for parts of *Brideshead Revisited*. Here, in between holidays at Brideshead, Sebastian and Charles attend dinner parties, watch the rowing at Eights Week and, of course, study. In that inter-war period particularly, the lifestyle at Oxford and Cambridge was in many ways an extension of a public-school existence, replete with upper-class convention as well as scholarly stimulation.

▼ **The setting**
The magnificent Castle Howard in Yorkshire was used as stately Brideshead for the television series. Tourism to the region boomed in the wake of the broadcast.

Did you know?
Evelyn Waugh worked as a schoolteacher, but did not enjoy the job. In 1925, during his first teaching post at a boys' school in Wales, the young writer attempted suicide by swimming out to sea. He managed to swim some distance from the shore, but was forced to turn back after he was stung by a jellyfish. He was also dismissed from one teaching post for drunkenness.

"I regard writing not as an investigation of character but as an exercise in the use of language, and with this I am obsessed... It is drama, speech and events that interest me."

Evelyn Waugh

ANIMAL FARM
GEORGE ORWELL

Publication date 1945–46

First edition

Arguably the finest political satire in modern literature, this story of a farmyard revolution betrayed by its leaders is a witty, funny, tragic but highly entertaining allegory about the former Soviet regime, and of political tyranny wherever it still rears its head.

GEORGE ORWELL
See page 40

▶ **Propaganda poster**
The revolutionary Bolsheviks in Russia used propaganda to keep the people loyal to the cause. This poster implores their followers to show no mercy to the Tsarists.

▲ **Stalin**
In the book, the character of Napoleon was based on the Soviet leader, Josef Stalin. Stalin became one of the most powerful dictators in history.

▲ **Trotsky**
Leon Trotsky, represented by Snowball in *Animal Farm*, was a key figure in the Russian revolution. After a power struggle with Stalin, he was exiled and eventually murdered.

POLITICAL ANIMALS

Orwell wanted to turn his political thoughts into a fiction that everyone could understand. The result was *Animal Farm*, mischievously subtitled "A Fairy Story" (the truth being that it was anything but). Despite being a worldwide bestseller, Orwell's anti-Soviet work was unwelcome in Britain at the time, as Stalin had been a vital ally in the war against Hitler. But the book was especially popular in Eastern Europe, where its cautionary tale of revolutionaries becoming tyrants rang true for many people.

Did you know?
Orwell's portrayal of life "down on the farm" is based on his own farming experiences in Hertfordshire, where he lived from 1936 to 1940. He kept a goat called Muriel.

THE STORY IN A NUTSHELL

The animals of **Mr Jones'** farm revolt against their human masters and drive them out, provoked by hunger and the rousing words of **Old Major**, the prize boar. Led by the pigs, the animals look forward to a life of equality, summed up by the maxim, "Four legs good, two legs bad". But gradually human tyranny is replaced by animal tyranny as the pigs are corrupted by power. Soon a titanic struggle erupts between the two leading pigs, **Napoleon** and the idealistic **Snowball**, for supremacy over all the animals.

"What I have most wanted to do throughout the past 10 years is to make political writing into an art. My starting point is always a feeling of partisanship, a sense of injustice."

George Orwell, 1945

◀ **On the big screen**
The animated version of *Animal Farm*, made in 1955 by Halas & Batchelor, was Britain's first full-length animated feature production. All the animals were voiced by Maurice Denham. However, the film was not entirely faithful to the original text, tagging on a hopeful ending by having Benjamin the donkey lead a new revolution in order to overthrow Napoleon and the pigs.

First edition

In Britain's best-loved Yuletide feast, Dickens single-handedly invents the spirit of Christmas past, present and future with this ghostly tale of miserly redemption. Such is its universal appeal that it has been dramatised dozens of times – but it never loses its magic.

CHARLES DICKENS
See page 24

▼ **On the small screen**
The Cratchit family enjoy a turkey dinner, thanks to Ebenezer Scrooge, in the 1977 BBC adaptation of *A Christmas Carol*. This production starred Zelah Clarke (far left), Michael Hordern, Bernard Lee and John Le Mesurier.

▼ **Marley's ghost**
This illustration of Scrooge's night-time visit from the ghost of his former business partner, Jacob Marley, is by S. J. Woolf. The haunting image was published in *The Century* magazine in 1911.

A HEARTWARMING TALE

Scrooge's path to redemption is a hugely satisfying affirmation of what it is to be human, a celebration of moral values as well as of the pleasures that life has to offer. At the time of writing the book Dickens was in financial difficulty – his family was growing ever larger, his previous novels were being published illicitly and he was in dispute with his (legitimate) publisher. He had to make money, and quickly. He wrote *A Christmas Carol* in two months, dividing the book into five "staves" rather than chapters, following musical notation – a Christmas carol, of course, is a song.

"'IT IS REQUIRED OF EVERY MAN', THE GHOST RETURNED, 'THAT THE SPIRIT WITHIN HIM SHOULD WALK ABROAD AMONG HIS FELLOW MEN, AND TRAVEL FAR AND WIDE; AND IF THAT SPIRIT GOES NOT FORTH IN LIFE, IT IS CONDEMNED TO DO SO AFTER DEATH.'"

"Bah, humbug!"

THE STORY IN A NUTSHELL

The miserly **Ebenezer Scrooge** is wealthy, but has little joy in life, in contrast to the **Cratchit** family, materially poor but emotionally rich, sustained by mutual love and support. On Christmas Eve, Scrooge is visited by the ghost of his business partner, **Jacob Marley**, who is condemned to wander the world. Marley warns Scrooge that to help him avoid the same fate, three spirits are to appear to him. That night Scrooge encounters **The Ghost of Christmas Past**, **The Ghost of Christmas Present** and **The Ghost of Christmas Yet to Come**. Scrooge has been offered a chance to change his ways, but can he redeem himself before it is too late?

48

FAR FROM THE MADDING CROWD
THOMAS HARDY

Publication date 1874

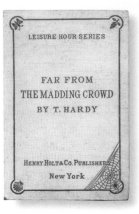

LEISURE HOUR SERIES

FAR FROM
THE MADDING CROWD
BY T. HARDY

HENRY HOLT & CO. PUBLISHER
New York

This meditation on passion and the Wessex countryside was Thomas Hardy's first real success, the book completely selling out just two months after publication. Hardy's story of wilful love and rivalry is set in a rural world that was beginning to vanish even when he was writing about it – a glimpse into a past forever lost.

THOMAS HARDY
See page 64

▲ **Hardy's birthplace**
The cottage in Higher Bockhampton, Dorset, where Hardy was born and lived for many years was built by his great-grandfather. It is now a National Trust property.

A PASTORAL SYMPHONY

Hardy took his title from a line in Thomas Gray's 18th-century poem *Elegy in a Country Churchyard*, marking a distance from the frenetic clash and clamour of society, the "madding crowd". He was writing at a time when Britain's industry was at its height, seemingly unstoppable in its growth and power – and ugliness. The dwindling countryside became ever more precious, rural lives more threatened. Hardy writes from his roots, extolling the natural beauty and rhythms of the land and the wisdom of age-old traditions, but without an urbanite's sentimentality: he is well aware of the tough realities. Bathsheba represents the wiliness of the city, while Gabriel Oak stands for the virtues of the countryside, his name being a symbol of strength and permanence. His simple honesty is in stark contrast to her sophistication and caprice, her desire to charm and manipulate. In the story at least, his country ways win through.

▲ **First US edition**
Before the publication of *Far from the Madding Crowd* Hardy had published four novels and was eking out a living as a writer. But it was this book's success that brought him enough income, aged 34, to marry.

▼ **A cliff hanger**
The spectacular, wild coastline of Dorset forms a dramatic backdrop to the novel, shadowing the drama in the hearts of the protagonists. It would have been over cliffs such as these at Lulworth Cove, popular today with tourists, that Gabriel Oak's sheep plunged to their deaths.

"A RESOLUTION TO AVOID AN EVIL IS SELDOM FRAMED TILL THE EVIL IS SO FAR ADVANCED AS TO MAKE AVOIDANCE IMPOSSIBLE."

Julie Christie and Terence Stamp in the 1967 film

THE STORY IN A NUTSHELL

When beautiful **Bathsheba Everdene** visits her aunt in the country, the shepherd **Gabriel Oak** falls in love with her and asks for her hand in marriage. She refuses, disappearing to the town of Weatherbury and taking over her late uncle's estate. To add to his woes, Gabriel's dog drives his sheep over a cliff, dashing his hopes of owning a farm. Desperate for work, he wanders to Weatherbury, where he fights a fire on a farm and asks the mistress, who is hidden behind a veil, for a job. She agrees – it is Bathsheba, of course. For fun, Bathsheba sends a Valentine to the only man who seems oblivious to her beauty, wealthy farmer **William Boldwood**. But then she falls for an arrogant soldier, **Frank Troy**. Boldwood tries to intervene, knowing Troy is having an affair with poor **Fanny Robin**, but Bathsheba quickly marries Troy – and just as quickly regrets it. Fanny's tragic death exposes Troy's duplicity: he rejects Bathsheba and then disappears. Worn down by Boldwood's persistence, Bathsheba agrees to marry him once Troy can be presumed dead. Delighted, Boldwood throws a lavish party, but the engagement festivities are interrupted by a sensational event.

▶ **On the big screen**
The 1967 film of the book starred Julie Christie as Bathsheba, Alan Bates as Gabriel, Terence Stamp as Troy and Peter Finch as Boldwood.

"Far from the madding crowd's ignoble strife
Their sober wishes never learn'd to stray;
Along the cool, sequester'd vale of life
They kept the noiseless tenor of their way."

From *Elegy in a Country Churchyard* by Thomas Gray

49 GOODNIGHT MISTER TOM
MICHELLE MAGORIAN

'A marvellous story that knows just how to grab the emotions' - GUARDIAN

Goodnight Mister Tom

Michelle Magorian

Early edition

Publication date 1981

This is one of those rare books that become an instant, award-winning classic, loved by both children and adults. It's a powerfully emotional tale set during the Second World War, but its depiction of a troubled child rescued by love is timeless.

MICHELLE MAGORIAN
1947–

Michelle Magorian was born in Portsmouth. As a child she lived abroad for several years, in Singapore and Australia, returning to England when she was nine, by which time she was already writing short stories. Her first ambition was to be an actress. At 19 she began a course at Bruford College of Speech and Drama in London, then attended mime school for a year in Paris. She continued to write poetry and short stories, becoming interested in children's fiction. *Goodnight Mister Tom* was her first novel. She has since written several novels, often set around the Second World War, as well as publishing picture books, poetry and short stories. At the same time, she pursues her acting career.

Other books by Michelle Magorian:

Back Home

Waiting for My Shoes to Dry

Who's Going to Take Care of Me?

A Little Love Song

Orange Paw Marks In Deep Water and Other Stories

Jump

Not a Swan

Cuckoo in the Nest

A Spoonful of Jam

▲ **Life in wartime**
Taking shelter from air raids became a familiar routine, but the frequent raids over big cities led many parents to send their children to the country.

GROWING PAINS – AND PLEASURES

Michelle Magorian describes with great sensitivity the typical anxieties of growing up, exacerbated by the upheavals of wartime. Her story immerses the reader in a past world while detailing all the unchanging pleasures of life: birthdays, pets, presents and family. The horrors of a young boy's life in war-torn London contrast sharply with the healing powers of the rural village in which he finds himself. This is at heart a moving and gentle tale of a growing friendship between a man and a boy who embark on a voyage of discovery. But it also paints a revealing picture of England during the war. At times funny, at times painfully sad, it is an optimistic portrayal of childhood that earned the author the *Guardian* Children's Fiction Award.

THE STORY IN A NUTSHELL

Just before the outbreak of the Second World War, eight-year-old **Willie Beech** is evacuated from London to the village of Little Weirwold. Taken in by grumpy old widower **Tom Oakley**, Willie slowly begins to flourish. He forms a close friendship with fellow evacuee **Zach**, a Jewish boy from a theatrical background with a fondness for long words. He is also befriended by local children and **Sammy** the dog. Willie finds happiness in Little Weirwold as he learns to write and uncovers a talent for drawing, while Mister Tom Oakley finds his own scars beginning to heal. Then Willie's new-found life is abruptly shattered when he is called back to London.

▲ **On the small screen**
Goodnight Mister Tom was adapted for film by Brian Finch. The 1998 Carlton production starred John Thaw as Tom Oakley and Nick Robinson as Willie Beech. "It makes a perfect family film," said Thaw, who dramatically altered his appearance for the role so that he was barely recognisable, despite his familiarity from TV parts such as Inspector Morse.

Evacuees taking their treasured belongings with them to remind them of home

"Goodnight Mister Tom has something for everyone, because in a way it's about everyone. We've all been children. We've all felt frightened. We've all felt unloved – and loved... hopefully."
John Thaw

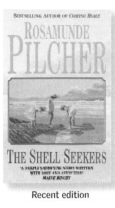

Recent edition

THE SHELL SEEKERS
ROSAMUNDE PILCHER

Publication date 1988

A beguiling saga of family life, *The Shell Seekers* charts the loves and losses of three generations in Cornwall and London. Beneath the story of the painting that gives the book its title is the search for something equally as precious and fragile as a shell: love.

ROSAMUNDE PILCHER
1924–

Described as "rich, famous and unknown", Rosamunde Pilcher has been a published author since she was 18. She grew up in Cornwall, her father overseas and her mother coping alone. When war broke out she left school, worked in the Foreign Office then joined the Women's Royal Naval Service, being posted to Ceylon. There, on the lookout for submarines, she wrote her first short story for *Woman and Home*. At 21 she married and moved to Scotland. As well as her highly popular novels, she also wrote romances for Mills & Boon and Collins under the pseudonym Jane Fraser, writing at the kitchen table so her children were free to interrupt. Her son Robin is also a novelist.

WOMEN AND HOME

At heart, *The Shell Seekers* evokes a woman's love: for family, for home – and for a man irretrievably lost. The novel came about after an American publisher asked for "something longer" than Pilcher's previous novels. The many-layered story that she produced moves fluidly back and forth over the years. It is peopled with engagingly flawed characters who draw the reader into their passions and heartbreaks. With Pilcher's talent for describing beautiful settings in loving detail, it adds up to an irresistible story of life, hope, children and loss.

"OUTSIDE, THE GARDEN WAS DROWNED IN A BLUE LIGHT, HEAVY WITH THE SCENT OF STOCK. AN EYELASH OF A MOON HUNG IN THE SKY. FAR BELOW, ON THE BEACH, THE SEA WHISPERED."

THE STORY IN A NUTSHELL

The novel sweeps from the Second World War to the present, over three generations. The family centres around **Penelope Keeling**, whose father's painting "The Shell Seekers" is now valuable. For Penelope this painting symbolises the ties between the generations, but its fate might tear the family apart. Two of her children, vulgar **Nancy** and on-the-make **Noel**, urge her to sell; only independent **Olivia** understands. As the story unfolds, we learn that Penelope and Olivia have each lost the only man they ever loved. Now Olivia's former lover has died and his daughter, **Antonia**, comes to stay. Penelope, meanwhile, takes on a young gardener, **Danus**. It is Danus and Antonia who will carry on a new love story, while the fate of "The Shell Seekers" is resolved.

▲ **On the big screen**
The 1989 film of *The Shell Seekers* was shot in Land's End, Lamorna Cove and Marazion in Cornwall. It starred Angela Lansbury, Sam Wanamaker and Patricia Hodge.

Other books by Rosamunde Pilcher include:

51 THE SECRET GARDEN
FRANCES HODGSON BURNETT

Publication date 1911

1960 edition

Unlock the door to *The Secret Garden* and step into a realm where the restorative power of nature can heal body and spirit. In this entrancing classic, children bring a neglected garden back to life, and by doing so help unhappy souls to bloom again.

FRANCES HODGSON BURNETT
1849–1924

Frances Hodgson was born and brought up in Manchester; her father died when she was three. When she was 16 the family emigrated to Knoxville, Tennessee. There Frances met Dr Swan Burnett; after he had courted her for seven years they married and settled in Washington, DC. By this time she had had several stories published in magazines. Leasing Maytham Hall in Kent, she began to divide her life between the US and Europe. In 1898 she divorced and remarried the actor Stephen Townsend. She started writing *The Secret Garden* in 1909 while laying out a garden for a house being built on Long Island. As well as her much-loved children's books, Frances wrote a number of popular novels for adults, several plays and a memoir of her childhood. She died aged 75 at her Long Island home.

Other books by Frances Hodgson Burnett include:

That Lass o'Lowrie's

Little Lord Fauntleroy

The Lost Prince

THE PATH TO THE SECRET GARDEN

The inspiration for *The Secret Garden* came from Frances Hodgson Burnett's rose garden at Maytham Hall, Kent. It was an old, overgrown orchard – entered by a wooden door – which she had cleared and planted with roses. She was devastated when she lost the house, but never forgot the garden. Her love for it flowered into a book years later when she was planting another garden at her new home on Long Island, New York.

THE STORY IN A NUTSHELL

When nine-year-old **Mary** is orphaned and sent from India to Yorkshire to live with her uncle, **Archibald**, she becomes wilful and disagreeable. The house is huge and mostly out of bounds, but Mary is allowed to play outside. She discovers an overgrown garden, locked for ten years since the death of Archibald's wife, and meets **Dickon**, a local boy. In the house Mary hears crying and finds **Colin**, Archibald's sickly son who believes he is dying, neglected by his grieving father. Mary and Dickon restore the garden, bringing life back to a house, a father and his stricken son.

"SHE... PUSHED BACK THE DOOR WHICH OPENED SLOWLY... THEN SHE SLIPPED THROUGH IT, AND SHUT IT BEHIND HER, AND STOOD WITH HER BACK AGAINST IT, LOOKING ABOUT HER AND BREATHING QUITE FAST WITH EXCITEMENT, AND WONDER, AND DELIGHT."

▲ **Letting the outside in**
The illustrations for the original 1911 edition, published by Grosset & Dunlap, were created by Charles Robinson. This one shows Mary throwing open a window to let fresh air into the stuffy room of her cousin, Colin Craven.

◄ **On the big screen**
When Mary and Dickon wheel the ailing Colin out into the sunshine to see their walled garden, its magic begins to work immediately. This charming film of *The Secret Garden*, directed by Agnieszka Holland in 1993, starred Kate Maberly, Andrew Knott, Heydon Prowse and the redoubtable Dame Maggie Smith.

First edition

OF MICE AND MEN
JOHN STEINBECK

52

Publication date 1937

Steinbeck, a powerhouse of 20th-century American literature, first tasted success with this drama. A vital read, in every sense, it portrays American labourers' struggle to balance pride and machismo with the need to care for the land. If they fail, they cannot survive.

JOHN STEINBECK
See page 70

▲ **Salinas, California**
This rich agricultural valley, which provided the setting for *Of Mice and Men*, is where Steinbeck was born and brought up.

"A man who writes a story is forced to put into it the best of his knowledge and the best of his feeling. The discipline of the written word punishes both stupidity and dishonesty."

John Steinbeck

LISTENING TO THE PEOPLE

The middle book in a trilogy about agricultural labourers in 1930s California, *Of Mice and Men* falls between *In Dubious Battle* (1935) and the mighty *The Grapes of Wrath* (1939). Steinbeck had worked the fields of the Salinas Valley, California, listening to the stories of the semi-literate migrant workers with whom he felt a close bond. His kinship for them is evident in much of his fiction – none more so than in this moving parable of male friendship and the failure of the American dream.

THE STORY IN A NUTSHELL

George and **Lennie** are buddies looking for casual farm work. Lennie is a clumsy, childlike giant, George his sharp-witted protector. They dream of owning some land where they will both "belong". But their bond for mutual survival sows the seeds of trouble. Lennie loves petting soft things, such as small animals and people's hair... but doesn't realise his own strength. **Candy**, an older ranch hand, offers to buy a half-share in the land, and the dream becomes tantalisingly close, until **Curley**, the boss's son, picks a fight with Lennie, and Curley's wife begins flirting. The ending is worthy of the highest Greek tragedy.

▲ **Migrant workers**
A pet was often the only source of warmth in a farm worker's life. Steinbeck based his novels on years spent living and working alongside these hard-pressed men.

▶ **On the big screen**
Steinbeck's novel has been made into a film twice. The Oscar-winning 1939 version (right), directed by Lewis Milestone, starred Lon Chaney Jr as Lennie and Burgess Meredith as George, with a great musical score by Aaron Copland. Hollywood censors deserve praise for their restraint, since the film was banned for offensive language in Australia in 1940. The 1992 film starred John Malkovich as Lennie and Gary Sinise as George.

Did you know?
Steinbeck's keen ear for naturalistic dialogue led to this book becoming one of the "most frequently banned" by school boards throughout the US for offensive language.

Hal Roach presents
"OF MICE AND MEN"
by JOHN STEINBECK

53

THE STAND
STEPHEN KING

Publication date 1978

STEPHEN KING
1947–

Born in Portland, Maine, US, Stephen King wrote from an early age. His first novel, *Carrie*, almost went unfinished when he decided to throw away the draft, but his wife persuaded him to persevere. *Carrie* brought immediate fame and was followed by more than 30 novels. These inspired many films, from horror classics such as *The Shining* to the prison drama *The Shawshank Redemption*, from the coming-of-age story *Stand by Me* to the futuristic thriller *The Running Man*. In 1999 King was seriously injured when he was hit by a truck while walking his dog. After a slow recovery he attempted self-publishing on the Internet, but in 2002 he announced that he would soon abandon writing altogether.

Other books by
Stephen King include:

The Shining
It
Misery
Salem's Lot
Desperation

An epic tale of post-apocalyptic horror, *The Stand* presents familiar themes of good versus evil, but with the verve of one of the greatest storytellers alive today. This powerful, often disturbing book, follows the near-total destruction of civilisation and the survivors' efforts to make a final stand against the evil that threatens them.

▲ **Current edition**
Stephen King's dedication to his wife reads, "For Tabby: This dark chest of wonders."

ARTICULATING THE APOCALYPSE

What compelled Stephen King to write *The Stand*? "I got a chance to scrub the whole human race, and man, it was fun! …the vicarious thrill of imagining an entire entrenched social order destroyed in one stroke." And imagine he did. The early stages of the book chronicle the terror and despair of a world disintegrating, with the shattered, near-empty planet rendered as only King knows how. As events never cease to remind us, this novel really concerns our paranoia about the end of the world – through technological disaster, disease or out-of-control military experiments. But as in all of his books, King never loses the human detail that drives his stories and gives his work its authenticity and emotional impact. All great stories, suggests King, are born of "real" lives facing universal challenges. It may not be the scariest of King's books, nor the most immediately accessible, but it has tremendous power and scope, and will probably endure as one of his most popular.

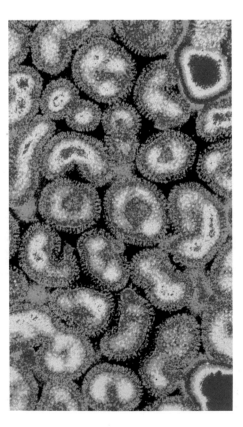

◀ **Paranoia is a virus**
In King's book, a viral terror wipes out most of mankind, but his work suggests that fear, too, spreads like a virus.

▲ **The Flatirons**
This jagged, ethereal mountain stands near Boulder, Colorado, where Mother Abigail sets up her ranch.

"This is the book that has everything – adventure, romance, prophecy, allegory, satire, fantasy, realism, apocalypse etc., etc. Even Roger Rabbit gets mentioned."

The New York Times

▶ On the small screen
The American TV mini-series telling the story of *The Stand* was directed by Mick Garris. Made in 1994, It starred Bill Fagerbakke, Gary Sinise and Molly Ringwald.

Did you know?
King's manuscript was much longer than the finished book. *The Stand: Complete and Uncut* restores much of the original text.

THE STORY IN A NUTSHELL

An accident at a top-secret government lab releases a deadly flu-like virus into the south-western United States. Despite the efforts of the military, the virus spreads worldwide, killing more than 90 per cent of humans and annihilating the existing social order. The few survivors start trying to rebuild society, taking on challenges from restoring the power supply to designing a new government. Many of the survivors also start having strange dreams: either of a 108-year-old prophetess, **Mother Abigail**, or of a demonic figure, **Randall Flagg**. The remnants of humanity gather into two groups around these figures, one good, the other evil. Flagg bases his growing empire of terror in Las Vegas; Mother Abigail sets up on a ranch in Boulder, Colorado. It becomes clear that mankind must choose either to let the whole tragic cycle of ignorance, evil and violence start again or to make a stand. The story builds to a titanic showdown.

"LIFE WAS SUCH A WHEEL THAT NO MAN COULD STAND UPON IT FOR LONG. AND IT ALWAYS, AT THE END, CAME ROUND TO THE SAME PLACE AGAIN."

54 ANNA KARENINA
LEO TOLSTOY

Publication date 1874–76

LEO TOLSTOY
See page 48

▲ **Tolstoy's study**
This is the room in a house in Moscow where Tolstoy wrote his final novel, *Resurrection*. The house is now a museum.

▲ **First US edition**
When *Anna Karenina* was first published in Russia, rival author Fyodor Dostoevsky congratulated Tolstoy on having created a "perfect work of art".

If Anna herself has everything, then so does this book – a timeless story of the search for happiness. It tells of two loves: the first, a sparkling adulterous affair that turns to tragedy, the second a timidly honest marriage that blossoms. This tale has a lighter touch than Tolstoy's others, and is regarded by many as his masterpiece.

A THOROUGHLY MODERN MASTER

The central themes of *Anna Karenina* are as relevant today as they were in the 1870s. Much of the story is taken from Tolstoy's own life: the ups and downs of his courtship and marriage, his pursuit of unattainably lofty ideals, his thoughts on fatherhood, his brother's death and his crisis of faith. The book is also strongly rooted in Russian themes of the time – devotion to the land, economic debates, religious ideas, the early stirrings of Communism and the changing status of women in society. The latter is reflected in the sympathetic portrayal of the adulterous Anna, which was revolutionary for the time. She is shown to be unhappy not because she disobeyed her husband, but because she has not found meaningful love. The character Levin is equally modern, desiring an equal partnership in marriage.

"ARE WE NOT ALL FLUNG INTO THE WORLD ONLY TO HATE EACH OTHER, AND THEREFORE TO TORMENT OURSELVES AND OTHERS?"

St Petersburg in the 19th century

"Happy families are all alike; every unhappy

METRO-GOLDWYN-MAYER PRÆSENTERER:

NY KOPI

GRETA GARBO · FREDRIC MARCH
ANNA KARENINA
ISCENESÆTTELSE: CLARENCE BROWN · PRODUCER: DAVID O. SELZNICK

The legendary Greta Garbo, 1935

THE STORY IN A NUTSHELL

Anna is a beautiful, entrancing woman, but she is trapped in a cold, unfulfilling marriage to government minister **Karenin**. Her only joy is her young son. Then she encounters a dashing soldier, **Count Vronsky**, and falls deeply in love. Tempted by the hope of true happiness, she is soon forced to make impossible choices between her love for Vronsky and her son, and the affair spirals out of control. Fate offers the three protagonists fleeting glimpses of a happy resolution, but they cannot seem to grasp them, and societal pressure adds to their personal anguish. As Anna is consumed by despair, even her passionate love for Vronsky cannot seem to sustain her. Meanwhile, another relationship is developing, less dramatic but equally engrossing. **Levin**, an enlightened landowner, falls in love with a young girl, **Kitty**; but finds that she is infatuated with Vronsky. Levin struggles, both to win Kitty's heart, and also to find some meaning in his life. As all the characters search for true happiness, Tolstoy reveals the double standards that govern the acceptable behaviour of aristocratic men and women. Controversially for the time, he shows that the only way to find true contentment is to follow your heart.

Vivienne Leigh as Anna, 1948

family is unhappy in its own way."

▶ **On the big screen**
This dramatic story has been adapted for film and television many times. The 1997 film version starred Sophie Marceau (right) in the title role with Sean Bean as Count Vronsky. It was filmed entirely on location in Russia, and featured the music of the great composers Tchaikovsky, Prokofiev and Rachmaninoff.

"Tolstoy is the greatest Russian writer of prose fiction...Tolstoy's prose keeps pace with our pulses, his characters seem to move with the same swing as the people passing under our window while we sit reading his book..."
Vladimir Nabokov

Did you know?
Tolstoy's wife Sofya (Sonya) used to help him with his work. She would make a neat copy of what he had written each day, so that he had something fresh to work from. She revelled in his genius and their partnership, and was heartbroken when, late in his career, he ended her involvement in his work. Tolstoy became a hermit towards the end of his life, and gave away most of his possessions.

55

A SUITABLE BOY
VIKRAM SETH

Publication date 1993

First edition

This astonishing debut is a huge, panoramic book, filled with thousands of voices lovingly captured. A simple declaration by a mother to her unmarried daughter leads to an unforgettable, epic journey into the heart of post-independence India.

VIKRAM SETH
1952–

The son of a judge and a businessman, Vikram Seth was born in Calcutta and raised in London and India. After attending exclusive Indian schools he graduated from Oxford in 1975, received a Master's degree in economics from Stanford University in 1978, and later studied at Nanking University in China. He worked for a while in demographic research, returning to New Delhi in 1987. Seth has published six collections of poetry, the first of which was *Mappings* (1980), as well as *From Heaven Lake* (winner of the Thomas Cook Travel Book Award in 1983), and three novels. He has also been awarded the Commonwealth Poetry Prize (1985) and the W. H. Smith Literary Award (1994). *A Suitable Boy* won the Commonwealth Writer's Prize and the Connect Award (1993).

▲ **Muslim migration**
In September 1947, huge numbers of Muslims gathered in New Delhi seeking transport from Hindu India to Muslim Pakistan. Conflict between Hindus and Muslims has a long and violent history, but the novel holds out hope for an era when there may be friendship rather than bloodshed
.

ROMANCE AMONG THE REALISM

For all its ambition and intricacy, *A Suitable Boy* is essentially a romantic novel with a satirical touch. It may be set on the stage of newly partitioned India, amid conflict and crisis, but at its heart is the story of the search for love. Its traditional realism harks back to the great novels of the 19th century, bringing to life a world that is unfamiliar to many of its readers. Part of Seth's achievement is his creation of the vast fictional metropolis of Brahmpur, a city that comes to represent the whole of India, with all its teeming life and drama.

THE STORY IN A NUTSHELL

Lata Mehra's mother insists that her daughter abide by Hindu custom and accept an arranged match, with a boy such as **Haresh**. But Lata is in love with fellow student **Kabir**, suitable in every way but one – he is a Muslim. The story of Lata's emotional struggle focuses on four families, the **Mehras**, the **Kapoors**, the **Chatterjis** and the **Khans**, as they indulge in intrigue, comic snobbery, violence, theft and adultery – all lovingly painted in Dickensian detail. Behind their tales is the bigger story of a new, more tolerant India, reaching its first general election as Lata makes her decision.

> "You should make time for it. It will keep you company for the rest of your life."
>
> The Times

Did you know?
Orion, which first published *A Suitable Boy*, paid £250,000 to acquire the book. This was an enormous sum for a literary novel, but the book has now sold more than one million copies worldwide. In 2003, Little, Brown offered Seth an advance of £1.4 million for his forthcoming book, *Two Lives*.

Other books by Vikram Seth:
The Golden Gate
An Equal Music

Current edition

THE BFG
ROALD DAHL
Publication date 1982

For the child in all of us, this enchantingly twisted story of a giant's friendship with an orphan is perhaps Dahl's funniest book. Its cast of bizarre characters, including the Fleshlumpeater and the Gizzard-Gulper, is a dark delight.

ROALD DAHL
See page 80

Did you know?
Roald Dahl wrote the screenplays for two films based on the novels of Ian Fleming: *Chitty Chitty Bang Bang,* in 1968, and the James Bond film *You Only Live Twice,* which was made in 1967.

A BIG FRIENDLY GIANT-SIZED RECEPTION

Grown-ups may groan at the gruesome bits, but young readers love them! Brilliantly illustrated by Quentin Blake, *The BFG* was an instant hit, winning prizes and accolades throughout the world. Dahl delights in making the adult world seem as monstrous as the creatures of myth and fable, here represented by a giant with massive ears who can hear all the secrets on the planet. His friendship with Sophie shows how children can overcome fear to take on the big, unfriendly world.

THE STORY IN A NUTSHELL

When orphan **Sophie** is snatched from her bed by a giant, she fears he is going to eat her for breakfast. Although he carries her off to Giant Country, he turns out to be a shorter, more benign and "jumbly" version of his neighbours. The **BFG** – Big Friendly Giant – explains that, while the other giants roam the globe to eat "human beans", he lives off "snozzcumbers", the most revolting vegetable in the world. So Sophie and the BFG set out to rid the world of the Bloodbottler, the Fleshlumpeater and other nasty giants, and hatch a plan to ask the Queen of England for help.

▲ **The BFG stamp**
In February 1993, the Royal Mail's special issue celebrating children's literature and its illustrators featured this illustration of the BFG by Quentin Blake.

Sophie Dahl

"Quentin Blake... based the drawings of Sophie on how I looked when I was five. I did have these enormous rather unattractive glasses and long straggly hair with a bad fringe."
Sophie Dahl

"'HOW MUCH DO GIANTS SLEEP?' SOPHIE ASKED. 'THEY IS NEVER WASTING MUCH TIME SOZZLING,' THE BFG SAID. 'TWO OR THREE HOURS IS ENOUGH.' 'WHEN DO YOU SLEEP?' SOPHIE ASKED. 'EVEN LESS,' THE BFG ANSWERED. 'I IS SLEEPING ONLY ONCE IN A BLUE BABOON.'"

Standing in the palm of his hand, Sophie talks to the BFG

57 SWALLOWS AND AMAZONS
ARTHUR RANSOME

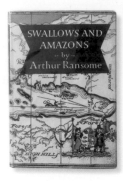

Publication date 1930

Here is every child's idea of the perfect holiday adventure. There is an island to explore, other children to play-fight with, boats to mess about in – and no parents in sight. *Swallows and Amazons* indulges everyone's escapist fantasy and yet is quite plausible; readers can imagine that these experiences might well be their own.

ARTHUR RANSOME
1884–1967

As a child, Arthur Ransome spent holidays at Coniston in the Lake District. After Rugby school and a few months at Leeds University, he went to London, aged 17. There he worked as an office boy in a publishing company and wrote for newspapers; by 20 he was writing essays and children's books full-time. His study of Oscar Wilde (1912) led Lord Alfred Douglas to sue for libel. In 1915 he became Russian correspondent for the *London Daily News*; he met Lenin and Trotsky, and married Trotsky's secretary. He also went to China and the Middle East for *The Manchester Guardian*. In later years he lived in the Lake District.

ECHOES OF AN INNOCENT AGE

The words "Swallows and Amazons" have come to mean more than the title of a favourite children's book that wins lifelong loyalty from fans: they conjure up an idyllic time when childhood was long and lazy and parents weren't afraid to let children loose to play unsupervised. Ransome's story is rooted in his own childhood memories of the Lake District and in the exploits of children he knew. His practical experience of sailing small boats, camping under the stars, fishing and outdoor life in general gives authenticity to the tale. The children's adventures don't happen in some fantastical realm, but spring from the thrilling possibilities of exploration and discovery in the real world and in natural surroundings. This theme continued in a series of 12 Swallows and Amazons titles, which included *Pigeon Post*, winner of the first Carnegie Medal for the best British children's book in 1937.

▲ **First edition**
When *Swallows and Amazons* was first published it sold slowly in the UK. But in the US a book club took a large quantity, and then Ransome's publishers on both sides of the Atlantic pressed him to write a sequel.

Did you know?
The children who inspired the book first met Arthur Ransome in 1928, when visiting their grandfather for a long stay in the Lake District.

Other Swallows and Amazons titles:

Swallowdale
Peter Duck
Winter Holiday
Coot Club
Pigeon Post
We Didn't Mean to Go to Sea
Secret Water
The Big Six
Missee Lee
The Picts and the Martyrs
Great Northern?

"BUT WITH A LAKE AS BIG AS A SMALL SEA, A FOURTEEN-FOOT DINGHY WITH A BROWN SAIL WAITING IN THE BOATHOUSE, AND THE LITTLE WOODED ISLAND WAITING FOR EXPLORERS, NOTHING BUT A SAILING VOYAGE OF DISCOVERY SEEMED WORTH THINKING ABOUT."

THE STORY IN A NUTSHELL

John, **Susan**, **Titty** and **Roger Walker** are spending their summer holiday on a lakeside farm. Their father is away in the navy and their mother has a toddler to look after, so the four older children are free to amuse themselves. Spotting an island in the huge lake, they make a plan to go camping on it. Their father gives permission by telegram: BETTER DROWNED THAN DUFFERS IF NOT DUFFERS WONT DROWN (that's pragmatic parenting!). Mother agrees too, so they gather supplies and set off in the *Swallow*, a sailing dinghy. After a couple of days on the island they are surprised to see the *Amazon* sailing towards them, hoisting a skull and crossbones. The two girls aboard, **Nancy** and **Peggy Blackett**, who discovered the island years ago, say they are pirates from the River Amazon and refer to their uncle, living on a nearby houseboat, as **Captain Flint**. After a brief battle, the children become allies and embark on several adventures that teach them about sailing, camping and life.

> "I was enjoying my own childhood all over again, all the best bits of it and the bits that might have been ever so much better if only something or other had been different."
>
> Arthur Ransome

◄ **On the big screen**
The 1974 film version of *Swallows and Amazons*, directed by Claude Whatham, captured the innocence and magic of long summer holidays described so vividly by Ransome in the book.

► **Roger on guard**
The book was illustrated by the author himself with, as he puts it, help from Miss Nancy Blackett. Here Roger sits guard over the *Swallow* by the landing stage, repelling marauding children and adults alike.

58

BLACK BEAUTY
ANNA SEWELL

Publication date 1877

The original title page of this adored perennial classic read: "Black Beauty, his grooms and companions; the autobiography of a horse, translated from the original equine, by Anna Sewell". Such was the author's empathy with horses, that children could almost believe her.

First edition

ANNA SEWELL
1820–78

Anna Sewell was born in Great Yarmouth, Norfolk, to Quaker parents. When Anna was two, they moved to London. Aged about 14, she was crippled in an accident, and became reliant on a pony-cart, developing a great love of animals, especially horses. She became interested in writing when helping to edit her mother's religious bestsellers for children. In 1871 the family returned to Norfolk. Anna's health was failing and she was given 18 months to live. Too weak to get out of bed, she began to write *Black Beauty*, a few lines at a time. The book was published five years later in 1877, and within a few months Anna had died. At her funeral, her mother ordered that bearing reins should be removed from the horses in the cortège.

PIONEERING ANIMAL RIGHTS

Anna Sewell wanted to call attention to the mistreatment of horses. As a result, almost every chapter of *Black Beauty* exposes a kind of cruelty or ignorance. The book was published well before the advent of the motor car, when horses were exploited for all forms of travel as well as work, and there was little in the way of animal protection. Sewell's only novel helped change the way people thought about horses, and was influential in putting an end to some of the cruelty towards them and other animals.

THE STORY IN A NUTSHELL

Black Beauty is a handsome, spirited colt. At the age of four he is sold to **Squire Gordon**. He makes friends with the horses **Merrylegs** and **Ginger**, and hears tales of cruelties with past masters, including the use of the bearing rein (which forces the neck back), the pain of tail-docking and the dangers of blinkers. One night Beauty saves his master's life by refusing to cross a bridge that he can sense is broken. Then he and Ginger escape a fire in which other horses perish. Eventually sold to a new master, Beauty endures the kindness and cruelty of man as a noble beast must.

▲ **Horsedrawn London**
In the late 19th century Londoners made much use of horsedrawn cabs. Some cabbies were kind to their horses, but most overworked them.

◄ **On the big screen**
Black Beauty has been filmed many times. The 1994 version featured Sean Bean, David Thewlis, Peter Davison, Eleanor Bron and Peter Cook. Alan Cumming was the voice of Black Beauty.

"IT'S NO USE; MEN ARE STRONGEST, AND IF THEY ARE CRUEL AND HAVE NO FEELING, THERE IS NOTHING THAT WE CAN DO, BUT JUST BEAR IT ON AND ON TO THE END. I WISH THE END WAS COME."

First edition

ARTEMIS FOWL
EOIN COLFER

Publication date 2001

Eoin Colfer's first book in the *Artemis Fowl* series took the whole bag of fairy lore and gave it a good shake. Colfer mixed traditional elements with technology, wit and pace to create a new genre that he described as *"Die Hard* with fairies".

EOIN COLFER
1965–

Eoin (pronounced Owen) Colfer was born in Wexford, Ireland, and spent his childhood there. He read a lot, especially fantasy. "I moved directly from Narnia to Middle Earth. Thanks to Aslan and the Hobbit, I spent two years off the planet." His parents were teachers and writers, and he followed in their footsteps. After teacher training in Dublin, he returned home to teach. He began writing plays and short stories in the 1990s, publishing several books; *Benny and Omar* established him as one of Ireland's leading children's authors. *Artemis Fowl* was his sixth book. His agent auctioned it, and the heated contest turned it into a rapid bestseller. The film option advance (£700,000) was the largest ever received by an "unknown" author. After 14 years in the classroom, Colfer took a break to continue writing full time.

FAIR MEANS OR FOWL

It's a story to give any Hollywood action movie a run for its money, with a plot that's complex, contemporary, fast-moving and ingenious – and with witty dialogue, too. This is a new breed of gung-ho techno-fairies, who are not about to let any old (or young) criminal mastermind walk all over them. *Artemis Fowl* won praise from readers and critics, scooping the 2002 W. H. Smith 'People's Choice' Children's Book of the Year award.

▲ **Oak tree, river, moon**
Artemis finds the secret of the fairies' renewal of their powers. " they must pick a seed from an ancient oak tree by the bend in a river. And they must do this during the full moon."

> "Fast-paced, tongue-in-cheek, with some laugh-out-loud jokes... the book is also underpinned by some feel-good lessons about the environmental damage wrought by humans."
>
> The Sunday Times

THE STORY IN A NUTSHELL

Artemis Fowl, a brilliant 12-year-old criminal, has discovered (via the Internet) that fairies exist. In a quest to steal gold, he tricks a drunken fairy out of her Book (the fairy bible) and translates it. He uses the knowledge to kidnap **Holly Short**, captain in the elite "recon" branch of the Lower Elements Police (LEPrecon), and foil elf **Commander Root** and a fairy Retrieval Squad. Then a dwarf called **Mulch** tunnels under Artemis' lair, precipitating a grand finale.

▲ **Giant's Causeway**
The Giant's Causeway is a unique rock formation that stretches from Ireland to Scotland. "It was here, 10,000 years ago, that the ancient fairy race... had battled against the demon Fomorians."

If you like this you may also enjoy books by:
Terry Pratchett
Roald Dahl
Catherine Fisher
Anthony Horowitz
Michael Hoeye

Other books by Eoin Colfer include:

Artemis Fowl: The Arctic Incident

Artemis Fowl: The Eternity Code

The Wish List

CRIME AND PUNISHMENT
FYODOR DOSTOYEVSKY

Publication date 1866

FYODOR DOSTOYEVSKY
1821–81

Fyodor Mikhailovich Dostoyevsky was born in Moscow. In 1837 his mother died; two years later his father was murdered. He studied at the Military Engineering Academy in St Petersburg, before translating novels from French. His own first short story, *Poor Folk*, was published in 1846. At that time he became involved with a utopian socialist circle, for which he was arrested in 1849. After months of solitary confinement he was sentenced to death, commuted to hard labour, followed by military service. The trauma led him to Orthodox Christianity, reflected in his later work. In 1859, Dostoyevsky returned to St Petersburg. He resumed writing, to great acclaim. The deaths of his wife and brother in 1864 triggered a phase of gambling. Between 1867 and 1871 he and his new wife escaped their debts by travelling in Europe.

The ultimate psychological novel, *Crime and Punishment* is a powerful story of doom versus redemption, set in motion by a savage act of murder. Despite the book's 19th-century roots, this is the original tale of rebellious youth, which in Dostoyevsky's day was beginning to make its presence felt, and it remains a dominant theme in fiction today.

▲ **1951 edition**
The first Penguin Books edition was translated into English by David Magarshack.

INSIDE THE MIND OF A MURDERER

Significantly, the Russian word for "crime" used in the title is *prestupleniye*, which means "stepping over a line". Dostoyevsky explores how complex, disillusioned and radical youth Rodion Raskolnikov ("Rodya") can step far over the boundaries of morality in the name of higher principles. His crime is depicted in grim detail and the novel as a whole is a dark and evocative drama. More than that, it is an exploration of youth, morality and self-doubt. Much of the book's power lies in its slow revelation of a murderer's soul from within, linking Rodya's crime to our own inner conflicts and boundaries. As Dostoyevsky was writing, powerful social movements encouraged the overthrow of the social order, making this a novel of relevance to all succeeding generations.

RUSSIAN CLASSICS

The 19th century – the heyday of the Russian novel – brought us some of the best-loved stories in literature. Writers such as Tolstoy, Pushkin, Turgenev and Dostoyevsky addressed the moral and social questions of the day, issues that still have resonance. These novels sought to represent real life in art and saw great historical events and intricate personal emotions as sides of the same coin.

Did you know?
Wherever he lived in St Petersburg, Dostoyevsky chose corner apartments, with at least one view of a church. A loving father, he tutored his children himself and read them bedtime stories from Pushkin, Dickens, Walter Scott or Karamzin's *History of Russia*. He would then work into the small hours, drinking tea from the samovar and smoking.

▲ **Setting the scene**
This painting by Thulstrup depicts an old-clothes market in the heart of a Russian city. With its intellectual intensity, *Crime and Punishment* shows how ordinary Russians like these were starting to face the challenges of poverty with a fierce and singular intelligence.

Other books by Fyodor Dostoyevsky include:

The Double
The House of the Dead
The Insulted and the Injured
The Possessed
The Gentle Maiden

> "Dostoyevsky gives me more than any scientist, more than Gauss!"
> Albert Einstein

"IT WASN'T A PERSON BUT A PRINCIPLE THAT I KILLED! I KILLED THE PRINCIPLE, BUT I DIDN'T STEP OVER IT, I REMAINED ON THIS SIDE OF IT ... ALL I WAS ABLE TO DO WAS TO KILL. AND THE WAY IT'S TURNING OUT, IT SEEMS I DIDN'T EVEN MANAGE TO DO THAT ... THE PRINCIPLE?"

"The more cunning a man is, the simpler the trap he must be caught in."

▲ On the small screen
The BBC adaptation of *Crime and Punishment* made in 2002 starred John Simm (seen here with Lara Belmont as Sonya) as the central character in Dostoyevsky's complex, dark thriller. One of Russia's most treasured and demanding of literary characters, Raskolnikov presents a challenge to any actor.

THE STORY IN A NUTSHELL

Rodion Raskolnikov is an impoverished law student in St Petersburg who has pawned some items to an old woman. His law studies have set him thinking about the psychology and morality of crime, and he has devised a theory that divides humanity into the masses and the elite, with moral law applicable only to the masses: the special few are above it and may act as they choose. What starts as theory gradually enters reality, and he decides to kill the old woman and steal from her, since her money will do greater good in his hands. It may also spare his mother and sister further sacrifice; his sister, **Dunya**, has taken demeaning work and is considering a loveless, financially motivated marriage.

Having carried out the murder, however, for all his rationalising and lack of conscience Raskolnikov cannot cope with what he has done. He has frequent bouts of illness and behaves strangely towards his family, his friend **Razumikhin**, the angelic prostitute **Sonya** and the detective investigating the murder, **Porphyry**. The detective seems to understand more than he reveals and may be playing cat-and-mouse with Raskolnikov. The story twists as Raskolnikov's mind turns. Can the tortured student keep his wits about him as his beliefs clash with his feelings and he strives to avoid discovery?

▲ On the big screen
The 1935 film version starred Peter Lorre as Raskolnikov, and was directed by Josef Von Sternberg. One of Lorre's great acting roles, this film of light and shadow showed how a great tale is endlessly reinvented by and for each generation.

NOUGHTS AND CROSSES
MALORIE BLACKMAN

Publication date 2001

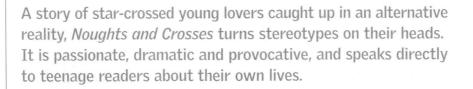

A story of star-crossed young lovers caught up in an alternative reality, *Noughts and Crosses* turns stereotypes on their heads. It is passionate, dramatic and provocative, and speaks directly to teenage readers about their own lives.

MALORIE BLACKMAN
1962–

Born in London, Malorie Blackman went to Honor Oak Grammar School. She took computer studies at Thames Polytechnic and then had various jobs before starting to write at the age of 26. After 82 rejection letters, her first book was published two years later in 2001. She has since written more than 20 books, for all age groups, and has won several awards including the WHS Mind Boggling Books Award, Young Telegraph/ Gimme 5 Award and Young Telegraph/Fully Booked Award. Her work has also been shortlisted for the Carnegie Medal. *Noughts & Crosses* won the Lancashire Children's Book Award. Blackman followed it with a sequel, *Knife Edge*, and a related novella, *An Eye for an Eye*. She still lives in south London.

Other books by Malorie Blackman include:

Hacker
Thief
Pig-Heart Boy
Knife Edge

▲▼ **Success stories**
The history lesson in the book draws attention to successful black people, such as Arctic explorer Matthew A. Henson (above) and Charles Drew (below), who started blood banks and was a director of the Red Cross.

BLACK AND WHITE

Like a photographic negative, *Noughts and Crosses* shows us a picture with black and white reversed. We recognise the descriptions of the inequalities between races in a segregated society, but the picture is startling because in this world the Noughts are the white underclass and the Crosses are the powerful black rulers. Malorie Blackman's challenging novel asks difficult questions and tackles discrimination in a way that no other book for teenagers has before.

THE STORY IN A NUTSHELL

Noughts are white people, second-class citizens in a world run by the black Crosses. **Callum** (a Nought) and **Sephy** (a Cross) are friends, so Sephy coaches Callum for the exam that lets token Noughts into the Cross-controlled high school. On their first day, Nought pupils are greeted with a hostile demo: Sephy is beaten up as a "Blanker-lover". Callum's father and brother join the Liberation Militia, and when a bomb goes off in a shopping centre it has shocking consequences for the whole family. As Callum becomes increasingly politicised, Sephy finds herself in terrible danger and events build to a truly shocking climax.

▲ **Equality is the only way**
A racial integration policy in Boston schools in 1975 quickly resulted in the establishment of inter-racial friendships and improved school attendance.

"MAYBE THINGS WOULD BE DIFFERENT FOR THEM, BETTER... MAGGIE FORCED HERSELF TO BELIEVE THAT THINGS WOULD BE BETTER FOR THE CHILDREN, OTHERWISE WHAT WAS THE POINT OF IT ALL?"

MEMOIRS OF A GEISHA
ARTHUR GOLDEN

Publication date 1997

This modern classic is so rich in detail and emotional depth that it reads like a genuine autobiography. In fact, a male American novelist has imagined this life of a Japanese woman who inhabits a closed and mysterious world full of ritual and ceremony.

Current edition

ARTHUR GOLDEN
1957

Arthur Golden was born in Chattanooga, Tennessee. After obtaining a degree from Harvard in art history, specialising in Japanese art, he spent a summer in Japan. Then came an MA in Japanese history at Columbia University, where he also learned Mandarin Chinese. Immersing himself in the culture of the East, he worked for two years in Tokyo, then returned to the United States and took an MA in English at Boston University. He was inspired to write *Memoirs of a Geisha* by meeting the illegitimate son of a renowned businessman and a geisha. Golden spent ten years researching the book, relying heavily on the experiences of retired geisha Mineko Iwasaki. He lives in Brookline, Massachusetts, and teaches literature and creative writing.

Did you know?

The word geisha means "art person" or "artist". These women undergo rigorous training to master the arts of traditional Japanese music and dance, as well as charming conversation. Widely misperceived in the West as prostitutes, they are in fact more like skilled society hostesses, and are mainly employed to provide an elegant female presence at private teahouse parties.

ART IMITATING LIFE

From the start of this, his only novel to date, Golden creates the illusion that it is a real life story, using "translator's notes" to provide a context for the woman and his relationship with her as the translator of her tale. Golden presents the reader with an extraordinary insight into the secretive world of the Japanese geisha – a world that, having become entrenched in society, was then battered by war and forced to adapt to the modern world. *Memoirs of a Geisha* is a eulogy to a dying art and a rich tradition.

> "WE DON'T BECOME GEISHA SO OUR LIVES WILL BE SATISFYING. WE BECOME GEISHA BECAUSE WE HAVE NO OTHER CHOICE."

THE STORY IN A NUTSHELL

In 1929, aged nine, **Sayuri**, a strikingly pretty child, leaves her poor fishing village with her sister. They are both sold into slavery but, while her sister ends up working as a prostitute, Sayuri is sent to a geisha house. Growing up in the geisha district of Kyoto, she learns the skills required for this way of life and endures a difficult but eventually triumphant metamorphosis into one of the most successful geishas in the land, despite the efforts of her vicious rival **Hatsumomo**. As the Second World War bursts into their rarefied world, Sayuri has to adapt quickly and apply all her practical skills to survive, slaving at menial work. Then an old flame reappears and life takes another unexpected turn.

Geisha learn the Shamisen

If you like this you may also enjoy books by:

Mineko Iwasaki
Lisa Dalby
James Clavell

A TALE OF TWO CITIES
CHARLES DICKENS

Publication date 1859

First edition

Dickens' second work of historical fiction is set against one of the most cataclysmic events in history: the French Revolution. He takes huge themes – violence, justice, redemption – and weaves them into a gripping human story of love and loyalty against the odds.

CHARLES DICKENS
See page 24

Did you know?
The subject matter and style of *A Tale of Two Cities* were heavily influenced by Thomas Carlyle's *The French Revolution* (1837), which Dickens acknowledges in the Preface as a "wonderful book".

A TALE OF OPPOSITES

"It was the best of times, it was the worst of times, it was the age of wisdom, it was the age of foolishness…". The opening lines of *A Tale of Two Cities* are some of the most famous in literature, and they set the tone for the book. This is a story of contrasts, of dramatic events that affect whole nations and personal encounters that change the lives of individuals. Dickens portrays the full range of human experience; love and hate, peace and violence, order and chaos, sobriety and drunkenness, compassion and cruelty… and, crucially, hope and despair. His underlying moral message is the possibility of redemption, embodied in Carton's self-sacrifice. However, despite the high ideals and historical context, *A Tale of Two Cities* is above all a great read and a wonderful story of love and compassion.

THE STORY IN A NUTSHELL

The two cities are London and Paris, before and during the French Revolution. After 18 years unjustly imprisoned in the Bastille, **Doctor Manette** is released and taken to England to start a new life with his daughter **Lucie**. A court case brings them into contact with two very different men: **Charles Darnay**, an exiled French aristocrat accused of spying, and **Sydney Carton**, a brilliant but disreputable and self-loathing barrister. Darnay is saved by Carton, who casts doubt on the prosecution. Both men love Lucie; she marries Darnay and has a child. Years later Darnay learns that a faithful servant has been imprisoned by association with him, and feels he must return. But he too is imprisoned and sentenced to death. His family is drawn to bloodstained Paris, where they fall under the guillotine's lengthening shadow. It is time for Carton to honour a longstanding pledge to Lucie…

▲ **On the big screen**
A Tale of Two Cities has been committed to celluloid many times, but the 1935 MGM production is a real classic. It starred Isabel Jewell as Lucie Manette and Ronald Colman as Sydney Carton.

"IT IS A FAR, FAR BETTER THING THAT I DO, THAN I HAVE EVER DONE; IT IS A FAR, FAR BETTER REST THAT I GO TO, THAN I HAVE EVER KNOWN."

◄ **The guillotine**
During the Revolution, aristocrats and enemies of the state were publicly beheaded at the guillotine.

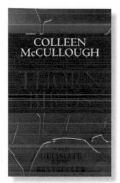

COLLEEN McCULLOUGH

Current edition

THE THORN BIRDS
COLLEEN McCULLOUGH

Publication date 1978

A family saga spanning three generations, with forbidden love at its heart, *The Thorn Birds* is set against the dramatic backdrop of the Second World War. Add the harsh but stunning landscape of the outback of Australia and the result is a true blockbuster.

COLLEEN McCULLOUGH
1937

Colleen McCullough was born in Wellington, New South Wales, Australia, then moved to Sydney. She tried working as a schoolteacher, a librarian and a journalist before deciding to retrain as a neurophysiologist at the age of 30. In 1974 she published her first novel, *Tim*. McCullough gave up work to concentrate on writing. The publication of her second novel, *The Thorn Birds*, justified her decision and catapulted her onto the bestseller lists. McCullough specialises in historical fiction, such as her blockbusting *Masters of Rome* series. She has also written lyrics for musical theatre, several cookbooks and a biography. She currently lives with her husband on Norfolk Island in the South Pacific.

THE AGONY AND THE ECSTASY

Thorn birds – who perch on thorn bushes to sing a brief but beautiful song – became synonymous with pain and fleeting happiness in this extraordinary love story about a young woman and her priest. Inevitably, the book attracted criticism from the Catholic Church when it was published. Not that this hampered sales: word-of-mouth ensured that *The Thorn Birds* went on to sell millions of copies. In 1983 the novel was adapted into to an award-winning TV mini-series watched by more than 100 million viewers worldwide.

▲ **On the small screen**
The adaptation of *The Thorn Birds*, starring Rachel Ward as Meggie and Richard Chamberlain as Ralph, gripped the nation when it was aired in 1983, and brought the book to a whole new audience.

THE STORY IN A NUTSHELL

The only girl in a family of boys, **Meggie Cleary** grows into a beautiful, spirited woman. For as long as she can remember, she has loved the kind but ambitious **Ralph de Bricassart**. Although Ralph is a Catholic priest, the two consummate their affair. However, when Ralph has to choose between Meggie and the Church, he chooses his vocation. A heartbroken Meggie gives birth to Ralph's son **Dane**. Years pass and Ralph rises through the ranks of the Church. As a young man, Dane decides that he, too, wants to become a priest. Consumed by bitterness, Meggie sends him to his father in Rome to be ordained – with tragic consequences.

"I DID IT ALL TO MYSELF, I HAVE NO ONE ELSE TO BLAME. AND I CANNOT REGRET ONE SINGLE MOMENT OF IT."

Other books by Colleen McCullough include:
Tim
An Indecent Obsession
The First Man in Rome
The Grass Crown
Fortune's Favorites
Caesar's Women
Caesar
The Song of Troy
Morgan's Run
The October Horse

65 MORT
TERRY PRATCHETT

Publication date 1987

Death never seemed such fun: only Terry Pratchett could make the Grim Reaper so endearing. In the fourth Discworld novel a great character gets his star turn, and the delights of going through the keyhole of The Grave of All Hope could make anyone laugh in the face of eternity.

▲ **Current edition**
A new Discworld novel usually sells more than 100,000 copies in hardback in the UK alone.

THE DEATH AND SOUL OF THE PARTY

Boundless imagination fuels the pages of *Mort*. Over four years and three hugely popular novels, Pratchett had given life to a tangible world with a wealth of characters, cultures and traditions. In the fourth instalment he turns to the exploration of Discworld's metaphysical realm. Written with characteristic dryness and wit, *Mort* takes us on the ultimate journey (in every sense) and appeals to the escapist in us all. This is a jewel in the Discworld crown.

TERRY PRATCHETT
1948–

Born in Beaconsfield, Buckinghamshire, Pratchett had his first short story commercially published when he was 15. His early Discworld novels were written in his spare time while working as a press officer for an electricity company. The instant popularity of the books meant that soon after the publication of *Mort* in 1987 Pratchett was able to take on writing full-time, and the next 15 years saw a string of successes and accolades. He was the best-selling British fiction writer of the 1990s, and in 1998 was given an OBE for services to literature. As well as the phenomenal Discworld series (28 titles so far, with the latest, *The Wee Free Men*, published in 2003), Pratchett has written numerous other books for children and adults. His prolific work continues to delight readers of all ages.

Other books by Terry Pratchett include:
Good Omens
(Big Read no. 68)
Guards! Guards!
(Big Read no. 69)
Night Watch
(Big Read no. 73)
The Colour of Magic
(Big Read no. 93)

THE STORY IN A NUTSHELL

Death needs an apprentice. A young lad called **Mort** needs a profession. So Mort leaves the local hiring fair in the company of a dark, bony stranger, having been reassured that being dead is not a requirement of the job. The two travel through the air on Death's white charger, **Binky**, to a black house in a realm outside time. The other inhabitants are **Albert**, a mysterious old servant, and Death's adopted daughter, the haughty, chocolate-eating **Ysabell**. Soon Mort is allowed to perform "The Duty" alone, but the trouble begins when his conscience intrudes in the job. Mort saves the life of the beautiful **Princess Keli**, thus changing the course of history. This has a terrible effect on reality, and the resulting paradox threatens the very fabric of the universe. The novel has a double climax involving Death and Mort on one side and a race to save the princess on the other.

JOSH KIRBY

Born Ronald Kirby in 1928, "Josh" acquired his nickname at a Liverpool art college where fellow students compared his work to that of the painter Sir Joshua Reynolds. Kirby was already an established name in Fantasy Art when he began producing vivid illustrations for Terry Pratchett's Discworld series. Kirby produced 25 covers for the series, defining the Discworld look and with Pratchett acknowledging: "I only invented the Discworld. Josh created it." Kirby died in his sleep in late 2001, aged 72.

▼ **Cover illustration**
Josh Kirby's colourful and fantastic designs capture the magical exuberance of the novels perfectly, and have become an essential part of the Discworld style.

"Discworld is more complicated and satisfactory than Oz, has the energy of The Hitchhiker's Guide to the Galaxy and the inventiveness of Alice in Wonderland."
A. S. Byatt

Did you know?
Pratchett's 30 Discworld novels have sold more than 10 million copies around the world and have been translated into 21 languages, including Japanese, Czech, Greek, Estonian, Bulgarian, Finnish and Hebrew.

"ONLY ONE CREATURE COULD HAVE DUPLICATED THE EXPRESSIONS ON THEIR FACES, AND THAT WOULD BE A PIGEON WHO HAS HEARD NOT ONLY THAT LORD NELSON HAS GOT DOWN OFF HIS COLUMN BUT HAS ALSO BEEN SEEN BUYING A 12-BORE REPEATER AND A BOX OF CARTRIDGES."

66

THE MAGIC FARAWAY TREE
ENID BLYTON

Publication date 1943

ENID BLYTON
1916–1990

Enid Blyton was born in London, the eldest of three children. She began writing children's stories and poems when she was a teacher in an infants' school. As her literary commitments grew, she left teaching to devote her time entirely to writing. In 1924 she married, and later had two daughters. She published more than 500 books for children in a career spanning over 40 years, inventing some of the best-loved stories in children's fiction. Many of her stories paint a picture of traditional English life at its most idyllic, achieving a timeless quality that accounts in part for their continued popularity today – along with the reliable series format of favourite characters setting off on exciting adventures that always have a happy ending.

Other books by Enid Blyton include:

The Mallory Towers series

The Amelia Jane series

The Adventures of the Wishing Chair

The Famous Five series

The Secret Seven series

There's a tree in the middle of a secret, sun-dappled wood, so tall that its branches reach beyond the clouds, into an ever-changing kaleidoscope of weird and wonderful lands where anything can happen. Magic and faraway indeed, the stories are a source of enchantment for millions of children – and fond memories for grown-ups.

▲ **Current edition**
In recent editions of the book, the children's names have been changed to Frannie, Beth and Rick. And Jo is now spelled with an "e".

THROUGH A CHILD'S EYES

Enid Blyton's talent for creating characters and adventures that spark the imagination of children – written as if she were thinking like a child herself – is perhaps best displayed in the "Faraway Tree" trilogy, which also includes *The Enchanted Wood* and *The Folk of the Faraway Tree*. "Real-life" child characters rub shoulders with gnomes, pixies, talkative rabbits and whispering trees, along with such fantastic folk as Moonface, Silky the fairy, Dame Washalot, Mr Whatzisname and the Saucepan Man. Free from adult restraint, they can have adventures to their hearts' content. The series continues to charm its readers and all three books have remained in print for more than 60 years.

"I don't think I would have become a novelist at all if it wasn't for Enid Blyton. She managed to create characters who lived on the page."
Ken Follett

The Saucepan Man, by Dorothy M. Wheeler

Did you know?
The Enchanted Wood and the Magic Faraway Tree first appeared in *The Yellow Fairy Book*, which was written in 1936 – two years before *The Enchanted Wood* was published, and seven years before *The Magic Faraway Tree*.

AN ENDURING FAVOURITE

Enid Blyton is one of the most popular children's authors of all time. Her books have been translated into more than 40 languages and have sold over 400 million copies worldwide. Blyton's style of writing regularly attracts criticism for its perceived snobbish attitudes, stereotypes and limited, undemanding vocabulary (not to mention sexism and racism). But the proof of the story is in the reading, and Enid Blyton's books continue to captivate children and transport them to a tantalising fantasy world.

THE STORY IN A NUTSHELL

Jo, Bessie and Fanny have moved to the country with their parents. In this, the second book of the series, they are visited by their city-dwelling cousin Dick, who is expecting to be bored. He is soon proved wrong when his cousins show him the Faraway Tree. The children visit mysterious worlds with their friends who live in the tree. Some of the lands that appear at the top of the tree are magical, happy places, such as the Land of Birthdays and the Nursery Rhyme Land. Others are more sinister, such as the Land of Dreams where the children meet the Sandman and fall into a deep sleep. But whichever land it is, and whatever you get up to, woe betide you if the land changes before you climb back down the ladder to the Faraway Tree!

"THE CHILDREN JUMPED OVER THE DITCH AND WALKED THROUGH THE WOOD, DOWN THE PATHS THEY KNEW SO WELL. THE WOOD WAS FULL OF FAIRY FOLK GOING ABOUT THEIR BUSINESS. THEY TOOK NO NOTICE OF THE CHILDREN".

67

THE MAGUS
JOHN FOWLES

Publication date 1966

▲ **First edition**
John Fowles worked on drafts of *The Magus* for more than ten years before it was finally published in the mid-60s.

JOHN FOWLES
1926–

John Fowles was born in Leigh-on-Sea, Essex. He was educated at Bedford School, then briefly at Edinburgh University, before two years' compulsory service in the Royal Marines. After the Second World War he read modern languages at New College, Oxford, and then taught English in France and Greece. On the island of Spetsai he met Elizabeth Whitton, whom he married. From 1954 to 1963 he taught English in London while establishing himself as a writer. His breakthrough novel, *The Collector*, was a bestseller when it was published in 1963 and enabled him to write full-time. *The Magus*, though written first, was his second published novel. There followed further novels, short stories, poems and essays. In 1966 he moved to Lyme Regis, where he has lived ever since. He plans to turn his home into a centre for teaching creative writing.

Other books by John Fowles:

The French Lieutenant's Woman

Daniel Martin

Mantissa

A Maggot

On a remote island a young graduate finds himself drawn into a peculiar sequence of events. Is this a novel of profound psychological and philosophical insight? Or an ingenious mind game? Whichever, it is a heady mixture of psychology, philosophy and mythology that casts the author as master conjurer and the readers as his dazzled audience.

A RIDDLE WRAPPED IN AN ENIGMA

In the same way that Prospero controls his island world in Shakespeare's *The Tempest*, the god-like figure of *The Magus* directs the world within the Villa Bourani where a young man's journey of self-discovery is unfolding. On publication, *The Magus* quickly developed a cult following, particularly in America. Its appeal seems to be perennial and cross-generational despite Fowles' acknowledgment in his foreword to the revised edition: "I now know the generation whose mind it most attracts and that it must always substantially remain a novel of adolescence written by a retarded adolescent." Fowles himself is notoriously non-committal about the "solution" of the novel. "Its very imperfections, its really not quite knowing where it is going, explains in part why it works. Most young people know they don't know; and the not knowing in this ephemeral, uncertain world is generally the nearest we shall ever get to the truth."

"THINK WHAT IT WOULD BE LIKE IF YOU GOT BACK TO YOUR ISLAND AND THERE WAS NO OLD MAN, NO GIRL ANY MORE. NO MYSTERIOUS FUN AND GAMES. THE WHOLE PLACE LOCKED UP FOR EVER. IT'S FINISHED FINISHED *FINISHED*."

▲ **Links to the ancients**
The ruined cliff-top city where Nicholas finds himself after his trial is based on Monemvasia in the southern Peloponnese in Greece.

Did you know?
The Magus draws heavily on Fowles' own life. Like Nicholas, he taught English in a school on a Greek island – Anargyrios College on Spetsai, which was "supposedly based on Eton and enshrining the spirit of Byron".

▶ **An ethereal world**
References to the play *The Tempest* abound in *The Magus*, and there are clear comparisons to be made between Prospero and Conchis. This 18th-century painting shows Ariel, Prospero and Miranda on Prospero's island.

► The Magician
Two of the symbols associated with the Magus or Magician in the Tarot are the Lily and the Rose, which are alternative names for the twins June and Julie in the novel. The novel has 78 chapters, and there are 78 cards in the Tarot pack.

THE STORY IN A NUTSHELL

The narrator and anti-hero of the novel is **Nicholas Urfe**, recently graduated from Oxford, young, arrogant and restless. He accepts a job as an English teacher on the Greek island of Phraxos. Shortly before his departure he has a brief affair with **Alison Kelly**, an Australian living in London. Once on Phraxos, Nicholas meets the mysterious and charismatic millionaire, **Maurice Conchis**. Conchis introduces him to two beautiful twin sisters, **June** and **Julie**, and begins spinning a web of intrigue and theatre into which Nicholas is drawn, at first willingly, then with increasing desperation. Conchis is the Magus, who masterminds everything that happens but whose motives remain unclear. In a series of elaborately staged tableaux, reality and illusion shift constantly, actors and audience change roles, and Nicholas is purposely tricked, frustrated and eventually put to a final test.

"... You are sick. You live by death, not by life"

"...what I hope readers of The Magus will realise is my deep love, half cultural and physical, half intense and very present, for all Greece itself, then and now."

John Fowles

► On the big screen
Anthony Quinn (above right) played Conchis in the 1968 movie and Michael Caine (below) played Nicholas. Caine commented that it was the worst movie he had been in because "nobody could figure out what it was about". Fowles admitted that the film was "a disaster all the way down the line".

68 GOOD OMENS
TERRY PRATCHETT AND NEIL GAIMAN

Publication date 1990

TERRY PRATCHETT
See page 124

NEIL GAIMAN
1960–

Current edition

The End is nigh, and it's funnier than mankind expected. A twist on 1990s millennial angst, *Good Omens* blends religious satire with a subversive, dark but wickedly funny tone in a story that takes us to the end of the earth.

ARMAGEDDON OUT OF HERE...

Terry Pratchett teams up with comic-book writer Neil Gaiman to produce a fantasy that only these two talents could create. Pratchett's gift for shaping comic characters out of supernatural beings is at its most vibrant in this outrageous tale of angels and demons, while Gaiman adds his trademark black humour; the result is a page-turning romp through Armageddon.

▼ **Original sin**
The relationship between Aziraphale and Crowley goes back to a certain event in the Garden of Eden. They have been rivals for so long that they've formed a bond of mutual tolerance.

THE STORY IN A NUTSHELL

Demon **Crowley**, an ex-angel "who did not so much fall as saunter vaguely downwards", and the angel **Aziraphale** have an understanding: Crowley can do things like develop Manchester, while Aziraphale has a free hand in places such as Shropshire. They have grown accustomed to Earth and neither is keen on the idea of Armageddon. So when the Antichrist is born, they resolve to find him and avert the End. Others are on the trail of the child, but is it the right one? Time is running out, and it's raining – fish.

◀ **Motorised horsemen**
As the End threatens, the apocalyptic Death, Famine, War and Pollution take to their motorbikes.

Did you know?
Terry Pratchett describes his collaboration with acclaimed comic-book writer Gaiman as "a lucky accident – right person, right subject, right time". Allegedly, Pratchett wrote the lighter chapters and the darker material was by Gaiman.

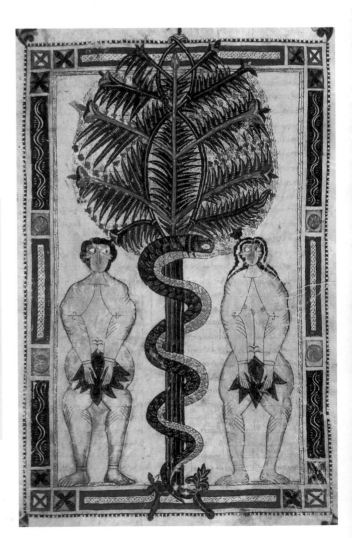

"CROWLEY REMEMBERED WHAT HEAVEN WAS LIKE, AND IT HAD QUITE A FEW THINGS IN COMMON WITH HELL. YOU COULDN'T GET A DECENT DRINK IN EITHER OF THEM, FOR A START."

Current edition

GUARDS! GUARDS!
TERRY PRATCHETT

Publication date 1989

Dragons might be big, flaming and extinct, but in one of the best-loved Discworld tales, they are summoned back to life with some magic words. Pratchett conjures up a lively tale in this fiery and comic addition to a series whose flights of fancy are unequalled.

TERRY PRATCHETT
See page 124

Did you know?
Pratchett's headmaster condemned the moral tone of his first story for the school magazine – it sold out immediately.

HERE BE DRAGONS

This eighth Discworld novel is filled with wit and fantastical comedy. It's dedicated to that hapless group of people – guards – whose traditional role in stories is to be slaughtered to make the hero look good. But for Pratchett, who revels in upending tradition, it's the little men who are the heroes. The guards of the Ankh-Morpork City Watch might be drunken, lazy, dirty and naive, but they are among Discworld's favourite sons.

> "I didn't go to university.
> Didn't even finish A-levels.
> But I have sympathy for
> those who did."
>
> Terry Pratchett

THE STORY IN A NUTSHELL

A secret brotherhood – the Elucidated Brethren of the Ebon Night – is stealing magic objects from Ankh-Morpork. They plan to summon a dragon to terrorise the citizens, and then install a puppet king (sole qualification: dragon-banishing). **Captain Vimes** of the Night Watch objects to people being incinerated on his turf. He is helped by his Night-Watchmen: fat and cowardly **Colon**; runtish **Nobby**; and a new recruit, **Carrot**, six foot six inches tall and raised to think he's a dwarf. Vimes reports to **Lord Vetinari**, the city's Patrician, who makes Machiavelli look sweet and simple, and he is aided by dragon-breeding **Lady Ramkin**. Titanic battles are played out above the city.

◄ **Cover illustration**
All the "little" people of Discworld have a story of their own in a tale that puts the spear-carriers centre stage and turns them into heroes. Again, Josh Kirby puts the faces to Pratchett's words.

70 LORD OF THE FLIES
WILLIAM GOLDING

Publication date 1954

First US edition

"Kill the beast! Cut his throat! Spill his blood!" This terrifying twist on a "boy's own" adventure is one of the greatest novels about children, and one of the bleakest. It is a haunting tale about the dark heart of mankind once civilisation has been stripped away.

STALKING THE BEAST WITHIN

Golding's novel describes the exploits of a band of schoolboys who become barbarians when stranded on a remote island. This pessimistic view of human nature, where evil triumphs over goodness, was formed by Golding's wartime experiences – his awareness of mankind's potential to descend into savage, tribal, almost animal behaviour. Civilisation may be just a camouflage, like the young warriors' war paint, but Golding recognises that an organised society keeps our basest instincts at bay.

"THE ROCK STRUCK PIGGY A GLANCING BLOW FROM CHIN TO KNEE; THE CONCH EXPLODED INTO A THOUSAND WHITE FRAGMENTS AND CEASED TO EXIST."

THE STORY IN A NUTSHELL

During the Second World War, a plane carrying a party of English schoolboys crash-lands on a deserted island. A tribal society evolves, but splits into warring factions: one marked by a willingness to cooperate and maintain a fire (led by **Ralph**); the other by worship of fun and ritual violence (led by **Jack**). By night their dreams are haunted by the image of a terrifying beast. As the boys' delicate sense of order fades, so their fears are transformed into something more primitive; behind a mask of war paint, their behaviour starts to take on a murderous significance.

▲ **On the big screen**
In the 1990 version of *The Lord of the Flies*, directed by Harry Hook, shipwrecked British schoolchildren were replaced by American military cadets whose plane crashes into the sea. The boys fight for survival on an island.

WILLIAM GOLDING
1911–93

Born in Cornwall, the son of a teacher and a suffragette, William Golding was educated at Marlborough Grammar School and Oxford University, studying science before switching to literature. He worked in amateur theatre and then became a teacher. After serving in the Royal Navy during the Second World War he resumed teaching. He published some poetry in the 1930s, but did not achieve success as a writer until he was 43 with his first novel, *Lord of the Flies*. His subsequent writings often dealt with people under extreme conditions and were characterised by their powerful narratives, moral subtext and dense symbolism. In 1980 he won the Booker Prize with *Rites of Passage*, the first part of a maritime trilogy set during a 19th-century voyage to Australia. In 1983 Golding was awarded the Nobel Prize for Literature, and in 1988 he was knighted.

Other books by William Golding include:
The Inheritors
Pincher Martin
The Spire
Darkness Visible

Did you know?
The title of the book is a literal translation of Beelzebub (from the Hebrew), which in Judaeo-Christianity denotes the personification of evil.

"THIS IS OUR ISLAND. IT'S A GOOD ISLAND. UNTIL THE GROWN-UPS COME TO FETCH US WE'LL HAVE FUN."

First edition

PERFUME
PATRICK SUSKIND

Publication date 1985

A dark tale of murder and obsession told with exhilarating zest, *Perfume* was a publishing sensation and an international bestseller. Its subject matter is sensational too – literally so, focusing on one of the five senses refined to an extreme by a depraved but brilliant anti-hero.

PATRICK SUSKIND
1949–

Patrick Süskind was born in Ambach, near Munich, in 1949. He studied medieval and modern history at the University of Munich, then became a television writer. His first work, a play entitled *The Double Bass*, was written in 1980 and has since been performed in Germany, Switzerland, New York, at the National Theatre in London and at the Edinburgh Festival. *Perfume* was Süskind's first novel, and was internationally acclaimed. As well as several other novels, he has written a volume of short stories. He is also the co-author of an enormously successful German television series, *Kir Royal*.

SCENTS AND SENSITIVITY

The story of a man's quest for the ultimate perfume, the whole novel revolves around smell – scent, aroma or stink. Part of the extraordinary magic of the book lies in the skill with which Süskind can use words to evoke the subtleties and extremes of olfactory experience, brilliantly conveying the atmosphere of 18th-century France as he does so. It is a virtuoso performance and one so vivid that many readers have been left feeling they are experiencing the world in a new way.

THE STORY IN A NUTSHELL

Jean-Baptiste Grenouille is born in Paris in 1738 with a mysterious quality: he has no smell of his own. He has a hunger for the aromas of the world, and an uncanny ability to recognise, analyse and remember every scent he experiences. But what begins as a rare gift crosses a boundary into psychopathology when he strangles a young girl in order to possess the "magic formula" of her scent. He starts an apprenticeship with the foremost perfumer in Paris, and learns the science of scent. In Grasse, he terrifies the town as he sets out to become the greatest perfumier of all time.

"A meditation on the nature of death, desire and decay, a remarkable debut."
Peter Ackroyd

▶ Perfumed paradise
For centuries Grasse, a small town in Provence, France, has been acknowledged as "the Rome of scents, the promised land of perfumers". This 1898 engraving shows factory workers breaking up flowers prior to making perfume.

If you like this you may also enjoy books by:

Umberto Eco
Franz Kafka
Thomas Harris
Will Self
Virginia Woolf

"AH! HE WANTED TO HAVE THAT SCENT...TO PEEL IT FROM HER SKIN AND MAKE HER SCENT HIS OWN..."

Other books by Patrick Süskind include:

The Pigeon
The Story of Mr Sommer
Three Stories and a Reflection

THE RAGGED TROUSERED PHILANTHROPISTS
ROBERT TRESSELL

Publication date 1914

Current edition

Part autobiographical novel, part socialist treatise, this is one of the few authentic novels of working-class England in the early 20th century. It changed minds, hearts and lives and, some say, influenced the development of the Welfare State.

ROBERT TRESSELL
1870–1911

Robert Tressell was born in Dublin but moved to South Africa when he was a child. He married in 1891 and had a daughter. After his wife died in 1895 he and his daughter moved to Johannesburg then back to Britain, to Hastings. The 1906 General Election brought him into contact with a group of socialists living in Hastings. A serious recession followed, and Tressell experienced long periods of unemployment. It was during this time that he wrote his novel. Tressell became depressed after it was rejected by three publishers, and on one occasion tried to burn it. After a brief period in Liverpool, Tressell and his daughter decided to emigrate to Canada. However, Tressell could only raise the money to buy one ticket. In 1910 he sent his daughter alone, promising to join her. A few months later he died of tuberculosis and was buried as a pauper. His book was published posthumously.

THE VOICE OF THE PEOPLE

The writer Alan Sillitoe called *The Ragged Trousered Philanthropists* "the first great English novel about the class war", and in it Robert Tressell takes no prisoners. While lambasting fat-cat employers and uncaring politicians he criticises fellow workers he believes are complicit in the capitalist conspiracy to keep the poor trapped in dreadful conditions, with shamefully low wages. With a Dickensian tendency to reveal character in people's names, Tressell gives us Crass the chargehand and Misery the foreman. In a clarion call to socialists, Tressell emphasises the need for workers to pull together in the trades union movement.

THE STORY IN A NUTSHELL

The story takes place during a year in the lives of a group of painters and decorators. They are joined by **Frank Owen**, a working man's prophet, who preaches to them about the benefits of socialism. He is appalled by their lack of political motivation and self-respect, their apathy in the face of great exploitation, so ironically dubs them "philanthropists" – benefactors in ragged trousers who willingly hand over the results of their labour to their capitalist masters. Owen attempts to enlighten his friends, encouraging them to abandon their culture of beer, football, betting and sex. He urges them to aspire to better lives for themselves and their children, to fight the capitalist system. But will they listen?

The rich lived in large, sumptuously furnished houses

▶ **Slum dwellings**
Living conditions for the working class at the start of the 20th century were often appalling.

Did you know?
Fred Ball rewrote his biography of Robert Tressell after he discovered that Tressell's daughter, Kathleen, who had been presumed dead in a car crash in Canada, was actually alive and living in Gloucestershire.

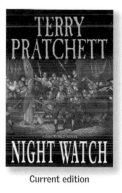

Current edition

Vimes, one of Terry Pratchett's most popular characters, has a long dark night of the soul in this hard-boiled episode from the Discworld series, which spins a tale of time-travel, psychopaths and the People's Republic of Treacle Mine Road.

TERRY PRATCHETT
See page 124

"The most interesting characters, from the point of view of a writer, are the ones who are screwed up in their head. That means people like Granny Weatherwax and Commander Vimes." Terry Pratchett

IN THE DARKER WATCHES OF THE NIGHT

The 27th Discworld novel is a mature work, casting off some of the frivolity of earlier books to concentrate on darker issues and pursue a powerful, intricate storyline. The hero of *Night Watch* is a world-weary veteran of many adventures, and Pratchett whisks him back in time to meet his younger, more impetuous self. The familiar landscape of Discworld is all there, but hidden in the narrative is a witty parody of London life and geography.

THE STORY IN A NUTSHELL

Sam Vimes has risen to the rank of Commander, and is now a Duke. His beloved wife **Sybil** is about to give birth to their first child. He passes the time with old Watch comrades: **Colon**, **Nobby** and **Carrot**. It's the anniversary of the death of seven of his fellow Night Watch officers and he yearns for more carefree days. But while he dreams, the psychopathic killer, **Carcer**, is cornered. Vimes confronts him on the roof of the library – but a sudden temporal disturbance sends them both back 30 years into the past, offering Vimes the chance to change history.

◀ **The giant turtle**
Discworld is supported by four elephants, riding on the back of a giant turtle. The gender of the turtle is something of a mystery to the inhabitants of the Disc, as they are not able to peer underneath it themselves.

"APART FROM THE CURFEW AND MANNING THE GATES, THE NIGHT WATCH DIDN'T DO A LOT. THIS WAS PARTLY BECAUSE THEY WERE INCOMPETENT."

▶ **The art of fantasy**
Josh Kirby claimed that illustrating the Discworld series was very liberating. Pratchett says he didn't know what the Discworld looked like until he saw Kirby's drawings.

74 MATILDA
ROALD DAHL

Publication date 1988

Current edition

ROALD DAHL
See page 80

"This story is one of his very best, displaying just the type of verbal fireworks that have encouraged children to choose him so consistently as their favourite author."
Nicholas Tucker

Rough Guide to Children's Books

Everyone loves Matilda. Adults love her because she is a child prodigy who prefers books and maths to watching telly. Children love her because she gets even with the horrible adults in her life – who are no match for the wits of this (very clever) child.

A CHANCE TO SETTLE SCORES

Roald Dahl obviously enjoyed creating the villains in *Matilda* – he aired some pet hates in their characters, especially patronising adults who dull children's spirits. He brought in some pet loves, too; Matilda confidently asserts that children's books ought to have "funny bits" in them: "Children are not so serious as grown-ups and they love to laugh." *Matilda* won the Children's Book Award in 1988, and in 1999 it was voted most popular children's book in a World Book Day survey of 15,000 children.

Miss Trunchbull has a way with children

MATILDA'S BIG READ

At the age of four Matilda read all the children's books in the library and liked *The Secret Garden** by Frances Hodgson Burnett best of all. Then she started on the adult books. Here's what she read in six months:

Great Expectations,* Nicholas Nickleby and *Oliver Twist* by Charles Dickens; *Jane Eyre** by Charlotte Brontë; *Pride and Prejudice** by Jane Austen; *Tess of the D'Urbervilles** by Thomas Hardy; *Gone to Earth* by Mary Webb; *Kim* by Rudyard Kipling; *The Invisible Man* by H. G. Wells; *The Old Man and the Sea* by Ernest Hemingway; *The Sound and the Fury* by William Faulkner; *The Grapes of Wrath** by John Steinbeck; *The Good Companions* by J. B. Priestley; *Brighton Rock* by Graham Greene; and *Animal Farm** by George Orwell.

* Big Read voters loved these too!

THE STORY IN A NUTSHELL

Matilda is a genius. By the age of 18 months she knew as many words as most grown-ups. But her parents did not appreciate her intelligence, and her father said, "What's wrong with the telly, for heaven's sake?" Reading books boosts Matilda's self-confidence. She decides to punish her parents and when her father makes her eat her dinner in front of the television she puts glue in his hat. At school Matilda's teacher, **Miss Honey**, discovers that she is a mathematical genius as well as a brilliant reader. Unfortunately, the headmistress, **Miss Trunchbull**, is a tyrant who hates children, especially clever ones. But Matilda has supernatural powers that stupid adults can only dream of.

BRIDGET JONES'S DIARY
HELEN FIELDING

Publication date 1996

First edition

Bridget Jones is the voice of the mid-1990s thirty-something singleton, waging an unending war against flab and over-indulgence, constantly in search of inner poise and a boyfriend. This is a brilliant evocation of life as a single girl in a particular time.

HELEN FIELDING
c. 1960–

Helen Fielding was born in Yorkshire. After reading English at Oxford University, she worked for the BBC on news, light entertainment and children's TV programmes. Her first novel, *Cause Celeb*, drew on her experience making documentaries for Comic Relief. *Bridget Jones's Diary* began as a weekly column in the *Independent* newspaper, and has since inspired two bestselling novels.

Suave but stiff. *(if only!?)*

Aloof. Unavailable. Ice queen. *(quite fancy a snog though...)*

Gorgeous and my boss. *(must NOT sleep with him!?)*

RENÉE ZELLWEGER   HUGH GRANT   COLIN FIRTH
BRIDGET JONES'S DIARY
For anyone who's ever been set up, stood up or felt up.

The poster for the film adaptation

"Helen Fielding is one of the funniest writers in Britain and Bridget Jones is a creation of comic genius."
Nick Hornby

DIARY OF AN EVERYWOMAN

Bridget is intelligent, witty and independent, she's also insecure, anxious and sometimes lonely. In other words, she's normal. Women recognise aspects of themselves in Bridget, just as men see traits of their wives or girlfriends (and perhaps something of themselves in the novel's male characters). *Bridget Jones's Diary* highlights the difference between what people are and what they think they should be.

THE STORY IN A NUTSHELL

Bridget begins with a list of New Year resolutions, including "I WILL go to gym three times a week not merely to buy sandwich". Her diary for the ensuing year records her battle against eating too much, drinking too much and smoking too much — and the progress of her love life. The story is a classic love triangle. Bridget's mother tries to pair her off with barrister **Mark Darcy**, seemingly a bit of a stuffed shirt. Bridget shows no interest and instead embarks on an affair with **Daniel Cleaver**, her flirtatious boss. As Bridget's personal and professional life lurch between triumph and disaster, she relies on friends for help, advice and Chardonnay. The story echoes *Pride and Prejudice*, as Fielding openly acknowledged: "I shamelessly stole the plot. I thought it had been v. well market-researched over a number of centuries".

▼ On the big screen
Texan Renée Zellweger had to work hard to lose her accent to play the English Bridget in the 2001 film adaptation. Colin Firth, who starred as Bridget's hero Mr Darcy in the BBC dramatisation of *Pride and Prejudice*, played Mark Darcy.

Other books by Helen Fielding:
Cause Celeb
Bridget Jones: The Edge of Reason

"MONDAY 2 JANUARY 2 A.M. OH, WHY AM I SO UNATTRACTIVE? WHY? EVEN A MAN WHO WEARS BUMBLEBEE SOCKS THINKS I AM HORRIBLE."

76 THE SECRET HISTORY
DONNA TARTT

Publication date 1992

First edition

DONNA TARTT
1963–

Donna Tartt was born in a small town in Mississippi in 1963. She read voraciously as a child, often skipping school to devour classic Victorian novels. She was a precocious writer too: her first sonnet was published in a literary magazine at the age of 13. In 1981 she went to the University of Mississippi but, after a year, moved on to Bennington, a small but well-known liberal arts college in Vermont. There she met Brett Easton Ellis, author of *American Psycho*, who encouraged her when she started writing *The Secret History*. The book took seven years to complete. It was auctioned to the Canadian publisher Knopf for an advance of $450,000 and, on publication, was an immediate success. Tartt did not write a second novel, however, until 2002 – some ten years later.

Other books by Donna Tartt:
The Little Friend

Before the publication of *The Secret History*, Donna Tartt was unknown. But the young American's bewitching story of an elite group of classics students that struggles with guilt and the ethics of its terrible deeds took Tartt to the top of the bestseller lists.

CLASSICAL TRAGEDY IN MODERN DRESS

Part murder mystery, part psychological suspense thriller, part philosophical treatise on the nature of good and evil and part history of ancient Greek mythology, *The Secret History* is hard to pigeonhole. Despite its complexity and Tartt's fear that the novel would be too highbrow for a wide readership – "the book's long… it's got Greek phrases, and it's not written in a style that's popular" – it has proved extraordinarily successful. Comparisons have been made with *Crime and Punishment* and *The Great Gatsby*; while there are echoes of these, *The Secret History* has its own distinct voice.

▲ **Model college**
Bennington College in Vermont was the inspiration for Hampden College where the action is set.

THE STORY IN A NUTSHELL

Richard Papen is a new student at Hampden College in Vermont. To fit in with his fellow students, he disguises the fact that he comes from a small suburban town in California. On campus, he becomes enchanted by one clique in particular, a group of five classics students: **Henry Winter**, tall, sophisticated, well-bred, manipulative and the group's natural leader; **Francis Abernath**, gay and urbane; **Charles** and **Camilla Macaulay**, twins who are intimately close; and **Bunny Corcoran**, rich, boorish and bullying. Their mentor is the mysterious and charismatic **Professor Julian Morrow**, who teaches them ancient Greek and reinforces their sense of moral and intellectual superiority. Richard gradually discovers that the group is concealing a gruesome secret, the consequences of which none of the members yet fully understand.

▲ **Dionysian excess**
The Greek god of wine and ecstasy epitomises the stripping away of civilised restraint. In Tartt's novel Dionysian frenzy turns to violence .

"A beautifully written story, well told, funny, sad, scary, and impossible to leave alone."
John Grisham

THE WOMAN IN WHITE
WILKIE COLLINS

Publication date 1860

First edition

This thrilling, suspense-filled tale of madness, murder and mistaken identity is a model example of the sensationalistic novel, blending horror with psychological realism. A Gothic masterpiece, *The Woman in White* is the best known of Wilkie Collins' work.

WILKIE COLLINS
1824–89

William Wilkie Collins was born in London, the son of William Collins, a noted landscape and figure painter. During the 1830s he spent some years in Italy with his parents. On returning to England he spent five years in the tea business and then entered Lincoln's Inn (to read for the bar) but was drawn to writing. He wrote 25 novels, plays, numerous short stories and more than 100 non fiction pieces. In 1851 Collins met Charles Dickens. They became friends, collaborating on *Household Words* and *All Year Round* A rift developed between them shortly before Dickens' death, when Collins' brother married Dickens' daughter.

A PIONEERING STYLE

In *The Woman in White* Collins used the innovative technique of having the various characters narrate the story from their own viewpoints – a technique that we tend to associate more with 20th-century writers. This method enabled him to reveal as much or as little of the plot as he liked, adjusting the pace of the narrative to crank up the mystery and tension that are vitally important ingredients of the novel. Collins' treatment of his female characters was revolutionary. Unlike the trend at the time towards idealising women or portraying them as childlike, as his friend Charles Dickens was prone to do, Collins' made his heroines strong and assertive individuals who strike an immediate chord with modern readers.

Other books by Wilkie Collins include:
The Moonstone
The Evil Genius
Poor Miss Finch
Hide and Seek

THE STORY IN A NUTSHELL

Walter Hartwright is employed as a drawing master to the innocent and sheltered **Laura Fairlie** and her feisty sister **Marian**. On his way to take up the post he has an eerie encounter with the mysterious **Woman in White** on a moonlit road. Walter falls in love with Laura but, abiding by her father's deathbed request, she will not renege on her betrothal to **Sir Percival Glyde**. Sir Percival is only after her fortune, however, and is aided and abetted in his dishonourable intentions by his villainous friend and adviser, **Count Fosco**. Glyde's disreputable past links him with the Woman in White, and this connection triggers a chain of events that sees great intrigue unravelled, lives put in peril and dark secrets revealed.

◄ **On the big screen**
The 1947 film version starred Eleanor Parker as Laura Fairlie and Sydney Greenstreet as the diabolical Count Fosco.

► **Inside the asylum**
This cartoon by Merry, based on Hogarth's "Bedlam", satirises the world of a Victorian asylum, into which one character is thrown.

78 ULYSSES
JAMES JOYCE

Publication date 1922

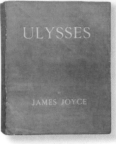

▲ **First edition**
Ulysses was initially denounced by the church for its profanity and wasn't published in the UK until 1936.

JAMES JOYCE
1916–1990

James Joyce was born in the suburbs of south Dublin into a chaotic middle-class Catholic family. He was educated by Jesuits and went on to university where he studied languages and philosophy and, briefly, medicine. As a young man, Joyce became disillusioned with the Catholic Church and with what he perceived as the narrow-mindedness of Irish nationalism. He left Ireland with his lover, Nora Barnacle, and never lived there again, preferring to live a nomadic life in European cities, such as Paris, Trieste and Berne. Despite this self-imposed exile, his subsequent work – including poetry, plays, short stories and novels – was almost exclusively concerned with Ireland, and particularly with Dublin. After several years of ill health and having all but lost his eyesight, Joyce died in 1941. He is buried in Zurich.

Other books by James Joyce include:

A Portrait of the Artist as a Young Man

Finnegan's Wake

Dubliners

Regarded by many people as the greatest novel of the 20th century, *Ulysses* traces a day in the life of a Dubliner by means of an innovative swirling stream of consciousness, myth and religion, alternating with interludes of gossip, sex, intellectual sparring and debate about the nobility of the ordinary man.

A DAY IN THE LIFE

The title refers to Homer's epic poem, the *Odyssey*, the story of wandering hero Ulysses striving to get home to his wife after a ten-year absence. In Joyce's epic, Leopold Bloom encounters a menagerie of Dublin characters in his quest to return to his wife Molly, culminating in an unpunctuated 60-page outpouring of passion that is one of the most extraordinary achievements in 20th-century literature. *Ulysses* is a parody of a heroic epic, but it has a deeper purpose: this day in the life of a city reveals, through one man, all of humanity in its infinite variety. This is a novel of possibilities: of language, of what "the novel" can be and of what any one of us can strive for. It is a difficult read, but a milestone of Modernist literature.

▲ **The original Ulysses**
This Grecian urn depicts a scene from Homer's *Odyssey*, the basis for Joyce's own epic story.

> "It is the book to which we are all indebted and from which none of us can escape."
> T. S. Eliot

▲ **Nora Joyce**
James Joyce's wife was the inspiration for Molly. "Bloomsday", 16th June 1904, is the anniversary of her first date with Joyce.

▶ **Davy Byrnes pub**
Bloom stopped at this Dublin bar for his lunch. Fans of the book meet here on 16th June each year to celebrate "Bloomsday".

▼ ▶ On the big screen
The 2003 film adaptation of *Ulysses*, called *Bl,.m* was filmed in Ireland. It stars Stephen Rea as Leopold Bloom and Hugh O'Conor as the young Stephen Dedalus. The screenplay and direction are by Sean Walsh.

THE STORY IN A NUTSHELL

On the morning of 16th June 1904, **Stephen Dedalus** and **Leopold Bloom** go about their business in Dublin, while Bloom's lusty wife **Molly** is waiting at home for an afternoon of sensuous delight with her lover. Bloom's journey takes him to many locations, from library to brothel to pub to maternity ward to funeral parlour. On the way, he encounters the voices and thoughts of a city of strangers, friends and acquaintances – housewives, lovers, gamblers, priests, pub philosophers, nationalists and prostitutes. As night falls, Bloom's path crosses that of young Stephen (a portrait of Joyce himself as a youth), whom he rescues from a beating in a mock-heroic manner. Finally, Bloom makes his way home to bed where Molly is thinking about him and waiting, promising a night of passion in her arms

"STEPHEN CLOSED HIS EYES TO HEAR HIS BOOTS CRUSH CRACKLING WRACK AND SHELLS. YOU ARE WALKING THROUGH IT HOWSOMEVER. I AM, A STRIDE AT A TIME. A VERY SHORT SPACE OF TIME THROUGH VERY SHORT TIMES OF SPACE."

BLEAK HOUSE
CHARLES DICKENS

Publication date 1853

CHARLES DICKENS
See page 24

This dark and brooding novel reveals a world that is rotten to its very core, but at the same time retains Dickens' characteristic warmth and humour, and is considered one of his greatest books. A gallery of droll grotesques unveil the history of *Bleak House* and deliver a searing indictment of British society in the mid-19th century.

▲ **Holiday home**
Set high on the cliffs at Broadstairs, Fort House – now renamed Bleak House – was Dickens' summer home. It is now a museum.

A RADICAL VOICE IN A COMPLACENT AGE

Dickens was the first major writer of his time to confront – with first-hand experience – the dark side of the early Victorian era. The industrial revolution had made land owners wealthier and created a prosperous middle class, but it had also given rise to extremes of poverty. At the centre of this unequal battle were the lawyers who, far from upholding the noblest principles of defending the poor, delighted in making money out of their misery. As Dickens says, "The one great principle of the English law is to make business for itself." Dickens' social and political commentary was radical for its time but, unlike some of his other tales, *Bleak House* still seems timely and relevant today. This is both a tragic story of doomed young love and a genuinely enthralling murder mystery – arguably, the first of a popular tradition that is stronger than ever today. But Dickens also implies that those who enter Bleak House should not abandon *all* hope.

▲ **First edition**
The novel was first published in serial form, between March 1852 and September 1853, then republished in book form in 1853.

◄ **The Great Exhibition**
Bleak House challenges the view of a prosperous Britain put forward by the 1851 Great Exhibition. The Archbishop of Canterbury expressed thanks that there was in England neither violence nor destruction, but "peace within our walls and plenteousness within our palaces".

THE STORY IN A NUTSHELL

There are three main stories, interwoven in Dickens' inimitable way with dozens of other incidents and characters. The first story is the case of "Jarndyce and Jarndyce" in the Court of Chancery. Young **Richard Carstone** is a ward of benefactor **John Jarndyce**, and expects money from the case, but he is exploited by ruthless predators. In secret he marries his fellow ward, **Ada Clare**, but, by now hopelessly trapped in a convoluted and apparently endless court case, he descends into poverty and ill health. Another Jarndyce ward is the virtuous **Esther Summerson**, who is pivotal to the second strand of the story. Unknowingly, she is a link to the aristocratic **Lady Dedlock**, whose lawyer, **Tulkinghorn**, scents a secret and tries to uncover it. There is a murder, which is doggedly investigated by the estimable **Inspector Bucket**. The third strand is narrated subjectively by Esther (the first time a male English writer used a female narrator). Like all other characters great and small, rich and poor, she has her part to play and her destiny to fulfil.

◀ **A dim view**
The central metaphor is fog, which symbolises legal obfuscation and ignorance. Some can see through it – "Snagsby sees it all", while others (Inspector Bucket) see it too late. Others see but don't understand. Jo possesses vital evidence but "never knowd what it wos all about".

> "If young people are interested in understanding the complex nature of their society; and if young people are at all interested in the history of their culture then Dickens is still fully relevant."
> Peter Ackroyd

DICKENS' MAIN ILLUSTRATOR

Hablot Knight Brown, known as "Phiz", is the illustrator most associated with Dickens, working first on a pamphlet called *Sunday Under Three Heads*, then on *The Pickwick Papers* after the suicide of the previous illustrator. Browne illustrated ten of Dickens' novels and the pair worked together for 23 years. At first, Browne used the pseudonym "N.E.M.O.", meaning "Nobody" in Latin. He later adopted the name "Phiz" while he was working on *The Pickwick Papers*. His relationship with Dickens deteriorated after a disappointing reaction to the illustrations for *A Tale of Two Cities*. He never worked with Dickens again.

▲ **On the small screen**
The 1985 BBC television mini-series, directed by Ross Devenish, starred Denholm Elliott (above) as John Jarndyce and Diana Rigg as Lady Dedlock.

If you like this you may also enjoy books by:

Joan Aiken
W. Somerset Maugham
Rohinton Mistry
Iain Sinclair
Anthony Trollope
Tom Wolfe

Did you know?
Dickens' descriptions of urban squalor were used by social reformers to highlight the unhealthy conditions in Victorian towns and the need for sanitary reforms. In 1851 life expectancy in British towns was less than 30 years. Edwin Chadwick, the author of the report on the sanitary conditions of British towns, consulted Dickens about the best way to present his findings and used his descriptions to draw the public's attention to the problem.

"FOG EVERYWHERE. FOG UP THE RIVER, WHERE IT FLOWS AMONG GREEN AITS AND MEADOWS; FOG DOWN THE RIVER, WHERE IT ROLLS DEFILED AMONG THE TIERS OF SHIPPING, AND THE WATERSIDE POLLUTIONS OF A GREAT (AND DIRTY) CITY."

DOUBLE ACT
JACQUELINE WILSON

Publication date 1995

First edition

This classic girls' story is told by two "first persons" – twins who go everywhere and do everything together. The reader is invited on a roller-coaster journey of discovery as the girls learn more about themselves, each other and life.

JACQUELINE WILSON
See page 74

▼ **On the small screen**
In the Channel 4 adaptation of *Double Act,* the twins were played by Chloe and Zoe Tempest-Jones.

TWO ARE BETTER THAN ONE

All of Jacqueline Wilson's talents are doubled in this book. There are two "unreliable narrators" who think they are very similar but don't realise how different they actually are. So there are at least two plots, and the emotional content is more than doubled. The author captures the pain and uncertainty of changing circumstances in life, as well as the unexpected pleasures.

> The Red Bookshop
> High Street
> Cussop
> 19 May
>
> Dear Madam - We are sorry, we don't know your name.
>
> We are ten-year-old identical twins, nearly eleven and we hate our school in this village. We don't fit in. The lessons are boring and there aren't any proper books and the only games we play are rounders.
>
> We went to the television audition for *The Twins at St Clare's.* We very nearly got the part actually. We were featured in the television coverage. Well, one of us was. And you were featured too and your wonderful school and we thought Oooh this is our idea of heaven, the stage and the swimming pool and the games and the animals and all that.
>
> So please can we come to your school in September? We promise to be good pupils and you don't have to worry about us being homesick because we hate our home. Yours faithfully
> Ruby Barker
> Garnet Barker.
>
> P.S. Please say yes. You won't regret it. Honestly.

Ruby's letter to the headteacher

What they read

The twins Ruby and Garnet reveal a lot about themselves and what they like when they tell us what they read. Ruby writes that "Garnet likes old books... stuff like *Little Women* and *What Katy Did* and all those E. Nesbit books. And she reads twin books too. Books like *The Twins at St Clare's.* And all the *Sweet Valley Twins.* I read them too, because you can read them nice and quickly. But the books I like best are true stories about flashy famous people".

Dad's bookshop has a whole shelf of school stories at the back. When Garnet is offered a place at a boarding school she swots up on the subject by reading a lot of school stories, including the *Chalet School* books by Elinor Brent-Dyer and *Mallory Towers* by Enid Blyton.

"GARNET IS USUALLY THE ONE WHO WRITES STUFF. HER WRITING'S NEATER THAN MINE. SO OFTEN I GET HER TO DO MY SCHOOLWORK. SHE DOESN'T MIND".
"YES I DO."

THE STORY IN A NUTSHELL

Ruby and **Garnet** are ten-year-old identical twins, but quite different: Ruby is wilful and extrovert, while Garnet is quiet and bookish. They have not really got over the death of their mother, but they are close to their **Gran**. Then everything in their lives changes. **Dad** meets a new woman, called **Rose**; Gran moves into sheltered housing and Dad is made redundant. He buys a bookshop in the country, and Rose moves with the family to the new area, but the girls don't like their new life, or their new school. They audition for parts in a TV adaptation of Enid Blyton's *The Twins at St Clare's* and apply to go to a boarding school. Then comes a series of events that force the girls to rethink who they are in relation to each other and to the rest of their family.

Current edition

This is a story of revenge: the revenge that Mr and Mrs Twit take on each other, and then the revenge their victims take on them. Young readers love this amusing, anarchic but deeply moral tale, in which the baddies get no less than they deserve.

ROALD DAHL
See page 80

CRIME AND PUNISHMENT, TWIT-STYLE

At first *The Twits* seem to be indulging in aimless nastiness. The tricks that Mr and Mrs Twit play on each other leave even the author speechless after a while: "But that's enough of that. We can't go on for ever watching these two disgusting people doing disgusting things to each other." Indeed, sighs the adult reader. But this short book is for children (aged seven and upwards), who are delighted by the slobbiness of the Twits and outraged by their treatment of animals.

The birds carry out their plan to foil the Twits

> "My crusade is to teach small children to love books so much that it becomes a habit... if you are able to read books and enjoy them and love them you've got the whole world of literature at your feet."
>
> Roald Dahl

THE STORY IN A NUTSHELL

Mr Twit is a nasty old man who has so many bits of food in his beard that whenever he gets hungry he just sticks out his tongue to collect a morsel. **Mrs Twit** hits animals and small children with her walking stick. The Twits are engaged in a constant tit-for-tat with each other, but they are even crueller to animals. They eat bird pie, catching the birds by putting glue all over the branches of a tree. The Twits also keep monkeys in a cage and force them to do everything upside-down. One day, the African Roly-Poly bird flies in and, while the Twits are out buying guns, a cunning plot is hatched to foil them.

"IF A PERSON HAS UGLY THOUGHTS, IT BEGINS TO SHOW ON THE FACE. AND WHEN THAT PERSON HAS UGLY THOUGHTS EVERY DAY, EVERY WEEK, EVERY YEAR, THE FACE GETS UGLIER AND UGLIER UNTIL IT GETS SO UGLY YOU CAN HARDLY BEAR TO LOOK AT IT."

Quentin Blake illustrates what will happen if you keep thinking ugly thoughts

82

I CAPTURE THE CASTLE
DODIE SMITH

Publication date 1948

Adored for its infectious humour and enthusiasm, *I Capture the Castle*'s charm lies in the voice of the inexperienced narrator, Cassandra, whose wonderful turn of phrase carries us through the absurd situations in which she finds herself.

Current edition

DODIE SMITH
1896–1990

Dodie Smith grew up in Manchester. Her first love was the theatre and she trained at RADA. She gave up acting in 1923 to become a toy buyer for Heal's, where she is thought to have had an affair with the owner, Sir Ambrose Heal. Her playwriting career was launched in 1931 with the hit *Autumn Crocus*, followed by four more plays. In 1939 she left for the US with her manager; they married that year, having been "married for seven years in every way but legally". Their beloved Dalmatians, including Pongo, were later immortalised in *The Hundred and One Dalmatians* (1956). In 1954 they returned to England. Smith obsessively reworked *I Capture the Castle* before it was published in 1948 to instant acclaim. She continued to write for adults and children, including four autobiograpical volumes, until her death aged 94.

Other books by Dodie Smith include:

The Hundred and One Dalmatians

The Town in Bloom

It Ends with Revelations

The Girl from the Candle-lit Bath

Look Back with Mixed Feelings

A CAPTIVATING CHRONICLE

From its famous opening (which finds the heroine sitting in the kitchen sink trying to find inspiration), *I Capture the Castle* is a period comedy that exposes and celebrates people's eccentricities. The idealisation of romantic bohemian life and intellectuals is coupled with a love of the humdrum and the everyday. In a witty and subtle story chronicled in the journal of Cassandra Mortmain, Dodie Smith has created some much-treasured characters, including a heroine whose own literary attempts are often unintentionally amusing.

Did you know?
Disney optioned the film rights to *I Capture the Castle* in 1949 as a vehicle for Hayley Mills, but never made the film. Smith's estate negotiated a swap for a remake of *101 Dalmatians*.

◄ **On the big screen**
I Capture the Castle was made into a film in 2002. Directed by Tim Fywell, it stars Romola Garai, Bill Nighy and Tara Fitzgerald.

THE STORY IN A NUTSHELL

Seventeen-year-old **Cassandra Mortmain** lives in a dilapidated castle, blessed with eccentric relations whose quirks and foibles she faithfully records in her journal. Her father, having produced one obscure masterpiece, is wrestling with writer's block after a spell in prison, and her stepmother **Topaz** is "a famous artist's model" with a fondness for wandering about in the nude. **Stephen**, the son of the maid (this being a rose-tinted time when even families living in genteel poverty had domestics), is in love with Cassandra. The lack of money is getting worse: nobody can pay the rent. All hope rests with Cassandra's elder sister **Rose**, a "pinkish" beauty who is determined to marry well. Along comes rich and eligible American **Simon Cotton** and his equally attractive brother Neil, and romantic traps are laid. Simon begins to succumb – but where will it all lead?

The castle provides a romantic setting but a drain on family finances

83

Publication date 1998

First edition

It is no surprise that this was awarded the Newbery Prize, America's highest honour for children's literature. The book's younger readers are hooked on its easy style, spiked with danger and intrigue, but it's also a richly rewarding read for adults.

LOUIS SACHAR
1954

Louis Sachar (pronounced Sacker) was born in New York. The family moved to southern California when he was nine. He began his university studies at Antioch College in Ohio, but when his father died suddenly he returned to California. While taking a degree in economics at the University of California, he took a teaching course, which inspired him to write children's books. Later he qualified as a lawyer, but he had already published a book and could not decide which career to follow. He worked part time at both until 1989, when he became a full-time writer. Sachar has won many awards in the US, including those voted for by children. His long list of US publications (such as *There's a Boy in the Girls' Bathroom*) is gradually being introduced in the UK after the success of *Holes*. He lives in Texas, where *Holes* is set.

DIGGING FOR VICTORY

For such a funny book, the elements are pretty dark: a generations-old curse, a children's prison camp and even a sinister female warden. But it is often the dark matter that makes up the universe of the best-loved children's literature – which is precisely where *Holes* belongs. The story of *Holes* proved so popular with readers that Sachar followed it with *Stanley Yelnats's Survival Guide to Camp Green Lake*. Yelnats (that's "Stanley" spelled backwards) is a true hero for all children.

Did you know

In the year and a half it took Sachar to write *Holes* no-one else knew anything about it, not even his wife or daughter. He writes alone in his office and his only companions are his two dogs, Lucky and Tippy, who, he says, are sworn to secrecy.

"'I'M NOT GOING TO RUN AWAY,' STANLEY SAID. 'GOOD THINKING,' SAID MR SIR. 'NOBODY RUNS AWAY FROM HERE. WE DON'T NEED A FENCE. KNOW WHY? BECAUSE WE'VE GOT THE ONLY WATER FOR A HUNDRED MILES. YOU WANT TO RUN AWAY? YOU'LL BE BUZZARD FOOD IN THREE DAYS.'"

"This is a story of friendship with the cleverest of plot twists, and descriptions so vivid you can feel the heat of Stanley's desert prison burning off the page. A total must read."

The Times

THE STORY IN A NUTSHELL

Wrongly convicted of theft, **Stanley Yelnats** is sent to a boys' juvenile detention centre. Camp Green Lake is not a camp, it is not green and there is no lake. It is in the Texas desert, baked by sun and infested with rattlesnakes, scorpions and poisonous lizards. Here the boys must dig a hole a day, five feet deep, five feet across, in ground so hard that it is almost impossible to break. **The Warden** claims the labour is character building – but she has her own reasons for wanting the holes dug, which relate to a legend going back 100 years, involving a feared outlaw of the Old West and Stanley's ancestor. The past is interwoven with the present, and Stanley sets out to discover the truth.

Other books by Louis Sachar include:

There's a Boy in the Girls' Bathroom

Dogs Don't Tell Jokes

Sideways Stories from Wayside School

Marvin Redpost: Why Pick on Me?

84 GORMENGHAST
MERVYN PEAKE

Publication date (Titus Groan) 1946 (Gormenghast) 1950 (Titus Alone) 1959

MERVYN PEAKE
1911–1968

Mervyn Peake was born in Kuling, China, to English missionary parents and grew up in Tientsin, where the declining world of ancient tradition made a deep impression on him. Peake came to England in 1923 and studied at Croydon School of Art, and then at the Royal Academy. After a productive couple of years at an artists' colony on Sark, Peake began teaching at Westminster School of Art. There he met his muse, the painter Maeve Gilmore. They married in 1937 and had three children. During the Second World War he suffered a nervous breakdown and was invalided out of the army. However, he went on to become a war artist and was one of the first civilians to enter Belsen. A celebrated illustrator, artist and poet, Peake also wrote plays and produced set and costume designs, but it is for the creation of Gormenghast that he is best remembered. He developed Parkinson's disease and died in an Oxford Hospice at the age of 57.

Other books by Mervyn Peake include:

Mr Pye

Shapes and Sounds

Letters from a Lost Uncle

For the sheer scale of its ambition the *Gormenghast* trilogy stands shoulder to shoulder with *The Lord of the Rings*. Conjuring up a grotesque and horribly funny world, the novels blend the Gothic, the Dickensian and the fantastic and draw the reader into the deepest recesses of Mervyn Peake's imagination.

AN ARTIST'S VISION OF HELL

The castle of Gormenghast itself is like a maze, full of paradoxes and visual jokes. Gormless, ghastly characters are born into an oppressive world whose very walls seem to fill the soul with gloom. Gothic nightmare, farce and foul deeds all fight for air among the crumbling stones. Peake's painter's eye allowed him to translate his own feelings of isolation into the architecture of a creation that satirised 19th-century establishments as they faced up to the onslaught of 20th-century wars. The castle draws its inspiration from many an institution buried deep under centuries of tradition, while Steerpike is the working boy who challenges the social order: a character very much of Peake's time.

▲ **First edition**
The trilogy took shape immediately after the war. Peake's cover for the first edition of *Gormenghast*, the central book, clearly shows Peake's wartime inspiration, rather than his more Gothic leanings.

◄ **The Peake family**
After the war the Peakes lived an idyllic life on Sark.

▲ ▶ **Bringing the characters to life**
Peake sketched all of his characters. Compare the drawing of Steerpike (with Fuschia) with actor Jonathan Rhys-Meyers (right) in part one of the recent TV production of the trilogy.

THE STORY IN A NUTSHELL

Titus Groan becomes the 77th Earl of Gormenghast after a series of gruesome events engineered by **Steerpike**, a Machiavellian upstart who is no longer content to be a mere kitchen boy. Steerpike becomes an apprentice to **Barquentine**, the Master of Ritual, in order to learn all the castle's innermost secrets and also in an attempt to seduce **Fuchsia**, Titus' sister. The vain and ugly **Irma Prunesquallor** throws a party to ensnare a husband and quickly falls in love with **Bellgrove**, Titus' headmaster. One day Titus gives Bellgrove the slip and escapes through a tunnel. For the first time he discovers that there is life beyond the castle walls. He is found by **Flay**, an old servant who has previously been banished from the castle. Flay secretly returns to Gormenghast to spy on Steerpike, who embarks upon a merciless campaign to do away with anyone in the way of his ambitions. As a huge flood overwhelms the castle and threatens to sweep everything away, Titus makes plans for his revenge on the ruthless Steerpike.

Steerpike and Barquentine

The headmaster, Bellgrove

> "PEAKE WRITES AS AN ARTIST, CONCERNING HIMSELF WITH COLOUR AND TEXTURE."

The Times Educational Supplement

Titus' aunts, the twins Cora and Clarice

"...THE ROOFSCAPE WAS NEITHER MORE NOR LESS THAN A CONGLOMERATION OF STONE STRUCTURES SPREADING TO RIGHT AND LEFT AND AWAY FROM HIM. IT WAS A MIST OF MASONRY. AS HE PEERED, TAKING EACH STRUCTURE INDIVIDUALLY, HE FOUND THAT HE WAS A SPECTATOR OF A STATIONARY GATHERING OF STONE PERSONALITIES."

Did you know?

Peake designed the logo for Pan Books. His friend, the author Graham Greene, advised Peake to take a single payment for the job rather than a royalty. This decision cost Peake a fortune, as Pan Books was a huge success, and the royalties would have made him far richer than his writings ever did.

THE GOD OF SMALL THINGS
ARUNDHATI ROY

Publication date 1997

First edition

This debut novel was received with rapture on its publication. Readers and critics alike were dazzled by its energy, diverted by its wordplay. With great skill and subtlety Roy constructs a complex story of small lives devastated by disaster.

ARUNDHATI ROY
1961–

Arundhati Roy was born in Bengal, the daughter of a Christian mother and a Hindu father. They divorced when Roy was still a child. At the age of 16, she left home to live in a squatters' colony in Delhi. She studied architecture, married a fellow student and moved to Goa. She later divorced and returned to Delhi, where she met the film director Pardeep Krishen, who encouraged her to write screenplays. They later married. Roy has said that she now intends to concentrate on political journalism. In 2000 she was arrested for protesting against the huge Narmada Valley dam-building project on poor villagers' lands in Madhya Pradesh.

The spices central to Kerala's culture

THROUGH THE EYES OF A CHILD

The novel is set in Kerala, India's southernmost state, where Arundhati Roy spent her childhood. Much of the novel draws on her own experience: "I grew up in very similar circumstances. My mother was divorced. I lived on the edge of the community in a very vulnerable fashion." Roy's story is written from a child's point of view, shadowed with adult awareness as a forbidden love affair stirs up the prejudices of a traditional community.

THE STORY IN A NUTSHELL

Estha and **Rahel** are seven-year-old twins, so close to each other that they comprise a "single Siamese soul". Their mother is **Ammu**, a Syrian Christian. They have been forced to return in disgrace to her parental home in Kerala after Ammu's divorce from the twins' father, the alcoholic Hindu owner of a tea plantation. One day in 1969, the twins' cousin, **Sophie Mol**, arrives from England. That day, Ammu begins a secret affair with **Velutha**, an "Untouchable" (an outcast from the then strict caste system, who was effectively a "non person"). When the affair is discovered, Ammu is locked in her room by her vindictive aunt. She vents her frustration on her children. As a result, the twins, together with Sophie Mol, decide to run away. As they are crossing the river their boat capsizes and Sophie Mol is drowned. This single tragedy sets in train a series of further personal disasters.

"...it's not just about small things, it's about how the smallest things connect to the biggest things – that's the important thing."

Arundhati Roy

"THE DAYS ARE LONG AND HUMID. THE RIVER SHRINKS AND BLACK CROWS GORGE ON BRIGHT MANGOES IN STILL, DUSTGREEN TREES. RED BANANAS RIPEN. JACKFRUITS BURST. DISSOLUTE BLUEBOTTLES HUM VACUOUSLY IN THE FRUITY AIR."

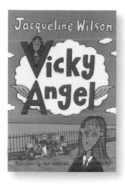

Current edition

JACQUELINE WILSON
See page 74

Jacqueline Wilson is known for writing about big emotional issues in a way that is accessible to children. And what could be more emotional than death? *Vicky Angel* deals with the grief and guilt of death, while all the time retaining a sense of humour.

TALKING ABOUT DEATH

How are children supposed to understand death, to find out what it really means? Many of them have never experienced the loss of someone close to them or attended a funeral. Yet they hear about death all the time, they see it on television and in the newspapers, both real deaths and fictional ones. In *Vicky Angel* the ultimate taboo subject for kids is confronted head-on, but in a thought-provoking yet warm and witty story that offers real advice and reassurance to everyone.

THE STORY IN A NUTSHELL

Jade's best friend, **Vicky**, is killed in a road accident. Jade misses her terribly. Then suddenly Vicky reappears. No one else sees her, but Jade and Vicky do all the things together they used to do. Vicky goes to school with Jade because she wants to see what everyone is saying about her. They go into London and wander around together. Jade wonders how this can happen: the science she has learned at school doesn't explain it; nor does Religious Instruction. Vicky seems to be a law unto herself. At the funeral Jade reads one of Vicky's English essays, "Reasons to be Cheerful", which finishes, "Life is short. You don't know how long you've got so make the most of it. Don't waste time moaning. Enjoy yourself." Jade must now find a way to enjoy life once again without her friend.

" 'WHAT DO YOU THINK IT'S LIKE FOR ME?' SAYS VICKY. 'IT'S BAD ENOUGH WHEN YOU SEE A GHOST. IT'S MUCH ODDER BEING ONE.' "

Did you know?
Jacqueline Wilson receives hundreds of letters each week from children who enjoy her books, or who have questions for her. She spends a couple of hours each evening replying to the letters from her young fans. She responds to every one personally.

87 BRAVE NEW WORLD
ALDOUS HUXLEY

Publication date 1932

ALDOUS HUXLEY
1894–1963

Aldous Huxley was born near Godalming, Surrey in 1894. His grandfather was the biologist and writer T. H. Huxley, who had worked with Darwin, and his mother's uncle was the poet Matthew Arnold. Huxley was educated at Eton and Oxford, and began writing soon after graduating. He was the first British editor of *House and Garden* magazine and worked on *Vogue*. His early novels satirised the shallow, "futilitarian" world of 1920s society. From 1923 he lived much of his life in Italy and France. In 1937 he went to work in Hollywood, but never really fitted in. Walt Disney is reputed to have turned down his proposal for an adaptation of *Alice in Wonderland* because he "could only understand every third word". In his later years, Huxley became increasingly interested in mysticism.

Other books by Aldous Huxley include:

Crome Yellow

Antic Hay

Point Counter Point

Eyeless in Gaza

Island

Ape and Essence

Time Must Have a Stop

Aldous Huxley wrote *Brave New World* as a sharp satirical fiction, but over 70 years later the novel stands as a chilling prophecy. In today's world of increasing state control and accelerating scientific development, Huxley's nightmare vision of an anaesthetised world does not seem so very distant.

▲ **First edition**
The Guardian described Huxley as a "brilliantly clever writer" but felt the book was too negative.

A WARNING TO THE FUTURE

Huxley began writing *Brave New World* before the rise of Nazism, the Second World War and the worst atrocities of Stalin's Communist pogroms. Much of his inspiration came from his first trip to America in 1926. What he saw troubled him – the rise of capitalism, the dehumanising demands of the factory production line, the worship of consumerism and the culture of instant gratification. He wrote, "The thing which is happening in America is a revaluation of values, a radical alteration (for the worse) of established standards." Huxley met the leading intellectuals and scientists of the time and he interpreted their most radical speculations and greatest fears to create his own warning to the world.

STORY IN A NUTSHELL

The novel is set in the seventh century AF ("After Ford") – 632 years after the birth of the inventor of the Model T. The World State is ordered and peaceful, controlled in every detail under the slogan "Community. Identity. Stability". The population is divided into five classes from the Alpha intellectual elite to the semi-moronic drones, the Epsilons. Eugenics has replaced biological reproduction and babies are bred in factories, their social class predetermined. Yet everyone is happy, lulled by drugs, games and recreational sex. **Bernard Marx** feels he doesn't quite fit in, and when he encounters **John**, who has been raised as a savage, Bernard's life changes. He brings John to the World State, and in time they both come to challenge the accepted wisdom of the brave new world.

Genetic engineering

"EVERYONE BELONGS TO EVERYONE ELSE, AFTER ALL."

▲ On the small screen
The 1980 US television version of *Brave New World* was directed by Burt Brikerhoff from an adaptation by Doran William Cannon and Robert E. Thompson. It starred Bud Cort as Bernard Marx and Jonelle as Fanny Crowne.

Did you know?

Huxley's book, *The Doors of Perception* (1954), about his experiments with the hallucinogenic drugs mescaline and lysergic acid, became a cult book for both the Beat generation of the 50s and the hippies of the 60s. Jim Morrison named his band The Doors after it, and Huxley was immortalised on the sleeve of The Beatles' *Sergeant Pepper's Lonely Hearts Club Band*.

◄ In the year of our Ford
Henry Ford symbolised everything that concerned Huxley about American capitalism. As every new Model T rolled off Ford's automated factory production lines, Huxley saw the subjection of humanity to the mechanistic demands of scientific progress.

"IN THE FOUR THOUSAND ROOMS OF THE CENTRE THE FOUR THOUSAND ELECTRIC CLOCKS SIMULTANEOUSLY STRUCK FOUR. DISCARNATE VOICES CALLED FROM THE TRUMPET MOUTHS."

"Technological progress has merely provided us with more efficient means of going backwards."

Aldous Huxley

88

COLD COMFORT FARM
STELLA GIBBONS

Publication date 1932

Playful and ironic, witty and warm hearted, Gibbons' comedy is a wicked parody of the rural novel, as an earthy and passionate group of country folk are confronted by a brisk, sensible young Londoner hell-bent on teaching them a little urban sophistication.

Early edition

STELLA GIBBONS
1902–1989

Gibbons was born and grew up in north London, where her father was a doctor. Educated at North London Collegiate School, she studied journalism at University College. She joined the British United Press news agency in 1924, but was sacked for miscalculating the exchange rate in 1926 and triggering a brief quiver in the financial markets. She joined the *London Evening Standard* in 1926, and finally *The Lady* in 1930. At this time her collection of poetry, *The Mountain Beast*, was published to much acclaim, and she began writing novels in her spare time – as well as in her not-so-spare time at work, where her tendency to reduce colleagues to laughter saw her banished to a back room. *Cold Comfort Farm* was her first novel, winning France's prestigious Prix Femina Vie Heureuse. In 1933 she married the actor and singer Allan Webb, with whom she had one daughter.

Other books by Stella Gibbons include:

Nightingale Wood

Westwood

Conference at Cold Comfort Farm

▲ **On the big screen**
Rufus Sewell played Seth in John Schlesinger's 1996 TV dramatisation, which was later released in the cinema. Kate Beckinsale starred as Flora.

"WHEN YOU WERE VERY SMALL – SO SMALL THAT THE LIGHTEST PUFF OF BREEZE BLEW YOUR LITTLE CRINOLINE SKIRT OVER YOUR HEAD – YOU HAD SEEN SOMETHING NASTY IN THE WOODSHED."

INTO THE MADDING CROWD

The target of *Cold Comfort Farm*'s satire was lusty nature and the rural idiosyncrasies of the novels of Thomas Hardy, D. H. Lawrence and Emily Brontë. Inspiration came also from Gibbons' family life; her parents' tendency to have highly emotional scenes made their home a hotbed of melodrama. She pokes fun with an invented rural vocabulary, but the caricatures are far from superficial: her characters are explored with genuine humanity and depth.

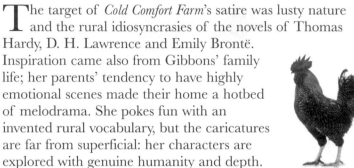

THE STORY IN A NUTSHELL

When sophisticated, educated **Flora Poste** is orphaned at the age of 19, she is left with little in the way of an income, so she descends upon her country relatives, the Starkadders, at their farm in the wilds of Sussex. There she finds **Aunt Ada Doom**, haunted by childhood secrets; cowed **Cousin Judith**, racked by inner demons; **Amos** the fiery lay preacher; lustful, movie-mad **Seth**; farming-obsessed **Reuben**; ethereal teenage dreamer **Elfine**; and many more. Flora, eminently sane and strong-willed, is determined to "tidy up" their rural lives.

Current edition

MAGICIAN
RAYMOND E. FEIST

Publication date 1982

The first instalment in the Riftwar series became a global bestseller. This vivid and original take on alien worlds and wizard lore casts its spell from the very first page as magic powers are tested to their limits in an action-packed battle.

RAYMOND E. FEIST
1945–

Born in Los Angeles, Raymond E. Feist now lives in San Diego with his wife and daughter. He began creating magical worlds in an extracurricular fantasy role-playing group he joined at the University of California, where he also obtained a degree in Communication Arts. After leaving unversity he worked for the state of California, until a tax revolt cut funding for his health service job. While unemployed he wrote *Magician*. Building on its immediate and massive success, he became a computer games writer, using the novel's imaginary world of Midkemia as the background for his games. Since then, he has written a series of Riftwar novels, all of which have been bestsellers.

"THE MAGICIAN WAS ENGULFED IN AN EERIE LIGHT, PULSATING WITH ENERGY. HE STOOD AT THE CENTER OF THE STORM, A TERRIBLE FIGURE IN THE DARK."

CONJURING UP NEW WORLDS

Feist's imaginary worlds are immensely rich in detail and texture, made real by their own logic, history and landscape – sometimes recalling fragments of our own earth and seeming all the stranger for it. The Riftwar books have the imaginative sweep to rival the great literary fantasies. The author contrasts traditional heroism with unfamiliar worlds as boundaries fall – not just between different civilisations, but between different dimensions.

THE STORY IN A NUTSHELL

On the planet Midkemia the lives of two boyhood friends are destined to be linked. Each has profound powers that he will discover as the story unfolds. At Crydee, a frontier outpost in the peaceful Kingdom of the Isles, **Tomas** is apprenticed to the Duke's army while his adopted brother, the orphan **Pug**, is apprenticed to a master magician. Pug uses his newfound magic skills to rescue the Duke's daughter **Carline** from trolls, and they begin to fall in love. Then the boys' comfortable world is swept away after they discover a ship wrecked on a nearby shore. Alien beings with superior magic have entered the boys' world through a rift in the fabric of the universe. A quest to find the root of all evil begins.

"I don't write fantasy, I write historical novels about an imaginary place."

Raymond E. Feist

Other books by Raymond Feist include:

Faerie Tale
Serpentine Queen
Riftwar: The World on the Other Side
Riftwar: Serpentwar
Riftwar: Legacy
Legends of the Riftwar

ON THE ROAD
JACK KEROUAC

Publication date 1957

JACK KEROUAC
1922–69

Born to French-Canadian parents in Lowell, Massachusetts, Kerouac was educated at local Catholic schools until he enrolled at Columbia University in New York City. There he met Neal Cassady, Allen Ginsberg and William Burroughs. He left Columbia before graduating, joined the merchant navy for a while and famously travelled backwards and forwards across America. His first novel, the somewhat conventional *The Town and the City*, was published in 1950. Seven years later, it was followed by *On the Road*. Its frantic pace and jazz-influenced prose style set the tone for a series of further heavily autobiographical novels. Together they make up what Kerouac called "the Legend of Duluoz", in which he mythologised his own life as a "strange, solitary, crazy, Catholic, mystic". Kerouac's continuing heavy intake of alcohol and drugs took its toll. He died in 1969, at the age of only 47.

Other books by Jack Kerouac include:

The Town and the City
The Subterraneans
The Dharma Bums
Big Sur
Desolation Angels

A cult classic that captures the spirit of an entire generation, *On the Road* crackles with restless energy, with a thirst for freedom and experience, and a hunger for the American dream. After almost 50 years it still challenges readers to defy convention and discover new emotional territories.

▲ **First edition**
The New York Times called the book's publication "a historic occasion".

PUSHING THE BOUNDARIES

Dissatisfied with the conformist style of his first novel, *The Town and the City*, Jack Kerouac wanted to invent a new language, one that would capture the energy of the lives he was trying to portray. He called it "kickwriting" and defined it in a letter to his friend Neal Cassady: "Write only what kicks you and keeps you overtime awake from sheer mad joy". Convinced that speed and spontaneity were the key to success, and influenced by the improvisational techniques of jazz musicians, Kerouac wrote fast and frenziedly, fuelled by a mixture of benzedrine and coffee. He produced the first version of *On the Road* as early as 1948, but then wrote the second major draft in just three weeks in the spring of 1951. The response of his publisher did not match this pace: the book was not published for another six years.

▲ **On a roll**
Kerouac typed the second draft of his novel onto ten 12-foot sheets of paper, which he taped together to make a roll 120 feet long. In 2001, the roll was bought at auction for $2.4 million.

THE STORY IN A NUTSHELL

The story is narrated by **Sal Paradise**, an ambitious young writer. Not long after he and his wife split up, he meets the charismatic **Dean Moriarty** in New York City. Disillusioned with the American dream and all it represents, they set off on trips by car and bus across the United States in pursuit of freedom and pleasure fuelled by drink, drugs and jazz. As they make their way through sprawling cities, small towns and endlessly unfolding country, they try to grasp the moment and live every day as if it were their last. The characters they encounter include **Carlo Marx**, an intense, energetic poet and **Bull Lee**, who owns a rundown ranch in the swamp country. From here they head to San Francisco – driving naked, stealing gas and bumming food and cigarettes.

> "On the Road sold a trillion Levis and a million espresso machines, and also sent countless kids on the road."
> William Burroughs

THE BEAT GENERATION

Kerouac first coined the term "beat" as an abbreviation of "beatific". But, according to a Times Square junkie called Herbert Huncke, it also meant "exhausted, at the bottom of the world, looking up or out, sleepless, wide-eyed, perceptive, rejected by society, on our own, streetwise." The Beat generation was a loose collection of writers, poets, musicians and artists who emerged in the 1940s and whose bohemian style was in part a reaction to the austerity of the war years. Key members were Kerouac, Allen Ginsberg, William Burroughs, Lucien Carr and Edie Parker. In the 1950s, the Beats spread from New York to San Francisco, where they centred on the City Lights bookstore. Eventually Kerouac tired of being a spokesman for the Beat generation. "I'm not a beatnik," he said, "I'm a Catholic."

▶ **Icons of the Beat generation**
In this thinly disguised autobiography, the narrator Sal Paradise is Kerouac himself, while the wild Dean Moriarty is his real-life friend Neal Cassady. The poet Carlo Marx is based on Allen Ginsberg and Bull Lee is William Burroughs.

Neal Cassady

Allen Ginsberg

William Burroughs

"WHEE. SAL, WE GOTTA GO AND NEVER STOP GOING TILL WE GET THERE."
"WHERE WE GOING, MAN?"
"I DON'T KNOW BUT WE GOTTA GO."

91 THE GODFATHER
MARIO PUZO

Publication date 1969

MARIO PUZO
1920–99

Mario Puzo was born in Hell's Kitchen, New York, the son of Italian immigrants. After military service in the Second World War, he returned to New York and attended the New School for Social Research and Columbia University. He worked as a government clerk and magazine writer and published two novels before *The Godfather*. Referring to the change in style after his first two books, he stated, "Before, I wanted to be [James] Joyce but I'm really more of a storyteller than an artist of language like Joyce." In spite of the financial rewards he reaped from *The Godfather*, he felt that he had sold out his literary abilities. Puzo wrote the screenplays for *The Godfather* trilogy, and won Academy Awards for the first two. He also wrote the screenplays for Superman and Superman II.

Other books by Mario Puzo:

The Dark Arena

The Fortunate Pilgrim

Fools Die

The Sicilian

The Fourth K

The Last Don

Omerta

This is the mother of all gangster tales. An epic saga of the Corleone family's struggle to establish and maintain power in 20th-century America, it augments the mythology of the Mafia while at the same time presenting its human face. *The Godfather* is the guidebook for every wannabe hood.

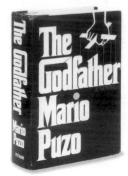

▲ **First edition**
The image of the puppeteer has become synonymous with *The Godfather*. The Don exerts control from behind the scenes, pulling the strings but without ever making his presence obvious.

IT'S A FAMILY AFFAIR

In 1965 Mario Puzo was a penniless writer of action stories for men's magazines, when a Putnam editor overheard him relating anecdotes about the Mafia. He offered him a $5,000 advance to write a book about the Sicilian underworld in America. Wowed by the money, Puzo, who had previously written two critically acclaimed but commercially unsuccessful novels, set out to write a blockbuster. He created a cross-generational portait of an Italian-American family in crime, which emphasised the solidarity as well as the glamour of the Mafia lifestyle. By the end of 1968 he had completed his penultimate draft and headed off to Europe, leaving the manuscript with his publisher. By the time he returned, the paperback rights had been sold for $450,000. He didn't dare to ask for time to rewrite it. Despite Puzo's worries that *The Godfather* wasn't as good as it could have been, it was a publishing phenomenon. It was the bestselling novel of the 1970s and has now sold more than 21 million copies.

▲ **Sinatra's suspicions**
Although Puzo always denied it, Frank Sinatra was convinced that he was the inspiration for the womanising, hard-drinking singer and actor Johnny Fontane who features in the book.

Did you know?
Mario Puzo based the character of Don Corleone on his own mother. "Whenever the Godfather opened his mouth, in my own mind I heard the voice of my mother," he claimed.

▲ **New York, New York**
The Godfather is set in the vibrant New York city of the 1950s, a society enjoying prosperity after the austere years of the Second World War.

"It might have been preferable to be in the Mafia. I'm glad I'm a writer, but it's hard work. Nobody likes to work hard."

Mario Puzo

LA COSA NOSTRA

The term Cosa Nostra ("our thing" or "our cause") is a criminal network based on familial ties that originated in medieval Sicily. In the 19th century it became involved in organised crime and spread to America. At the end of the 1920s two rival factions fought for control of crime in New York City. The death of one of the leaders united the factions and the modern American Mafia was born, although Salvatore Maranzano, the first Mafia Don, was himself murdered six months later. Maranzano established the code of conduct ("omerta"), set up the "family" divisions and structure, and established procedures for resolving disputes. In 1957, around the time *The Godfather* was set, the New York State Police uncovered a meeting of major Mafia figures in the upstate town of Apalachin. In 1963, two years before Puzo's book was published, ex-Cosa Nostra member Joseph Valachi exposed the name, structure, codes and members of the organisation for the first time.

THE STORY IN A NUTSHELL

The Godfather tells the story of the gang war between the **Corleones** and four other New York Cosa Nostra (Mafia) families in the 1950s. It recalls **Don Corleone's** arrival in America and his establishment of the Corleone dynasty, as well as the expansion of its interests in New York, Las Vegas and elsewhere. Sick of being disenfranchised by mainstream America, Corleone and the Mafia find a voice for the immigrant population – a people cast to the margins of society. Corleone does whatever is necessary to preserve his power and help his people – he settles their grievances and buys their allegiance for life. The Mafia lives by its own rules, and violence is an everyday reality. The Don prides himself on being a friendly, just and reasonable man, but at the same time he presides over a world of power struggles, blackmail, corruption and brutality. **Michael Corleone**, the Don's youngest son, is a law-abiding Ivy League graduate who is determined to avoid entering the family business and to find his own way in the world. However, he gradually learns that breaking away is not as simple as he would like and that he can never truly escape from his family ties. From the top to the bottom of society, Don Corleone wields a terrifying influence – but his position and power come at a very high price, both for him and for many members of his family.

Film poster, 1974

"WHO IS TO SAY WE SHOULD OBEY THE LAWS THEY MAKE FOR THEIR OWN INTEREST AND TO OUR HURT? AND WHO ARE THEY THEN TO MEDDLE WHEN WE LOOK AFTER OUR OWN AFFAIRS? WE WILL MANAGE OUR WORLD FOR OURSELVES BECAUSE IT IS OUR WORLD, COSA NOSTRA"

▼ **On the big screen**
The *Godfather* films are consistently voted some of the best films of all time in audience polls. The first, directed by Frances Ford Coppola and starring Al Pacino as Michael Corleone and Marlon Brando as Don Corleone, won three Academy Awards in 1972, including one for Best Picture.

If you like this you may also enjoy books by:

Lorenzo Carcaterra

Richard Condon

James Ellroy

George V. Higgins

Harold Robbins

Joseph Wambaugh

"I'll make him an offer he can't refuse."

THE CLAN OF THE CAVE BEAR
JEAN AUEL

Publication date 1980

First edition

The first book in Jean Auel's "Earth's Children" series revealed the author's passion for prehistory, and has held readers spellbound ever since. The world that she portrays is strange and compelling, but at the same time also comfortingly familiar.

JEAN AUEL
1936–

Born Jean Marie Untinen in Chicago, Illinois, Jean Auel was one of five children. She worked as a circuit board designer, technical writer and credit manager for an electronics firm. After joining Mensa aged 28, she studied for a master's degree at night school and, upon graduating at the age of 40, left her job. She had the idea for a short story and, in half an hour, she wrote an outline that later became the novels of her "Earth's Children" series. Jean Auel lives near Portland, Oregon, where she sponsored the first-ever "Oregon Archeological Retreat" in 1993. Auel's extensive research has earned her the respect of many renowned scientists, archaeologists and anthropologists around the world.

ECHOES OF A PRIMORDIAL PAST

Although the story takes place 30,000 years ago, the characters display a range of human traits and emotions that the modern reader can readily identify with. Ayla is an outsider who must adapt to her new life in order to survive. She swiftly became a popular heroine for readers around the world, sparking renewed interest in Stone Age culture and even creating a new genre of prehistoric fiction that remains popular today.

THE STORY IN A NUTSHELL

Ayla, a five-year-old girl, is orphaned during an earthquake. She is discovered by a band of Neanderthals, who are seeking a new cave; they are of the Clan of the Cave Bear. Thanks to the compassion of their medicine woman, Iza, the tall, blonde, blue-eyed, Cro-Magnon girl is saved and taken under the wing of Iza and her brother, the wise Shaman Creb, and eventually she is accepted by the clan. As Ayla grows up, she makes a powerful and dangerous enemy, a young man called Broud, the group's future leader. He tries to destroy Ayla, but she is a born survivor.

▼ **On the big screen**
The 1986 film, *The Clan of the Cave Bear*, starred Daryl Hannah as the Cro-Magnon Ayla. It was directed by Michael Chapman. Shot in British Columbia, the film was panned by the author and critics.

Other books by Jean Auel:

The Valley of Horses
The Mammoth Hunters
The Plains of Passage
The Shelters of Stone

A cave painting of a bison, showing the importance of animals to the earliest cultures

If you like this you may also enjoy books by:

Louise Cooper
Stephen Donaldson
Diana Gabaldon
Pauline Gedge
Christian Jacq
Edward Rutherfurd
Linda Lay Shuler

THE COLOUR OF MAGIC
TERRY PRATCHETT

Publication date 1983

In the first of the phenomenally successful Discworld series, the author fills his flat world with rounded characters, wild imaginings and ribald humour. *The Colour of Magic* was the literary Big Bang that began one of the best-selling series of books in the universe.

Current edition

TERRY PRATCHETT
See page 124

If you like this you may also enjoy books by:

Douglas Adams
Piers Anthony
Robert Asprin
Rob Grant
Simon R. Green
Andrew Harman
Barry Hughart
Tom Holt
Tanith Lee

"AT THIS ANGLE THE DRAGONFOLK LOOKED REASONABLY BEARABLE, BUT THE DRAGONS THEMSELVES, HANGING FROM THEIR PERCHES, LOOMED OVER THE SCENE LIKE IMMENSE GARGOYLES. THEIR EYES GLOWED WITH INTEREST."

THE START OF A LEGEND

Discworld seemed to spring fully formed into the mind of Terry Pratchett, setting the scene for a series of wild and wonderful adventures with a cast of characters to match. Pratchett's comic voice is wry, inventive and highly literate, improbably merging knockabout farce with philosophical musings that satirise our own world. There are 28 Discworld novels to date, as well as countless spin-offs: testament to the enduring appeal of the book that started it all.

THE STORY IN A NUTSHELL

Somewhere on the magical surface of Discworld – including the fetid metropolis of Ankh-Morpork – three characters meet: **Rincewind**, a wizard for whom the word "inept" was coined; **Twoflower**, the Disc's first ever Tourist (a word meaning "Idiot"); and **The Luggage** (which is what it says, only with teeth, lots of little legs, and a fanatical devotion to its master). Twoflower's wealth makes him a target for undesirables, so Rincewind is unwillingly drafted in as protector. Together with The Luggage, they set out on a journey determined by the gambling of the gods, who like a laugh as much as the next entity. They embark on the kind of adventures and mishaps that inevitably befall a cynical coward, a naive clown and their pet. The story ends with a powerful cliff-hanger, providing the impetus for the dozens of books to follow, and securing a captive audience.

"Fantasy is taking a different look at the everyday."
Terry Pratchett

Did you know?
The Colour of Magic was serialised on BBC Radio 4 soon after its publication. It was broadcast during *Woman's Hour* in 1983. This adaptation sparked a huge surge of interest in Terry Pratchett's work.

94 THE ALCHEMIST
PAULO COELHO

Publication date 1988 (English edition 1993)

During the 1990s, *The Alchemist* grew from a cult novel with a relatively small following into an international phenomenon. Its simple, life-enhancing message touched people across continents, inspiring them to listen to their heart and follow their dreams.

First edition

PAULO COELHO
1947–

Paulo Coelho was born in Brazil. Before the age of 20, he was committed three times to a psychiatric institution by his father, who couldn't understand his son's rebellious attitude. In the late 1960s and early 1970s he worked in the theatre and as a journalist. He was also a successful lyricist and comic-strip writer. In the latter role he incurred the wrath of the military dictatorship, and was imprisoned and tortured. After his release on grounds of insanity, he worked briefly as a record company executive, then travelled in Europe. In 1987 he published *The Pilgrimage (The Diary of a Magus)*. Since the success of *The Alchemist*, all his books have become international bestsellers. His many awards include France's Legion d'Honneur.

Other books by Paulo Coelho include:

The Pilgrimage

The Valkyries

By the River San Piedra I Sat Down and Wept

The Fifth Mountain

Veronika Decides to Die

The Devil and Miss Prym

Manual of the Warrior of Light

Alchemical processes and receipts, 15th century

A SLOW BURNER

When this, Paulo Coelho's second book, was published, it received a lukewarm reception – after only 900 copies of the first edition were sold, the publishers decided against a reprint. It was only when his subsequent book, *Brida* (1990), garnered widespread press attention that *The Alchemist* enjoyed increased exposure and an explosion of interest. It is now the most successful Brazilian and Portuguese-language book of all time and has sold more than 27 million copies worldwide.

THE STORY IN A NUTSHELL

Prompted by an old gypsy woman's interpretation of his recurrent dream and the wise words of a mysterious old man, **Santiago**, an Andalusian shepherd boy, sets out to fulfil his destiny by journeying from Spain to the pyramids in Egypt. Overcoming various challenges as he travels, he learns about the Soul of the World, the Universal Language and the importance of listening to his heart. By refusing to give up on his dreams, he comes to understand his purpose in life and his relation to the universe around him. Through his encounter with an alchemist in the Egyptian desert, he realises that he too is an alchemist. In this deeply symbolic book, the shepherd boy's journey serves as a metaphor for the journey that each person travels in search of his or her destiny.

"It's like music, really, the way he writes, it's so beautiful. It's a gift that I envy above all others."
Julia Roberts

Did you know?

Paulo Coelho studied alchemy for 11 years, attracted by the idea of the Elixir of Life. "When I learned of the possibility of finding a liquid that could prolong my life by many years, I decided to dedicate myself body and soul to making it."

"TO REALISE ONE'S DESTINY IS A PERSON'S ONLY REAL OBLIGATION. ALL THINGS ARE ONE. AND, WHEN YOU WANT SOMETHING, ALL THE UNIVERSE CONSPIRES IN HELPING YOU ACHIEVE IT."

Current edition

A true love story with all the pageantry, chivalry, jousting, falconry, bodice-ripping and tears that any reader could wish for, *Katherine* vividly recreates the world of 14th-century English royalty. Romantics around the world have taken this story to their hearts.

TRUE ROMANCE

Although Anya Seton preferred to think of her books as "biographical novels", they are usually categorised as historical romances. *Katherine* was originally branded "obscene and evil" for its portrayal of the lovers as good people, with Seton's own well-publicised affairs adding to the scandal. Ironically, today's readers are attracted to its romantic avowal of old-fashioned love.

THE STORY IN A NUTSHELL

In 1366, 15-year-old **Katherine de Roet** visits her sister, **Philippa**, at the royal court. Katherine's bewitching beauty brings her an offer of marriage from a choleric knight, **Hugh Swynford**, and the attention of one of the sons of Edward III, **John of Gaunt**, Duke of Lancaster, who is happily married to **Blanche**. Persuaded by her sister and John, Katherine marries Hugh, but is unhappy. When Blanche dies from plague, Katherine refuses to become John's mistress while Hugh is alive. When Hugh dies, Katherine and John embark on a passionate affair, and have four children. But John must marry politically, and this is far from the end of their story.

▲ 14th-century noblewoman

Did you know?
Anya Seton was a compulsive diary writer from an early age. During her adolescence her journals dwelt on her sexual escapades and her appearance.

ANYA SETON
1904–1990

Ann (later known as Anya) Seton was the only child of two successful writers. Her English father, Ernest Thompson Seton, wrote over 50 books. Her American mother, Grace, accompanied him on expeditions and wrote travel books. A renowned beauty, Anya was brought up to be a New York socialite but shared her parents' wanderlust, travelling widely to research her books. In 1923 she married, settling at first in Oxford then Princeton. After a much-publicised divorce, she remarried, later to divorce again. Having written many magazine articles on home-making, she sold her first short story in 1938. Her debut novel, *My Theodosia*, was published in 1941 and became an instant bestseller. Nine further novels were all hugely successful.

▲ **A dashing royal prince**
"Old John of Gaunt, time-honoured Lancaster", begins Shakespeare's *Richard II*. In *Katherine*, John bears "the Plantagenet stamp of long nose, narrow cheeks" and "his eyes were as bright blue as his father's".

▶ **The royal court of Windsor Castle**
Windsor Castle is the scene of romance and pageantry, where Katherine first meets John of Gaunt.

Other books by Anya Seton include:
Avalon
Green Darkness
Dragonwyck
Devil Water
The Winthrop Woman

96

KANE AND ABEL
JEFFREY ARCHER

Publication date 1979

Current edition

With their compelling plots Archer's novels never fail to sell in their millions, and *Kane and Abel* was no exception. It encapsulates Archer's favourite themes: the use and abuse of power and money, and an uncompromising clash of two strong-willed individuals.

JEFFREY ARCHER
1940–

Jeffrey Archer was born in Weston-super-Mare in 1940. He attended Wellington School in Somerset, then took a teacher training certificate in Oxford. A talented athlete, he represented the country as a sprinter. In 1969 he became an MP but resigned from Parliament in 1974 after being declared bankrupt, returning to public life after the success of his first novel. In 1985 he became Deputy Chairman of the Conservative Party, but resigned in 1986 over allegations that he had consorted with a prostitute. Having sued the *Daily Star* over the reports, he returned to politics and in 1992 he was made a peer. But amid further scandal about the case he withdrew his candidacy for Mayor of London 1999. In 2001 he was convicted of perjury and perverting the course of justice. He was released from prison in 2003.

Other books by Jeffrey Archer include:
Not a Penny More, Not a Penny Less
First Among Equals
A Matter of Honour
Honour Among Thieves

A TALE OF TWO TITANS

Jeffrey Archer's third book, *Kane and Abel* was a huge success, particularly in America where it topped the *New York Times* bestseller list. Its story of the personal duel between the privileged WASP (White Anglo-Saxon Protestant) William Lowell Kane and the immigrant Abel Rosnovski epitomised the clash between old and new interpretations of the American Dream. Archer wrote a sequel to *Kane and Abel*, *The Prodigal Daughter* (another biblical reference). This was also highly popular with readers, if not with Archer's persistent critics.

Towers of the Boston banking district

THE STORY IN A NUTSHELL

William Lowell Kane and **Abel Rosnovski** are born on the same day into completely different lives. Kane is the son of a Boston millionaire whose life is insulated by luxury and ease; Rosnovski is a poor Pole and later a concentration camp inmate, scarred by his suffering. Their paths cross years later as Rosnovski tries to save his hotel chain from going under and Kane's bank refuses to lend him the money. Rosnovski decides that he must destroy Kane at all costs. Fuelled by enmity, their duel becomes a fight to the death.

"...SO WHEN YOU GO TO BED AT NIGHT, MR KANE, BE SURE TO THINK ABOUT ME. WHEN YOU WAKE UP IN THE MORNING, THINK ABOUT ME AGAIN, BECAUSE I'LL NEVER CEASE THINKING ABOUT MY PLANS FOR YOU."

◄ **Brotherly hate**
In the book of Genesis, the rivalry between the two brothers results in Cain killing Abel.

GABRIEL GARCIA MARQUEZ

Publication date 1985

First edition

Colombian literary colossus García Márquez fills his magical landscapes with joyous life and the sickly smell of decay, crowding them with vivid characters and stories. This is a tale of unrequited passion revisited in the autumn of life – and another masterpiece.

GABRIEL GARCIA MARQUEZ
See page 76

CLOSE TO HOME
While García Márquez's other great novel, *One Hundred Years of Solitude*, was inspired by the lives of his grandparents, *Love in the Time of Cholera* owes much of its story to the way his father courted his mother. García Márquez himself has written that "the history of their forbidden love was one of the wonders of my youth"; he heard it recounted so often that by the time he came to write the novel, "I couldn't distinguish between life and poetry."

THE STORY IN A NUTSHELL
Dr Juvenal Urbino falls to his death climbing a tree while trying to recapture his pet parrot. His widow, **Fermina Daza**, to whom he has been married for over fifty years, is distraught. At the funeral, she is approached by **Florentino Ariza**, the man with whom she fell in love when young but whom she rejected. In spite of the fact that they are both now in their seventies, Florentino restates his "eternal fidelity and everlasting love" for her. The novel tells the story of their earlier love and tracks the course taken by their lives. As the novel comes back to the present day, they embark on a riverboat journey to rekindle the old flame.

Did you know?
Gabriel García Márquez contrasts the grim symptoms of the disease cholera, the outpouring and chilling of the body, with the release of love and the heat of passion. In so much of the author's work, people express life through their closeness to and defiance of death.

"Love in the Time of Cholera is an absolutely beautiful book. I like it very much at my age because it's all about old-age sex They end up going up and down the river pretending that the ship has got cholera and having it off for all eternity, and that appeals to me."
John Mortimer

"THE CAPTAIN LOOKED AT FERMINA DAZA AND SAW ON HER EYELASHES THE FIRST GLIMMER OF WINTRY FROST. THEN HE LOOKED AT FLORENTINO ARIZA, HIS INVINCIBLE POWER, HIS INTREPID LOVE, AND HE WAS OVERWHELMED BY THE BELATED SUSPICION THAT IT IS LIFE, MORE THAN DEATH, THAT HAS NO LIMITS."

98 GIRLS IN LOVE
JACQUELINE WILSON

Publication date 1997

JACQUELINE WILSON
See page 74

The first in Jacqueline Wilson's series of books "for older readers", *Girls in Love* is for girls who have already sampled the delights of *The Story of Tracy Beaker* and *Double Act* and are ready to read sharp, funny stories about boys, romance and sex.

First edition

Girls in Love

GROWING UP

A girl who started reading Jacqueline Wilson's books at the age of eight or ten can continue to be devoted to her favourite author well into her teenage years. Wilson understands teenagers just as well as she understands children, and the four books about Ellie, Nadine and Magda prepare young teens for new life experiences and problems. *Girls in Love* was followed by *Girls Under Pressure* and *Girls Out Late*. *Girls in Tears*, the fourth book in this series, won the W. H. Smith Children's Book Award in 2003.

▲ **On the small screen**
Girls in Love became a popular ITV series in 2003. Certain changes had to be made for the television as much of the book is developed through letters or takes place in Ellie's head.

THE STORY IN A NUTSHELL

Ellie is starting year nine at school, with her friends **Nadine** and **Magda**. She's almost forgotten about **Dan**, the rather unusual but nerdy boy she met during the summer holidays. But when the other girls start bragging about their boyfriends, suddenly Dan's name springs to Ellie's lips and she spins a wild romantic tale about him. Boyfriends are so much easier to deal with when they live far away. Just when the others are beginning to wonder whether Ellie's boyfriend really exists, Dan shows up at a party. Ellie is embarrassed, as he's not exactly the Dreamboat she had described. But Dan proves to have qualities that Ellie's friends appreciate, and Ellie comes to recognise them as well. Sub-plots involve Nadine's problems with her boyfriend, who is only after one thing, Magda's attempts at pulling boys and Ellie's relationship with her stepmother and stepbrother.

▶ **Ellie's lists**
Ellie makes lots of lists of "nines" (because she is in year nine), including nine heroes and heroines, nine things she hates about school, nine most embarrassing moments and nine romantic couples. Ellie wants to be an artist, and "illustrates" her lists, with a little help from Nick Sharratt, who has illustrated many of Wilson's books.

Nine Romantic Couples

1. Romeo and Juliet.
2. John Lennon and Yoko Ono.
3. Queen Victoria and Prince Albert.
4. Kermit and Miss Piggy.
5. Julian Clary and Fanny the Wonder Dog.
6. Jane Eyre and Mr Rochester.
7. Elizabeth Bennett and Mr Darcy.
8. Morticia and Gomez Addams.
9. Ellie and Dan ???

"DAN ISN'T MY BOYFRIEND. OK OK, HE'S FUN. AND I HAVE A GOOD TIME WITH HIM. AND I CAN SAY ALL SORTS OF STUFF TO HIM. AND THOUGH HE'S A HOPELESS NERD HE'S ALSO BRAVE. AND QUICK-WITTED. AND IMAGINATIVE. AND IT DOESN'T REALLY MATTER ONE HUNDRED PER CENT IF HE LOOKS STUPID."

The PRINCESS DIARIES
Meg Cabot

Current edition

THE PRINCESS DIARIES
MEG CABOT

Publication date 2000

A modern fairy tale – played for laughs. This newly revealed princess is a regular American teenager, a sassy New Yorker who tells it how it is: "I am so NOT a princess". Her comic trials and tribulations are told with warmth, wit and panache.

A ROYAL PROGRESSION
When Meg Cabot started writing this book it didn't have a princess in it and it didn't have this title. But once she thought about including a princess, the idea took over. *The Princess Diaries* went to the top of *The New York Times* bestseller list and was quickly bought up by Disney for a film version, which was released in 2001. In September 2002 the fourth title in the series, *Mia Goes Fourth*, topped the list of bestselling paperbacks for children in the UK.

▲ **On the big screen**
Disney's film version of *The Princess Diaries* – with Anne Hathaway (as Mia), Julie Andrews and Larry Miller – allowed director Garry Marshall to return to a familiar and much-loved theme, the total transformation of a young girl's life.

"My parents used to joke that when I was little, I did a lot of insisting that my 'real' parents, the king and queen, were coming to get me soon, and that everyone had better start being a lot nicer to me." Meg Cabot

▶ **Playground of the rich**
The fictional kingdom of Genovia is a very small country between Italy and France, and is based on Monaco.

THE STORY IN A NUTSHELL
Mia's parents split up before she was born. She lives in New York with her mother, and sees her European father once a year. One day he turns up unexpectedly and announces that he cannot have any more children because he has been diagnosed with cancer. Mia doesn't immediately understand the implications of this. But then no one had ever told her that her father is a prince. As Mia is the only child he will ever have, she is the heir to the throne of the kingdom of Genovia. Mia is shocked. She neither looks nor acts like a princess, so her grandmother arrives to transform her into a beauty and give her "princess lessons". Mia tries to keep her royalty a secret from her school friends, but soon everyone finds out, which causes big problems...

"GEEZ! WHATEVER HAPPENED TO NICE GRANDMOTHERS, WHO BAKE BROWNIES FOR YOU AND TELL YOU HOW PRECIOUS YOU ARE? IT'S JUST MY LUCK I GET ONE WHO HAS TATTOOED EYELINER AND TELLS ME I LOOK LIKE A HOOKER."

MEG CABOT
1967–

Meggin Patricia Cabot was born and brought up in Bloomington, Indiana. As a child she read the complete works of Jane Austen, Judy Blume and Barbara Cartland. She took a BA in fine arts at Indiana University and trained as an illustrator. In 1989 she moved to New York to pursue a career in illustration, but she was more interested in writing. She took a job at New York University as the assistant manager of an undergraduate dormitory. This gave her time to write, and she began to produce adult historical romances under the name Patricia Cabot. She also wrote contemporary adult novels under the name Meggin Cabot, and when she started writing books for teenagers she became Meg Cabot. She decided to use yet another name, Jenny Carroll, for her "paranormal" books. Many of her novels have been optioned for film or TV.

Other books by Meg Cabot include:

The Princess Diaries: Take Two

The Princess Diaries: Third Time Lucky

The Princess Diaries: Mia Goes Fourth

100

SALMAN RUSHDIE
1947–

Salman Rushdie was born in Mumbai (Bombay) in India into a middle-class Muslim family. He was sent to England to study: first to Rugby and then to King's College, Cambridge, where he read history. After graduating in 1968 he returned to the Indian subcontinent and worked for a time in Pakistani television. Back in England again, he joined a south London Theatre group as an actor. Rushdie's first novel, *Grimus*, was published in 1975, but he found fame in 1981 with the award-winning *Midnight's Children*. His glittering career took an unexpected turn when his novel *The Satanic Verses* (1989) offended many Muslims, and a *fatwa* (order of death) for blasphemy was issued against him by Iran's Ayatollah Khomeini. Forced to live in hiding for many years, Rushdie has continued writing undeterred, and continues living with his unique brand of celebrity.

Other books by Salman Rushdie include:

The Ground Beneath Her Feet

The Unexpected

Haroun and the Sea of Stories

East, West

MIDNIGHT'S CHILDREN
SALMAN RUSHDIE

Publication date 1981

Opening with a tumultuous, midnight birth, Salman Rushdie's novel pulls us into a world of noise and colours, poised between the end of one day and the beginning of another: the story of Indian Independence and one remarkable family.

A NEW LITERARY TRADITION

With *Midnight's Children*, Rushdie blazes a trail for a new type of post-colonial literature. From the shadow of the Western tradition he looks into the glare of a modern, complex, confident India, and sees a vibrant and independent identity. Bollywood mingles with Hollywood, traditional Indian culture and imported fashions – a heady, spicy blend, like the chutney he so lovingly describes. Words and cultures tumble over each other and compete for attention in a novel that is by turns idiosyncratic, playful, scholarly and filled with history as witnessed from the inside. Rushdie's extraordinary work won him fame, the 1981 Booker Prize and the James Tait Black Prize. In 1995 *Midnight's Children* was named as the outstanding Booker winner of the first 25 years, and it was adapted for the stage in 2002.

> "How do you tell the story of a crowd? How do you tell the story of a multitude? The central narrative has to push its way through the crowd."
>
> Salman Rushdie

The ingredients for Rushdie's favourite chutney

▲ **Current edition**
The publication of *Midnight's Children* catapulted Salman Rushdie to instant fame. *The New York Review of Books* described it as "one of the most important books to come out of the English-speaking world in this generation".

Did you know?
Salman Rushdie used to be an advertising copywriter in the 1970s and early 1980s, and came up with the slogan "Naughty, but nice" to advertise fresh cream cakes on UK television.

▶ **The last Viceroy**
On 15 August 1947, India's Viceroy and Viceroyine – Lord and Lady Mountbatten – were driven through the streets of Delhi by a six-horse state coach to the Indian Constituent Assembly to announce the Independence Proclamation. This was the first time in India's history that such dignitaries had shaken hands with the people while in proccession.

"THE NOSE ASSUMED A PATRIARCHAL ASPECT. ON MY MOTHER, IT LOOKED NOBLE AND A LITTLE LONG-SUFFERING; ON MY AUNT EMERALD, SNOBBISH; ON MY AUNT ALIA, INTELLECTUAL; ON MY UNCLE HANIF IT WAS THE ORGAN OF AN UNSUCCESSFUL GENIUS...."

THE STORY IN A NUTSHELL

In the first hour of India's independence, on 15 August 1947, 1,001 children are born, their lives destined to be entwined with that of their nation. Among them is **Saleem Sinai**, or rather the baby who assumes the identity of Saleem after a midwife swaps the real Saleem with the poor, orphaned baby – named **Shiva** – of a Western woman. By a twist of fate, the assumed Saleem's already large nose and blue eyes are attributed to Kashmiri heritage and his identity is never questioned as he grows up in a middle-class Mumbai home amid an eccentric family and neighbours. At the age of nine – triggered by a violent sneeze – Saleem discovers that he has the power to see inside other people's minds, a skill he applies within ever-widening parameters, from cheating at school to exploring all corners of the land. This leads him eventually to all the other "midnight's children", each of whom has a supernatural power of their own, and over the years Saleem begins to mould the children into a force that can shape the nation's future. But things do not turn out as planned, and Saleem's life becomes increasingly troubled when he encounters his bitter "alter ego", Shiva. He finds that his gifts have destroyed far more happiness than they have created.

A HISTORY OF THREE NATIONS

Spanning the years 1915 to 1977, *Midnight's Children* charts the birth and development of the modern Indian nation. India was considered the jewel in the crown of the British Empire, so the British were unwilling to relinquish control even as the empire diminished. However, after the Second World War, Britain lacked the resources to maintain its far-flung territories and, on 15 August 1947, 300 million Indians won independence. The transition was far from smooth, as the Muslim League and the Indian National Congress could not agree a settlement. Amid ethnic, religious and territorial violence, the states of India and Pakistan were born.

THE ONES THAT ALMOST MADE IT: 101–200

INDEX OF BOOK TITLES

INDEX OF AUTHORS

Acknowledgements

Dorling Kindersley would like to thank the following for their help with this book:

Contributors: Marian Broderick, Alan Buckingham, Amy Corzine, Benjamin Davis, Linda Davis, Jessie Grimond, Christy Hawkins, Thomas Marshall, Annalee Mather, Charlie Miller, Joe Munro, Nigel Ritchie, Catherine Rubinstein, Rebecca Yolland
Editorial: Corinne Asghar, Jane Chapman, May Corfield, Antonia Cunningham, Anna Fischel, Jude Garlick, Christine King, Chris Middleton, Catherine Rubinstein
Design: Sarah Cowley, Michael Duffy, Jenisa Patel, Amzie Vilamot
DTP: Gemma Casajuana Filella, Adam Shepherd
Picture Research: Alison Prior, Romaine Werblow

We are grateful to LISU – The Library and Information Statistics Unit at Loughborough University – for permission to include material from their two publications: *Who Else Writes Like...? A Reader's Guide to Fiction Authors*, and *Who Next...? A Guide to Children's Authors* to compile the lists for further reading.

Page 34 *The Lion, the Witch and the Wardrobe* by C. S. Lewis copyright © C. S. Lewis Pte. Ltd. 1950. Extract reprinted by permission
Pages 74, 144, 166 Extracts from *Double Act; Girls in Love* and *The Story of Tracy Beaker* by Jacqueline Wilson, published by Doubleday. Reprinted by permission of The Random House Group Ltd
Page 80 Extract from *Charlie and the Chocolate Factory* by Roald Dahl, published by Penguin Books Ltd reproduced with permission of David Higham Associates
Page 84 Extract from *Gormenghast* by Mervyn Peake, published by Random House reproduced with permission of David Higham Associates
Page 91 Extract from *Anne of Green Gables* reproduced with permission of The Heirs of L. M. Montgomery Inc.
Page 92 Extract from *Watership Down* by Richard Adams, published by Penguin Books Ltd reproduced with permission of David Higham Associates
Page 113 Extract from *The BFG* by Roald Dahl, published by Jonathan Cape Ltd and Penguin Books Ltd reproduced with permission of David Higham Associates
Page 145 Extract from *The Twits* by Roald Dahl, published by Jonathan Cape Ltd and Penguin Books Ltd reproduced with permission of David Higham Associates
Page 151 Extract from *Vicky Angel* by Jacqueline Wilson, published by Random House Children's Books reproduced with permission of David Higham Associates

Picture Credits

Key: l = left, r = right, c = centre, t = top. b = bottom, A = above, B = below.
Abbreviations **AI:** Alamy; **AA:** Art Archive; **BBC:** BBC Photo Library; **BTC:** Between the Covers Rare Books Inc. **BAL:** Bridgeman Art Library; **DK:** DK Picture Library; **MEPL:** Mary Evans Picture Library; **Getty:** Getty Images; **Hulton:** Hulton Getty; **NPG:** National Portrait Gallery, London; **Rex:** Rex Features.

Many of the following illustrations come from stills issued to publicise film and television productions made or distributed by the companies listed below. We apologise in advance for any unintentional omission or neglect and will be pleased to insert the appropriate acknowledgement to companies or individuals in any subsequent edition of this work.

14/15 **AA:** Imperial War Museum tr; **DK:** cr, Max Alexander br; Imperial War Museum, London tl; **Hulton:** Archive bl; **Rex:** HEP tl; Courtesy of **Vintage** cl. 16/17 **AI:** Rob Rayworth c; **Christie's Images** cl; **DK** tlB; **Hulton:** Keystone bl; **Kobal:** Universal / Canal / Ph: Peter Mountain br; **Rex:** David Hartley tl. 18/19 **BTC** tclB; **Corbis:** Bettmann bc; KJ Historical blA; **Corbis Sygma:** Jonathan Torgovnik tl; **Kobal:** US Army / Archive Photos br; **Kobal:** Paramount / Ph: Jack Gereghty tr; **VinMag** tcl. 20/21 **BTC** tcl; **Corbis:** Bettmann tl, tr; **Getty:** Stone / Sylvain Grandadam bl; **Hulton** tclB; **Getty:** bl; **Rex:** SNAP (SYP) bcl, tr. 24/25 **AI:** ImageState / Alex Howe tcl; **Rex:** Bettmann; **Corbis:** Hulton-Deutsch Collection tl; Peter Johnson tr; **Dickens House Museum, London** tlBr; **Hulton:** crB; Picture Post br. 26/27 Courtesy of **Bloomsbury:** cl, tc; **Corbis:** Angelo Hornak bc; **DK:** cAr; **PA Photos:** Australian Associated Press br; **Rex:** Colin Edwards tr; Ray Tang tl; Kevin Wisniewski bl. 28/29 **AI:** ImageState / David Tipling bl; **Corbis:** Historical Picture Archive cr; Staffan Widstrand c; **Rex:** Francesco Guidicini tl; Courtesy of **Scholastic** clr. 30/31 **BAL:** bl, tr, crA, br; **Corbis:** Ron Lowery bc; Roger Ressmeyer tl; Courtesy of **Pan** tcl. 32/33 **AA:** Tate Gallery, London / Eileen Tweedy bl; **BBC** bl; **Hulton** c, cr; **NPG:** *Charlotte Brontë (Mrs A.B. Nicholls)*, 1850 by George Richmond. Medium: chalk; Measurements 23 5/8 in. x 18 3/4 in. (600 mm x 476 mm) tl; Courtesy of **Penguin** cl. 34/35 Courtesy of **Collins** tcl; **Hulton:** Picture Post tl; Illustrations by Pauline Baynes © C.S.Lewis Pte Ltd from THE CHRONICLES OF NARNIA by C.S. Lewis copyright © C.S. Lewis Pte Ltd. Reprinted by permission bl, tcr, bcl, br. 36/37 **Corbis:** Robert Holmes bcl; **Corbis Sygma:** Kraft Brooks tl; **MEPL** tcr; **Kobal:** Columbia / Ph: Joseph Lederer br; Used by permission of Orchard House/The Louisa May Alcott Memorial Association tcl, cl (x 4), bcl(below); **Rex:** SNAP (SYP) tl. 38/39 **Corbis:** Bettmann tcl; Courtesy of **Harper Collins** tcl; **Kobal:** UA bl; Newline Cinema br; **VinMag** tr. 40/41 **BTC** tcl; **Corbis:** Philip Harvey tr; **Corbis Sygma** tl; **Kobal:** Columbia tcr, cr; Umbrella / Rossenblum / Virgin / Ph: Sarah Quill bc; Warner Bros br. 42/43 **BBC** tr; **Christie's Images** tcl; **DK:** Liz McAulay tlB; **MEPL** cBr; **Kobal:** MGM br; **NPG:** *Jane Austen*, circa 1810 by Cassandra Austen. Medium: pencil and watercolour; Measurements: 4 1/2 in. x 3 1/8 in. (114 mm x 80 mm) tl; **National Trust Photographic Library:** Andrew Butler bl. 44/45 **BTC** tlB; **Corbis:** Stapleton Collection tr; **Ronald Grant Archive** br; **Hulton:** Keystone Features bl; **Kobal:** Selznick / UA cB; **NPG:** *Dame Daphne du Maurier*, 24 July 1930 by Bassano. Medium: whole-plate glass negative tl.
46/47 **BTC** tcl; **Corbis:** Bettmann tl, tcr; The Corcoran Gallery of Art clA; Roger Tidman clB; **Kobal:** Universal bc. 48/49 **BTC** tlB; **Corbis:** Archivo Iconografica, S.A. tl; Bettmann tcl; Historical Picture Archive tcrB; Jose Fuste Raga cr; **Corbis Sygma:** Thierry Pratt br; Demetrio Carrasco blA; **Kobal:** Paramount tr. 50/51 **Corbis:** Robert Holmes bl; Hulton-Deutsch Collection tl; **Christie's Images** tcl; © Estate of EH Shepard 2003 Licensed by ©opyrights Group tlB, bcl, tr, brA. 52/53 **AI:** Gus tl; **Corbis:** Bettmann cr; Line Illustrations copyright E.H. Shepard under the Berne Convention, colouring Copyright © 1970, 1973 E.H. Shepard and Egmont Books Ltd, reproduced by permission of Curtis Brown Group Ltd, London tr, bc; **DK:** © Curtis Brown/Methuen - copyright tcr; Judith Miller & Dorling Kindersley & Biblion tcl; **NPG:** *Alan Alexander ('A. A.') Milne*, 1926 by Howard Coster. Medium: half-plate film negative tl; From the collection of The Central Children's Room, Donnell Library Center, **The New York Public Library**, all rights reserved br. 54/55 **AI:** James Callaghan tl; Leslie Garland Picture Library / Paul Ridsdale clA; **Corbis:** CinemaPhoto crB; **Kobal:** United Artists bcr; **NPG:** *Emily Brontë*, circa 1833 by Patrick Branwell Brontë. Medium: oil on canvas, arched top; Measurements: 21 1/2 in. x 13 3/4 in. (546 mm x 349 mm) tl; *The Brontë Sisters (Anne Brontë; Emily Brontë; Charlotte Brontë (Mrs A.B. Nicholls))*, circa 1834 by Patrick Branwell Brontë. Medium: oil on canvas; Measurements: 35 1/2 in. x 29 3/8 in. (902 mm x 746 mm) bl; Courtesy of **Penguin:** clB. 58/59 Courtesy of **Bloomsbury** bl; **DK:** Jane Burton blA; Andy Crawford tl; Barrie Watts clA; **Rex:** Tony Kyriacou blr; Mark Pinder br; Ray Tang tl. 60/61 **AA:** Tate Gallery, London / Eileen Tweedy clB; Courtesy of **Bloomsbury** tl, tcr; **DK:** bcr; Steve Shott tclB; Jerry Young bcl; **Getty:** Stone / Tony Garcia tcrB; Taxi / David Sacks cr; **Rex:** Ray Tang tl, tr. 62/63 **BTC** tcl; **Camera Press:** Lord Snowdon bcl; **Corbis:** Bettmann tl; **Getty:** Image Bank / Wilfried Krecichwost bcr; Courtesy of **Harper Collins** tl; **Newline Cinema** cr. 64/65 **AI:** Jim Zuckerman bl; **BTC** tcl; **British Library:** Add. 38282, f.1 tclB; **Corbis:** The Corcoran Gallery of Art tr; **Getty:** Taxi / Guy Edwardes tcrB; **Kobal:** Renn/ Burrill / SFP cr; **NPG:** *Thomas Hardy*, 1893 by William Strang. Medium: oil on panel Measurements: 17 in. x 15 in. (432 mm x 381 mm) tl. 66/67 **AKG London** tl; **BBC:** cr; **BTC** bcl; **BAL:** Herbert Art Gallery & Museum, *Coventry St. Michael's and Holy Trinity Churches, from the North East, Coventry*, 1849 by David Gee (1793-1872). Oil on canvas c; Courtesy of **The Eliot Society:** Ph John Burton tlB; **MEPL** tclB. 68/69 **BTC** tcl; **DK** tlB; **Getty:** Allsport / Zoran Milich tcr; Photographer's Choice / Gavin Heller br; Taxi / Arthur Tilley bl; **Rex:** Action Press tl. 70/71 **BTC** tcl; **Corbis:** Bettmann tl; Horace Bristol tr; Philip James Corwin tlB; Dorothea Lange tcr; **Hulton:** American Stock / Archive Photos bc; **Kobal:** 20th Century Fox br. 72/73 **AA:** Christ Church College, Oxford / Eileen Tweedy tl; **Christie's Images** tcl; **DK:** British Library, London bc; **MEPL:** bl, tr; **Hulton:** cr; Lewis Carroll tl; **Kobal:** Joseph Shaftel Productions tclB. 74/75 **BBC** bcr, br; Courtesy of **Random House** tl, tcl; Courtesy of **Nick Sharratt** tlB, cBl, bl, tr. 76/77 **AI:** Bill Bachmann tr; **BTC** tclB; **Corbis:** Enzo & Paolo Ragazzini bl; **DK:** British Museum, London / Alan Hills bcl; National Maritime Museum, London / James Stevenson cl; **Getty:** Image Bank / Gary Braasch c; **Hulton** br; **Magnum:** Rene Burri tl. 78/79 **BBC** tcr; **Christie's Images** tcr; **Corbis:** Gianni Dagli Orti bl; Hulton-Deutsch Collection br; **Corbis Sygma:** Dan Burn-Forti tl; **DK:** Joe Cornish tclB; **Hulton:** Topical Press Agency br; **MEPL** trB; Courtesy of **Pan** tcl. 80/81 **Jan Baldwin:** tl; © **Quentin Blake, 1995:** Images courtesy of **Penguin** tlB, tcrB, c, bcr, bcrA, br; **Camera Press:** Stewart Mark tr; **The Roald Dahl Centre** tclB; **Hulton:** Horst Tappe / Archive Photos tl; Courtesy of **Puffin** tcl. 82/83 **AA:** Illustration by Roland Hilder tr; **Corbis:** Michael Nicholson tl; Craig Tuttle br; **DK:** Tina Chambers tcl, tclB; **MEPL** tcl, tclB; **Kobal:** © Disney bl. 84/85 **Corbis:** Hulton-Deutsch Collection clB; Paul A Souders tr; **Hulton:** Picture Post tl; **Kobal:** PBS Masterpiece Theater bc; Rank (Carlton Intl.) br; Courtesy of **Stratus** tl. 86/87 **AA** bc; **BTC** tcl; **British Library:** Egerton 3038 f.14v cl; **Ronald Grant Archive** cr, br; **NPG:** *Jane Austen*, circa 1810 by Cassandra Austen. Medium: pencil and watercolour; Measurements: 4 1/2 in. x 3 1/8 in. (114 mm x 80 mm) tl. 88/89 **BTC** tl; **Blixa Film Produktion GmbH & Co. KG and Touchstone Television Productions, LLC** cr; **Corbis:** Tim Bird bcl; Universal/DeLaurentiis Corp c, bl; **Rex:** Sipa Press tl; **VinMag.** 90/91 **AA:** Bibliothèque des Arts Décoratifs Paris / Dagli Orti tcl; **Christie's Images** tl, tcr; **Corbis:** Jan Butchofsky-Houser tl; Dave G Houser cBr; Kevin R Morris tlB; *Anne of Green Gables* © 1908 L.C. Page and Son. Entered at Stationers' Hall, London. © 1986 David Macdonald, trustee, and Ruth Macdonald. *L.M. Montgomery* is a trademark of **Heirs of L.M. Montgomery Inc.** *Anne of Green Gables* and other indicia of "Anne" are trademarks and Canadian official marks of the Anne of Green Gables Licensing Authority Inc tr; **Kobal:** Columbia / Ph: David Appleby tl; RKO br; **NPG:** *Jane Austen*, circa 1810 by Cassandra Austen. Medium: pencil and watercolour; Measurements: 4 1/2 in. x 3 1/8 in. (114 mm x 80 mm) tl. 92/93 Photograph courtesy of **Chris Boyce** tcl; **DK:** Dave King tcrB; **Kobal:** Nepenthe/Avco-Embassy tr; **Frank Lane Picture Agency:** David Hosking br; **National Geographic Image Collection:** Steven L Raymer bc; **National Trust Photo Library:** Rob Judges cl; **Rex:** David Hartley tl. 94/95 **The Advertising Archive** bl; **BTC** tcl; **Corbis:** Bettmann tl, cBl; Leonard de Selva blA; **DK:** Beaulieu Motor Museum cl; **Kobal:** Paramount br; **VinMag** tcr. 96/97 **Corbis:** Bettmann tl; Marc Garanger tcr; Franc Marc-Frei cl; **Kobal:** Touchstone / Spyglass / Ph: Jonathon Hession br; Courtesy of **Penguin** tcl; **VinMag.** 98/99 **AI:** Jon Bower tr; Castle Howard br; **Christie's Images** tlB; **DK** blA; **Granada Television Limited** tc; **NPG:** *Evelyn Waugh*, 1930 by Howard Coster. Medium: half-plate film negative tl. 100/101 **BBC** cr; **BTC** tcl, br; **Corbis:** Bettmann tlB; cBl, Hulton-Deutsch Collection tr; **Corbis Sygma:** **MEPL** bl, bcr; **Kobal:** Halas & Batchelor (Blue Dolphin) bcl. 102/103 **BTC** tcl; **Corbis:** Cordaiy Photo Library Ltd/Chris North bl; Philadelphia Museum of Art tr; **Kobal:** VIC / Appia (Turner) Cb, br; **NPG:** *Thomas Hardy*, 1893 by William Strang. Medium: oil on panel Measurements: 17 in. x 15 in. (432 mm x 381 mm) tl; **National Trust Photo Library:** Eric Crichton tlB. 104/105 **AI:** Robert Harding Picture Library cAr; Courtesy of **Carlton** cBl; Courtesy of **Coronet** tcr; **DK:** Steve Gorton cBr; **Ronald Grant Archive** br; **Hulton:** tlB; Fox Photos bl; Courtesy of **Puffin** tl; **Rex:** Geoff Wilkinson tr. 106/107 **BTC** tcr; **Corbis:** Bettmann tl, tr; Craig Lovell cAr; **DK:** Cyril Laubscher cl; **Hulton:** LR Legwin / Archive Photos cr; **MEPL** c; **Kobal:** Zoetrope / Warner Bros / Ph: Murray Close bl; United Artists br; Courtesy of **Puffin** tcl. 108/109 **AI:** Imagina / Atsushi Tsunoda br; **Corbis:** W Perry Conway cBr; **DK:** Peter Chadwick clB; **Kobal:** Greengrass / Laurel Enterprises tcr; Courtesy of **NEL** bl; **Rex:** Crollalanza tcl; **Science Photo Library:** Dr Gopal Murti bl. 110/111 **BTC** tcl; **Corbis:** Archivo Iconografico, S.A. tl; Milepost 92 1/2 / Colin Garratt bc; John Springer Collection tr; **DK:** Demetrio Carrasco tlB; **Hulton:** Spencer Arnold bl; **Kobal:** Icon / Warner Bros / Ph: Keith Hamsphere cr; **Rex:** SNAP (SYP) tcr. 112/113 © **Quentin Blake, 1982:** Courtesy of **Random House** trB, br; **Camera Press:** Stewart Mark bcr; **Corbis:** Bettmann tlB; **Getty:** Stone / Paul Harris bcl; **Hulton:** Horst Tappe / Archive Photos tr; Courtesy of **Phoenix** tcl; Courtesy of **Random House** tcr; **Rex:** Nils Jorgensen tl. 114/115 **Corbis:** Jon Sparks bl; Judith Miller & Dorling Kindersley tcl; **Kobal:** Theatre Projects / EMI c; Courtesy of **Puffin** tl; **NPG:** *Arthur Michell Ransome*, 1932 by Howard Coster. Medium: half-plate film negative tl. 116/117 **BTC** bcl; **MEPL** tl, tlB, bcl; Fortean Picture Library br; **Getty:** Image Bank / Ryan Beyer tcrB; **Hulton:** Paul Martin tclB; **Kobal:** Warner Bros / Ph: Keith Hamshere bl; **National Trust Photo Library:** Joe Cornish cr; Courtesy of **Puffin** tcr; **Rex:** Crispin Rodwell tr. 118/119 **BBC** tr; **Corbis:** Archivo Iconografico, S.A. tl; Sean Sexton Collection cBl; **DK:** Mark Hamilton bcr; **MEPL** blA; **Kobal:** Columbia brA; Courtesy of **Penguin** tlB. 120/121 **Corbis:** Bettmann tlB; cBl; Christie's Images br; Courtesy of **Corgi** tl, tcl; **DK:** Dave King bcr; Courtesy of **The Red Cross** blA; Courtesy of **Vintage** tcr, tr. 122/123 **Christie's Images** tcl; **Corbis:** Gianni Dagli Orti bl; Hulton-Deutsch Collection tl; Paul A Souders bcr; **DK:** Westminster Cathedral / Andy Crawford trB; **Kobal:** MGM tclB; **Magnum:** Rex bcr; Mike Lawn tl; Courtesy of **TimeWarner** tr. 124/125 **Corbis:** Rune Hellestad tr; Courtesy of **The Estate of Josh Kirby** tr, b; Courtesy of **Transworld Publishers** tcl. 126/127 **AI:** Andrew Kornylak tlB; **Corbis:** Reinhard Eisele br; Courtesy of **Egmont Books** tcl, bl, tr; **Hulton:** Evening Standard tl; George Konig tcr. 128/129 **Advertising Archive** tcr; **AI:** Rob Rayworth c; **BTC** tcl; **BAL:** Yale Center for British Art / *Prospero, Miranda and Ariel, from "The Tempest"*, c. 1780 Artist unknown. Oil on canvas; 27 3/4 x 36 3/8 in (70.5 x 92.4 cm) bcl; **Corbis:** Dave Bartruff bl; **Kobal:** 20th Century Fox / Blazer Films / **Rex:** LWI tl; SNAP (SYP) br. 130/131 **AA:** Real biblioteca de lo Escorial / Dagli Orti bcl; **Corbis:** Rune Hellestad tl, tr; **DK:** Dave King bl; Jules Selmes tlB; Courtesy of **The Estate of Josh Kirby** bcr; Courtesy of **Writers House:** Ph: Sigrid Estrada tlB; Courtesy of **Transworld Publishers** tcl, tcr. 132/133 **BTC** tcl, tcr; **Camera Press:** B/S tr; **Corbis:** Gail Mooney trB; Bill Ross bcl; **DK:** bcr; Matthew Ward tlB; **MEPL** br; **Kobal:** Castle Rock / Columbia / Ph: John Bramley cr; **Rex:** Sten Rosenlund tl. 134/135 **Catalyst TV:** cr; **Corbis:** Rune Hellestad tr; Courtesy of **Flamingo** tcl; **Hulton:** clB; George Eastman House / Lewis W Hine / Archive Photos bl; George Eastman House / Oscar Rejlander / Archive Photos tl; Courtesy of **Reg Johnson** tl; Courtesy of **The Josh Kirby Estate** br; Courtesy of **Transworld Publishers** tcr. 136/137 © **Quentin Blake, 1988:** Courtesy of **Random House** cBl, bl; **DK:** cr; **Hulton:** Horst Tappe / Archive Photos tl; **Kobal:** Miramax / Universal / Ph: Alex Bailey cAr, br; Courtesy of **Picador** tcr; Courtesy of **Random House** tcl; **Rex:** Nils Jorgensen tr. 138/139 **AI:** Andre Jenny tclB; **BTC** tcl, tcr; **Corbis:** Hulton-Deutsch Collection tr; Araldo de Luca cBl; David H Wells bl; **DK:** Florence Nightingale Museum / Geoff Dann trB; **Getty:** Photodisc Green cl; **Hulton** bl; **Kobal:** Warner Bros bcr; **Rex:** Julian Makey tl. 140/141 **Christie's Images** tcl; **Corbis:** Bettmann blA, Macduff Everton bcl; **DK:** British Museum, London / Ivor Kerslake cAl; **MEPL** tl; Courtesy of **Odyssey Pictures** tcr, br. 142/143 **BBC** cBr; **BTC** cBl; **BAL:** Chris Beetles Ltd, London *Big Ben*, 1894 by Rose Maynard Barton (1856-1929) tc; Dickens House Museum, London *Illustration from Bleak House*, 1853 by Hablot Knight Browne (Phiz) bcr; **Corbis:** Hulton-Deutsch Collection tl; **Hulton** bl; **Rex:** Richard Gardner tlB. 144/145 © **Quentin Blake, 1980:** Courtesy of **Random House** cr, br; **Channel 4 Stills:** Stuart Wood cl; **Hulton:** Horst Tappe / Archive Photos tr; Courtesy of **Random House** tl, tcl, tcr; Courtesy of **Nick Sharratt** cAl, bcl. 146/147 Courtesy of **Bloomsbury** cr; **Corbis:** Frank Lane Picture Agency / Martin B Withers bcr; **DK:** Geoff Dann cr; **Getty:** Brand X Pictures bl; **Hulton:** cl; **Kobal:** Trademark / BBC cAl; **Rex:** E Charbonneau / BEI tr; Courtesy of **Virago** tcl. 148/149 **BBC** bc; Courtesy of **Sebastian Peake** tl, tcl, tc, r, cAl, bl; br. 150/151 **AI:** Robert Harding Picture Library tlBr; **Corbis:** Macduff Everton bl; Pablo Corral tr; **Corbis Sygma:** Sophie Bassouls tl; **DK:** cAr; Steve Gorton cBr; Colin Keates cl; Courtesy of **Random House** tcr; **Rex:** 152/153 **BTC** tlB; **Corbis:** Ted Horowitz cBl; Underwood & Underwood br; **Getty:** Stone / Paul Edmondson c; / Andrew Hall bl; **Kobal:** Universal TV tr; **NPG:** *Aldous Huxley*, 1934 by Howard Coster. Medium: half-plate film negative tl. 154/155 **AI:** Robert Harding Picture Library bl; **BBC** cBr; Courtesy of **Collins** tcr; br; **Rex:** Gordon Clayton cAl; **Getty:** Image Bank / Donald C Landwehrle cAr; Photodisc Green br; Courtesy of **Penguin** tcl; Courtesy of **Reggie Oliver** tl. 156/157 **BTC** tcl; **Christie's Images** cBl; **Corbis:** Bettmann cBrr; Allen Ginsberg tl; Ted Streshinsky cbR; Demetrio Carrasco br; **Hulton:** Evening Standard cr; Orlando tr. 158/159 **BTC** tcl; **Getty:** Time Life Pictures tl; **Hulton:** Ernst Haas blA; Weegee (Arthur Fellig) / International Centre of Photography tclA; **Kobal:** Paramount tr, br; **Rex:** SNAP (SYP) tlBr. 160/161 **BTC** tcl; **Catalyst TV** bcl; **Corbis:** Rune Hellestad br; Gianni Dagli Orti bl; Roger Ressmeyer tl; **Hulton** tlBr; **Kobal:** Warner Bros / Ph: Joseph Lederer cBl; Courtesy of **Transworld Publishers** tcr. 162/163 **AI:** Art Kowalsky bl; **AA:** Castello di Manta Asti / Dagli Orti trBl; **BAL:** Private Collection *John of Gaunt, Duke of Lancaster (1340-99) 4th Son of Edward III* Annonymous cBr; **Corbis:** Pawel Libera br; Courtesy of **Harper Collins** tcl; **Historical Society of the Town of Greenwich:** William E Finch Jr Archives MS2 Anya Seton Papers, box 47, folder 321 tr; Courtesy of **Penguin** tcr; **Rex:** Karl Shondorfer tl; **Wellcome Library, London** tlBr. 164/165 **AI:** Gary Cook br; Doug Wilson tcrB; **BTC:** tcr; **Corbis:** Geoffrey Clements bl; Kevin Fleming tclB; Courtesy of **Harper Collins** tcl; **Magnum:** Rene Burri tr; **Rex:** Nils Fleming tl. 166/167 **AI:** Robert Harding Picture Library cAr; **DK:** Andy Crawford c; **Kobal:** © Disney / Ph: Ron Bartzdorff cAr, cr; Courtesy of **Macmillan** tr; Courtesy of **Random House** tl, tcl; Courtesy of **Nick Sharratt** bcl; **Granada Media Group Limited** tlB, cr. 168/169 **Corbis:** Bettmann bc; Michael Boys bl; Catherine Karnow tr; Royalty-Free crl, crr; **Rex:** Dave Allocca tl; Courtesy of **Vintage** tcl.